SAINTE-BEUVE

NORBERT GUTERMAN, who holds several degrees from the Sorbonne, is the author (with Henri Lefebvre) of *La Conscience Mystifiée* and the editor of the bilingual *Book of French Quotations*. He has contributed articles to French and American magazines, and has been active as a translator.

FRANCIS STEEGMULLER is the author of such biographies as *Apollinaire: Poet Among the Painters; Flaubert and Madame Bovary; Maupassant: A Lion in the Path;* and *The Grand Mademoiselle.* He has translated *Madame Bovary* into English and *The Owl and the Pussycat* into French. His translation into French (in collaboration with Norbert Guterman) of *Wynken, Blynken, and Nod* will appear shortly.

SAINTE-BEUVE
SELECTED ESSAYS

TRANSLATED AND EDITED BY
FRANCIS STEEGMULLER
AND
NORBERT GUTERMAN

Anchor Books
Doubleday & Company, Inc.
Garden City, New York

Sainte-Beuve: Selected Essays was originally published by Doubleday & Company, Inc., in 1963.

Anchor Books edition: 1964

CONTENTS

Introduction   vii

What Is a Classic?   1

Montaigne   13

Corneille (*Le Cid*)   31

Racine   67

Molière   99

Madame de Sévigné   129

Voltaire and the Président de Brosses   145

Madame Geoffrin   163

Grimm   179

Jean-Jacques Rousseau's *Confessions*   207

Stendhal   223

Balzac   257

Madame Bovary by M. Gustave Flaubert   275

Baudelaire   293

On Sainte-Beuve's Method   299

Biographical Index   313

INTRODUCTION

CHARLES AUGUSTIN Sainte-Beuve was born in Boulogne in 1804 and died in Paris in 1869, mourned by Flaubert in the words: "Who is there left to talk with about literature now? Sainte-Beuve loved literature . . . He is an irreparable loss to every writer in France. He left behind him a vast body of writings on literature, best known among which is the long series of his *Lundis*—his weekly newspaper articles which appeared Monday morning over a span of several decades and which have since been collected in many volumes. There are no non-literary biographical facts of any consequence. Even his love affair with Adèle Hugo might properly be called a literary episode, so inextricably was it linked to Sainte-Beuve's psychologically complex literary relationship with her husband.

Sainte-Beuve wrote verse from an early age: he hoped to be one of France's great poets. However, after attending classes in Boulogne and Paris, having no independent means, he had to think of preparing himself to earn a living, and at nineteen, at his mother's urging, he entered medical school. While there, he began another apprenticeship—this one as a professional writer, with modest, and even more modestly paid, contributions to the newspaper *Le Globe*. His employers were rapidly convinced of his talent, and before long he found himself a literary critic. The turning point in his life came when he had been with the newspaper two years: he was assigned a two-part article on *Odes et Ballades,* by Victor Hugo, a revolutionary young poet already in public view. On the appearance of the article the grateful Hugo invited the twenty-two-year-old critic to his house, and he soon became a close friend of the poet and his young wife. They gave him enough self-confidence to abandon his medical studies. Devoting himself entirely to literature, he became the champion of the Romantic movement, writing for various magazines and in 1828 publishing his *Tableau historique et critique de la poésie française et du théâtre français au XVIe siècle.* This essay, which was supplemented by a volume of selections from Ronsard, was pioneering in the sense that it called attention to a rich and long-neglected period of French poetry, and placed the new Romanticism in the continuity of French letters.

In 1829 came his first volume of verse, *Vie, Poésies et Pensées de Joseph Delorme.* Like all his poetry, and like his novel, *Volupté* (1834), this was not published under his own name. The proximity of the demigod Hugo, and the great man's words of praise for his poetic and novelistic talent, served perhaps to increase rather than to diminish his diffidence in these fields. For all his longing to excel, like his friend, as poet and novelist, he knew he could never equal him. This made him bitter but not less lucid. The friendship began to degenerate even before Hugo discovered the relationship between Sainte-Beuve and his wife.

With the publication of *Critiques et Portraits littéraires,* begun in 1832, Sainte-Beuve established his critical authority, which was to continue undiminished until his death. A favorable Monday-morning article by Sainte-Beuve could do much for a new author. In 1837, lonely after the end of his affair with Adèle Hugo, and embittered by the savage reception of his volume of poems, *Pensées d'août,* he was glad of an opportunity to deliver a course of lectures at the University of Lausanne. He chose as his subject Port-Royal, the name given to a movement of religious and moral renovation in seventeenth-century France, which is associated with the names of Pascal,

Racine, and others of the period. He had become interested in Port-Royal some time before, when he was probing his own religious beliefs. The Lausanne lectures, which involved considerable research, were the foundation of his masterpiece, the five-volume *Port-Royal* (1840–59). In this work he brilliantly displays his greatest virtues as critic and historian: conscientiousness, a spirit of objectivity and impartiality that may reflect his medical studies, subtlety of expression, psychological understanding, and the ability to bring to life past epochs and personalities. Other works include a study of *Chateaubriand et son groupe littéraire*. In 1844 he was elected to the French Academy; in 1865 he was appointed Senator.

He never married. Adèle Hugo was to remain the only oasis in a life which was otherwise bare of intimate affectionate relationships. In a letter to a friend (1845) he laments the "death of his heart," and describes himself as having become "a purely critical intelligence." For all his renown, he never consoled himself for his shortcomings as poet and novelist: he poured out his bile in private notes, which were published only in 1926, more than fifty years after his death.

During his lifetime Sainte-Beuve's authority as a critic went all but unchallenged. The most famous of his adversaries was Balzac, who abused him in an article about *Port-Royal*. He was much admired in England. Matthew Arnold called on him in Paris, and in the present century critics as unlike as George Saintsbury and D. H. Lawrence thought him great. During the last two generations, however, an increasing number of literary men seem to have felt that Sainte-Beuve's contribution as a critic was valueless, and that his reputation is grotesquely overblown. This feeling has been most prominently voiced in a number of essays by Proust, written in 1908 and published only in 1954 under the title *Contre Sainte-Beuve* (the title of an article Proust had planned to write but never wrote). Proust's objections seem to center chiefly around Sainte-Beuve's failure to recognize the genius of such contemporaries as Balzac, Stendhal, and Baudelaire, and his reliance on "analysis" and biographical background rather than on intuition.

At the same time, interest in Sainte-Beuve has continued unabated. New critical methods have been evolved since his day, but his approach is still widely used. It would be difficult to name any other critic who has produced so vast and varied an *oeuvre,* so much of which retains its interest a hundred years after his death. It is characterized above all by an unflinching love of the very phenomenon of literature: "It is the glory and eternal honor of the domain of thought, of art," he once wrote, "that charlatanism never penetrates it. That is why this noble part of man is inviolable." It displays a rejection of all fanaticisms, a love of truth, the spirit of liberalism at its best—qualities that go far toward counterbalancing undoubted shortcomings. Sainte-Beuve still retains his position as a French classic. New editions of his works continue to appear, complete with scholarly introductions. Many persons, if asked "Who was the greatest French critic?" would still answer "Sainte-Beuve"—even though some of them might be tempted to add, as did Gide about Victor Hugo, *"Hélas!"*

The present volume of selections will perhaps enable the reader to form an opinion of his own. It is confined to French subjects, and includes, next to a number of essays long considered models of their kinds, several of those in which Sainte-Beuve's judgment has been found wanting. We have not included any of the laudatory essays devoted to mediocrities today forgotten—a kind of which any prolific critic might be guilty. Comments on the individual selections will be found in the notes.

Norbert Guterman
Francis Steegmuller

NOTE

BETWEEN 1849 and 1869 Sainte-Beuve published, almost every Monday morning, a literary or historical article in a Parisian newspaper, at various times the *Constitutionnel*, the *Moniteur*, or the *Temps*. These were collected into volumes, some of them during his lifetime, and published in three series: *Premiers lundis*, *Causeries du lundi*, and *Nouveaux lundis*. Earlier articles were reprinted in series entitled *Portraits littéraires*, *Portraits de femmes*, etc. In the present volume, each selection is accompanied by the date of its original publication, and by the name of the series in which it was subsequently republished and where the French text may be found. Most of the few footnotes are Sainte-Beuve's own. To supplement the biographical index, an occasional identification has been inserted in the text between brackets. From a number of the essays, portions have been omitted for the sake of greater readability —which is not to say that "readability" has been the editors' criterion. As Sainte-Beuve himself says in *Port-Royal*, when informing his readers that he quotes certain texts in abridged form: "Once and for all, I ask you to trust me: I have done nothing of this kind without good reason . . ." (*Port-Royal*, I, 459, n. 1.)

SAINTE-BEUVE

WHAT IS A CLASSIC?

A DIFFICULT question! One that could be answered in
many different ways, depending on the time and the place.
Today I shall try, if not to answer it, at least to examine it
and discuss it, if only to encourage my readers to answer
it for themselves, and to clarify, if possible, my own ideas
and theirs on this matter. Why, after all, should not the
critic venture now and then to treat a subject that is not
personal, to discuss not a given man, but a given thing?
Why should he not write something of the sort that our
neighbors, the English, modestly call an "essay" and have
developed into a genre? Of course, in order to treat such
subjects, which are always somewhat abstract and moral,
one must speak in an atmosphere of calm, one must be
sure of one's own and the reader's interest: one must, in
short, take advantage of one of those brief moments of
silence, moderation, and leisure which are rarely the lot of
lovely France—which, indeed, her brilliant genius bears
with impatience, even during periods when she is trying to
behave herself and is not engaged in making revolutions.

According to the usual definition, a classic is a uni-
versally admired old author, an authority in his field. The
term "classic" taken in this sense appeared first in ancient
Rome. There the name of *classici* was given, not to all
citizens of various classes, but only to those of the first
class, those who enjoyed an income above a certain figure.
Those whose income was inferior were referred to as *infra
classem*, i.e., as being below class as such. The word was

used in a figurative sense by Aulus Gellius. *Classicus assiduusque scriptor* was his term for a prominent writer of quality, a writer who counts, who has achievements to his credit, who is not swallowed up in the proletarian crowd. The expression presupposes a sufficiently advanced stage of development, a conscious differentiation within existing literature.

At first, the only true classics for the moderns were, of course, the ancients. The Greeks, by a singular good fortune, which greatly simplified matters for them, had only Greek classics, and they were the only classics for some time thereafter, in the eyes of the Romans who sought to imitate them. When the golden age of their own literature was reached, with Cicero and Virgil, the Romans in turn had their own classics, most of whom remained classics throughout the following centuries. The medieval epoch was less ignorant of Roman antiquity than might be supposed, but it lacked taste and moderation, as well as a sense of value. It preferred Ovid to Homer and ranked Boethius as a classic at least the equal of Plato. The revival of letters in the fifteenth and sixteenth centuries did away with this long confusion, and only then did admiration begin to acquire perspective. The genuinely classical Greek and Roman authors now stood out against a luminous background, and were harmoniously grouped in their two camps.

Meanwhile the modern literatures had come into being, and some of the most precocious among them, such as the Italian, had their own ancient period. There was Dante, soon hailed by his posterity as a "classic." Italian poetry since Dante has sometimes been less great, but it has often recovered greatness and has always preserved some of the impetus and resonance of its high origins. It is not without importance for a poetry to find its point of departure, its classical source, at such an altitude—to descend from a Dante rather than to develop laboriously from a Malherbe.

Modern Italy had her classics, and Spain had every right to think that she too had hers, at a time when France was still trying to discover herself. A few talented writers, endowed with originality and exceptional verve—scattered brilliant efforts, not followed up—are not enough to put a nation's literary fortunes on a solid foundation. The idea of the classical implies continuity and consistency, a tradition that forms a whole, is handed down, and endures. Not until after the golden age of Louis XIV did the French feel with a thrill of pride that such good fortune had finally come to them. The multitude of voices who kept proclaiming this advent to Louis XIV may have flattered the king and exaggerated the glory, yet at the same time they believed much of what they said, and rightly so. Now arose a curious, interesting difference of opinion. The very men who were most carried away by the marvels of the *grand siècle* and who went so far as to be willing to sacrifice the Ancients to the Moderns—the party, that is, whose leader was Perrault—tended paradoxically to exalt and to consecrate the very authors who most passionately contradicted and fought them. Boileau angrily took up the cudgels for the Ancients, defending them against Perrault, who was championing Corneille, Molière, Pascal, and other eminent men of the century, especially Boileau himself! The good-natured La Fontaine was on the side of the learned Huet in this quarrel, scarcely realizing that before long he himself would be a classic.

The best definition is by example. Once France had had her *grand siècle* and was able to look at it in perspective, she knew what the term "classic" meant better than by any theories. The eighteenth century, by its very variety, enriched this idea through the fine works we owe to its four great men. Read Voltaire's *Siècle de Louis XIV,* Montesquieu's *La Grandeur et la décadence des Romains,* Buffon's *Les Epoques de la Nature,* and Jean-Jacques Rousseau's *Le Vicaire savoyard* and his beautiful descriptions and meditations on nature, and tell me whether the eighteenth century did not, at its most memorable, reconcile tradition with freedom of development and independence.

At the beginning of the nineteenth century and during the Empire, when the first attempts at a decidedly new, rather adventurous literature were being made, certain peevish—rather than purist—opponents of the new style took it upon themselves to place severe restrictions on the term "classical." The first Dictionary of the Academy (1694) had defined a classical author merely as "an old author strongly approved, who is an authority in the matter he treats." The Dictionary of the Academy of 1835 goes much further: the originally rather vague definition has become narrower, much more exclusive. Classical authors are those "who have become *models* in a given language," and in the articles which follow, the term "models" is linked with "rules" set down for composition and style. There are repeated references to the "strict rules" which a writer must observe. Clearly, this definition of the classical was drawn up by worthy academicians in reaction to what was called at the time "the romantic." Theirs was a defense against a present enemy. It seems to me that the time has come to renounce such limiting, timorous definitions, and to suggest others, broader in spirit.

A true classic, as I should like the term to be defined, is an author who has enriched the human mind, who has actually added to its treasures and carried it a step forward, one who has discovered some unmistakable moral truth or recaptured some eternal passion in a human heart where everything seemed known and explored; who may have expressed his thought, observation, or discovery in any of a number of genres, but in a form at once great and sweeping, subtle and yet sensible, sound and beautiful in itself; who speaks to all in a style of his own, which happens also to be that of common speech, a style new but without neologisms, new and old at the same time, easily acceptable to any epoch.

A classic author such as this might well be revolutionary for a time, or at least seem so. But in truth, if he was violent at first and overthrew what stood in his way, he did so only in order quickly to right the scales in favor of order and beauty.

I should like to make this definition grandiose, broad, generous. If I were asked to illustrate it with names, I should mention first of all the Corneille of *Polyeucte,*

Cinna, and *Horace.* I should name Molière, the most complete and comprehensive French genius.

"Molière is so great," said Goethe (that king of critics), "that he surprises us every time we read him. He stands apart; his plays come close to the tragic, and no one dares imitate them. His *Avare,* where the vice depicted destroys all affection between father and son, is one of the sublimest of all works, and dramatic to the highest degree. . . . In a play, every action must be important in itself and point to one still greater. In this respect, *Le Tartufe* is a model. What an exposition, the first scene! From the beginning everything is significant and foreshadows something more important. There are beautiful expositions in several plays by Lessing, but that in *Le Tartufe* is unique, the greatest of its kind. . . . Every year I read a play by Molière, just as from time to time I pore over some engraving done from one of the great Italian masters."

[Goethe also said:] "I call the classic healthy, and the romantic sick. For me the poem of the Nibelungen is as classical as Homer; both are healthy and vigorous. The works of today are romantic not because they are new, but because they are weak, sickly or sick. The old works are classical not because they are old, but because they are energetic, hale and hearty. If we considered the classical and the romantic from these two points of view, we should all soon be in agreement."

Indeed, I should like every free mind, before he reaches a final decision in this matter, to make a tour of the world and to survey the various literatures in their primitive vigor and infinite diversity. What would he see? First of all Homer, the father of the classical world—who is certainly, however, less a simple and distinct individual than a vast living expression of a whole age of semibarbarian civilization. To make him a classic in the proper sense of the term, it was necessary to ascribe to him, after the fact, a design, a plan, literary intentions, and qualities of Atticism and urbanity which he certainly never dreamed of —his natural inspiration abundantly sufficed. Next to him, we see great and venerable figures like Aeschylus and

Sophocles, of whose works we possess only a small portion;
they stand there as though to remind us of others, who
deserved no doubt to survive as much as they, but who
succumbed to the ravages of time. This alone should teach
us not to oversimplify our view of literature, even of classical literature. We should recognize that the order which
has prevailed for so long, which is so exact and well-
proportioned, is a highly artificial creation, based on our
limited knowledge of the past.

This, of course, applies with even greater force to the
modern world. The greatest names we find at the beginnings of the various literatures are such as to upset our
most traditional concepts of what is beautiful and proper
in poetry. For instance, is Shakespeare a classic? Yes, today
he is one for England and for the world, but in the period
of Pope he was not. Pope and his friends were the only
"classics" par excellence; they seemed definitively so the
day they died. Today they are still classics, and they deserve the title, but they are classics of the second rank,
and they are forever dominated and put back in their
place by the one who has finally come into his own.

I am certainly not one to speak against Pope and his
excellent disciples, particularly when they are as gentle
and natural as Goldsmith; next to the greatest, they are
perhaps the most pleasant among the writers and poets,
those most apt to add charm to life. One day Pope added
a postscript to a letter Bolingbroke wrote to Swift saying
in effect: "I fancy that if we three were to spend only
three years together, some profit might result for our century." No, we must never speak lightly about those who
had the right to say such things about themselves without
bragging. We should rather envy the fortunate, favored
ages when talented men could propose to form such associations, which at the time had nothing chimerical about
them. Whether named after Louis XIV or Queen Anne,
such ages are the only truly classical ones in the broader
sense of the word, the only ones which provided superior
talents with a propitious climate and shelter. We know
this only too well, living as we do in an age without inner

unity, when talents, possibly equal to those of other ages, have been lost or frittered away because of the uncertainties and inclemencies of the times. Still, we must recognize that there are many kinds of greatness or superiority. The authentic sovereign geniuses surmount difficulties where others fail. Dante, Shakespeare, and Milton succeeded in rising to their full height and produced their imperishable works despite obstacles, oppression, and storms.

There has been a great deal of discussion on the subject of Byron's opinions about Pope, and attempts have been made to account for the apparent contradiction in the spectacle of the author of *Don Juan* and *Childe Harold* exalting the purely classical school and declaring it to be the only good one, while taking himself an entirely different tack. Once again, Goethe hit the nail on the head when he said that Byron, whose poetic inspiration was so great and noble, feared Shakespeare, who was so much more powerful in the creation and management of characters in action: "He would have been glad to ignore him; he was embarrassed by his sublimity completely devoid of egotism; he felt that he could never take wing beside him. He never wished to ignore Pope, because he did not fear him; he knew very well that Pope was a sheltering wall." If the school of Pope had retained, as Byron wished, its supremacy and a kind of honorary sway over the past, Byron would have been unique and uncontested in his genre; the erection of Pope's "wall" would mask our view of the great figure of Shakespeare, beside whom Byron is but second best.

In France we had no great classic author before the seventeenth century, no Dante or Shakespeare capable of giving guidance to every subsequent period of literary renewal. We had some potentially great poets, such as Mathurin Régnier and Rabelais, but they lacked ideas; they did not possess the required passion and gravity. Montaigne was a kind of premature classic in the Horatian tradition, but he was as capricious as an undisciplined child; he gave in to every passing libertine mood and fancy. Our ancestors provided us with scantier foundations to build upon than is the case with any other nation. When the day came to recover our literary freedoms and rights, it was more difficult for us to remain classical while emancipating ourselves. However, with Molière and La Fontaine among our seventeenth-century classics, we have models great enough to inspire daring and talented writers.

What seems to me the important thing today is to preserve and cherish the idea of classicism, while at the same time broadening it. There is no formula for producing a classic: this much must be recognized as self-evident.

The best and greatest classics are the most unexpected, as witness those virile geniuses who are truly born immortal and flourish forever. The seemingly least classical of the four great poets of the *grand siècle* was Molière; his contemporaries applauded him more than they respected him, enjoyed him without realizing his worth. Next to him the least classical seemed to be La Fontaine: and you see what happened to both of them two centuries later! Far above Boileau, even above Racine, are they not today unanimously recognized as the most fertile, the richest contributors to our knowledge of human nature?

This is not to say that we have to discard the rest or think less of them. I believe the Temple of Taste needs to be remodeled, but in rebuilding it our task is merely to enlarge it, to make it the Pantheon of all noble men, of all who have notably and durably increased the sum total of the human spirit, the enjoyments and conquests of the mind. For my part—and it is only too obvious that I could not in any degree lay claim to being the architect or designer of such a temple—I shall confine myself to expressing a few wishes, contributing to the blueprint, as it were. Above all, I should not exclude anyone among the worthy: I want everyone so entitled to have his place there, from that freest of creative geniuses, that greatest and least self-conscious of all the classics—Shakespeare—to the very least of the classics in miniature, to Andrieux. "My Father's house has many mansions"—let this be true of the Kingdom of the Beautiful no less than of the Kingdom of Heaven. Homer, as always and everywhere, would be the

first in such a realm, the most resembling a god; but behind him, like the procession of the Magi, would stand
those three magnificent poets, those three Homers so long
unknown to us, who composed immense revered epics for
the ancient nations of Asia: Valmiki and Vyasa the Hindus,
and Firdusi the Persian. In the domain of taste it is a good
thing to know at least that such men have existed, so that
the human race is seen as a whole. Having paid our respects, however, we should not linger in these distant
climes. Closer to home, we could find myriad attractions,
both pleasant and sublime, and we could enjoy a rich
variety of changing scenes, often enough startling, but in
whose seeming disorder we would never find disharmony.
The most ancient poets and sages who expressed human
morality in simply stated maxims would converse among
themselves in words "rare and suave" and would not be
surprised at understanding one another at once. Men like
Solon, Hesiod, Theognis, Job, Solomon—and why not Confucius, too?—would welcome to their company such ingenious moderns as La Rochefoucauld and La Bruyère.
Listening to the others, these latecomers would say, "They
already knew all we know; all we did was to give new life
to their wisdom." At the most prominent elevation, standing above broad and gently rising slopes, Virgil, surrounded by Menander, Tibullus, Terence, and Fénelon,
would engage them in conversation of great charm and
dignity. His radiant features ringed with modesty would
recall the distant day when he entered the theater in
Rome just after his verses had been recited, and the whole
audience rose as one man—giving him the same tribute as
it was accustomed to give Augustus. Not far away, un-
willing to be separated from so dear a friend, Horace would
in turn preside—in so far as a poet and so subtle a sage can
preside—over the group of witty worldly poets who speak
as other men sing: Pope become less irritable; Boileau
grown less of a scold; Montaigne, whose appearance here
in this charming corner would remove the last possibility
of any resemblance to a literary school. La Fontaine would
feel at ease here and, having lost much of his restlessness,

would never depart. Voltaire would stop by, but though
he would be fond of the place, he would not have the
patience to stay. On the same elevation as Virgil, a little
below him, one would see Xenophon, wearing an air of
simplicity that suggests nothing of the captain but rather a
priest of the Muses. Around him we would find the At-
ticists of all languages and countries—men like Addison,
Pellisson, Vauvenargues, all those who know the value of
easy persuasiveness, exquisite simplicity, and graceful casualness. At the center three great men would at last be
reunited in front of the main temple (for there would be
several temples in the precincts), and when they were together, no fourth man, however great, would dream of
drawing near to share either their words or their silence.
Such beauty would emanate from them, such unmistakable
grandeur, that no one would dare. Theirs is the perfection
of harmony which appears but for a day when the world
is young. Their names have become the ideal of art: Plato,
Sophocles, Demosthenes. And yet, when all due honor has
been paid these demigods, we may yet observe a familiar
throng of excellent minds who prefer to cluster around
Cervantes, Molière, and others of that class: the depicters
of ordinary life, friendly, indulgent benefactors of mankind
who see us steadily and whole, who teach us to laugh and
to be wise, and who do not find it beneath them to appeal
to our warmer feelings and love of pleasure.

I shall not prolong this description: to be complete, it
would require a book in itself. The Middle Ages, you may
well believe, would with Dante occupy hallowed heights;
at the feet of the poet of the Paradiso, most of Italy would
spread out like a garden. Boccaccio and Ariosto would dis-
port themselves there, and Tasso would rediscover the
orange groves of Sorrento. More generally, every nation
would have a corner of its own, but no one would feel
constrained to remain within it; I see the authors strolling
about in search of teachers and brothers and finding them
in the least likely places. Lucretius, for example, would
want to discuss with Milton the origin of the world and
the ordering of the primeval chaos; and while each of

them would argue in favor of his own theory, they would agree at least on the divine nature of poetry.

Such are our classics; the imagination of each reader may complete the drawing and pick out the group he prefers. For one must choose, and the first condition of taste—once one has understood the whole—is not to flit from group to group, but to settle permanently in one. Nothing blunts or extinguishes taste more than continual flitting about: the poetic spirit is no Wandering Jew. However, when I speak of choosing a place to settle down, I do not mean that we should imitate even those who are most congenial to us among the masters of old. Let us content ourselves with understanding them, admiring them, and let us, who have come along so much later, try at least to be ourselves. Let us make a choice on the basis of our own instincts. Let us keep the sincerity and the naturalness of our own thoughts and feelings, as surely as we can; let us add something more difficult, which is elevation, if this is possible, and orientation toward some high goal. Speaking our own language and governed by the conditions of the age in which we find ourselves, from which we derive our strengths as well as our shortcomings, let us ask ourselves from time to time, our heads lifted up to the peaks, our eyes on the group of mortals we most revere: "What would they say of us?"

But why always speak about being an author, about writing? Perhaps you have reached an age when you will write no more. Happy those who read and reread, who follow their own inclinations in perfect freedom! There comes a time in life when, having been everywhere and done everything, there is no intenser pleasure than to study the things we already know, going ever deeper into them, relishing the feelings we have already had, as we see over and over again the persons we most care for: these are the pure delights of maturity. It is then that the term "classic" takes on its true meaning—when every man of taste makes his choice on a basis of irresistible predilection. Then taste is formed and becomes definitive; then we achieve good sense, if we ever do. We have no more time to experiment, no more desire to set out on journeys of discovery. We confine ourselves to our friends, to those who have stood the test of time. Old wine, old books, old friends. Then we say to ourselves what Voltaire put into these delightful lines:

> Jouissons, écrivons, vivons, mon cher Horace!
>
> . . . .
>
> J'ai vécu plus que toi: mes vers dureront moins;
> Mais au bord du tombeau, je mettrai tous mes soins
> A suivre les leçons de ta philosophie,
> A mépriser la mort en savourant la vie,
> A lire tes écrits pleins de grâce et de sens,
> Comme on boit d'un vin vieux qui rajeunit les sens.

> [Let us enjoy life, let us write, my dear Horace!
>
> . . . .
>
> Though I have lived longer than you, my verses will
>   not live so long;
> But on edge of the grave, I shall do all I can
> To follow the lessons of your philosophy,
> To despise death while enjoying life,
> To read your writings full of grace and meaning,
> Just as we drink old wine to rejuvenate our senses.]

In short, whether it be Horace or another, whichever old author best renders our thought when we are ripe with years, he it is with whom we shall find ourselves in steady conversation, as with an old friend. His friendship will never fail or deceive us, and the cloudless serenity he brings to our lives will reconcile us with our fellow men and with ourselves.

24 October 1850 (*Causeries du lundi*).

Sainte-Beuve had a great love and understanding of the older literatures. This is reflected in his judgments of the classics, which are usually penetrating and sure and always tinged with a warm humanity.

MONTAIGNE

OVER the past two centuries a great deal has been written about Montaigne. Authors as important and brilliant as Pascal have spoken their minds, and yet there is one point that, in my opinion, has not been stressed enough. Namely, that Montaigne does not give us a philosophical system, is not primarily the Pyrrhonian skeptic—Montaigne is the very embodiment of nature.

He is nature in all her purity, yet civilized; nature in her broadest, most typical expressions as well as in her most individual moods, not excluding her aberrations. All of nature untouched by grace. What the Jansenists hated in Montaigne, above all, was the way he incarnates the natural man. Their instinct did not deceive them.

Montaigne was raised by an affectionate father who took pains with his education. However, he was never exposed to strong religious influence as a child. In his earliest years, he was taught Latin rather than the catechism. His father, who had been a soldier in Italy and had had a varied experience of life, was something of a philanthropist, with ideas of his own. His son was brought up like a sixteenth-century Emile, in the country; his sponsors in baptism, chosen by the older Montaigne, were of the humblest station. Thus he was taught never to look down upon anyone, however poor, but on the contrary filled with a sense of obligation and attachment to the common people. This admirable father carried his concern for his child's upbringing to such a point that he arranged for him to be wakened each morning to the sound of music. Montaigne's earliest studies were limited to languages and to observation of the life around him. Abstract and difficult subjects were eliminated. He grew up gentle and tractable, a trifle lazy. Apparently rather stolid and easygoing, the boy nonetheless possessed a bold imagination. At the Collège de Guyenne where he lived in comfort thanks to his father's generosity he showed the first signs of literary interest. He became fond of the *Metamorphoses* of Ovid, that Ariosto among the ancients. This wholly pagan book was his boyhood favorite. The tale of Achilles choosing his arms fired his imagination. After this, he "drank in," as he says, the *Aeneid,* Terence, Plautus, and the Italian comedy in quick succession. He took part in school performances of the Latin tragedies by Buchanan and by Muret, and even at this early date he rejected, as impertinent, objections to the frivolity of such an occupation. At the age of thirteen his formal studies were at an end. As for those other pleasures of youth, which pose such a problem to chastity, he tells us later that he could hardly remember a time when he had not enjoyed them. The natural freedom of his mind had been little constrained by his upbringing; however, easygoing as he was, it always had what he calls "well-settled motions," that is, he brought a sure and open intelligence to his judgment of things. He ruminated for himself, without feeling the need to communicate. He was little drawn to that kind of romanticism which is not present in nature but which a precocious imagination sometimes nurtures. Though anything but hostile to physical love, which he recognized as the greatest of natural pleasures, he never experienced love as an exclusive passion.

He preferred friendship, that less venturesome, less feverish, commoner, and more universal passion. We know how much friendship meant to him; in his writings he paid many a beautiful tribute to it. In all these respects —to mention no others—he strikes me as a complete specimen of the well-balanced natural man. His was a humanism only nominally Christian, but for all that public spirited, decent, and "sensible." In a period of civil war he kept his head and pursued no private ambitions. He discharged his duties honorably in several posts, though without overwhelming distinction. He readily returned to private life after his terms as counselor to the Parlement of Bordeaux and as mayor of that city. His real profession, his only "trade," was to be a human being. He made no deep study of any one subject, for fear he might be wholly caught up in it, for fear of exiling himself from common humanity.

He tells us that he did not have enough knowledge to supervise the lessons of a ten-year-old schoolboy, but when it came to testing the quality of a young mind with two or three questions—that was something he could do. His was a mind at once active and uncommitted, curious about everything, but forever ready to turn in upon itself for refreshment.

He changed as he grew older, but he grew old by easy stages. His favorite author after Ovid was Lucian, and after Lucian, Virgil: that is, the easygoing child became the Stoic rhetorician and the latter in turn gave way to the serene old man. Likewise, he was extravagant with money as a young man, sometimes requiring the assistance of friends; then there was a second stage when he was more careful with money, perhaps a bit too careful; and when more years had gone by, he attained a more balanced and relaxed attitude. "I measure my garment according to my cloth, and let my expences goe together with my comming in; sometimes the one, sometimes the other exceeds: But they are never farre a sunder." (*Essays*, I, 40; Florio trans.)

He married, at thirty-three, in compliance with the custom of his day. He became a father. These new responsibilities he rose to most honorably, for all the reputation he may have had as a wild young man. At all events, he was a better husband and father than he had expected or promised to be. Later, looking back on his life, he said: "I have seene the leaves, the blossomes, and the fruit; and now see the drooping and withering of it. Happily because naturally." (*Essays*, III, 2) The term "naturally"

comes naturally from his pen. The more I reflect about
Montaigne, the more I am convinced that he was the natural man par excellence.

Let me dwell on this point, if I may. The phrase is so
often and so vaguely used, I should like to analyze it more
carefully and to develop its fuller implications.

There is something of Montaigne in every one of us.
Every one of our inclinations, moods, and passions—every
one of our diversions, amusements, and flights of fancy
upon which Christianity has made no mark—all such states
of mind deserve to be called "Montaigne" states of mind.
To accept the "naturalness" of our lives, for all the operations of what is called "divine grace"—a sort of unreflective
nakedness into which we relapse when following our natural inclinations, as though the soul had never been re-
deemed—to accept this "Tahiti" of the soul is also to accept
Montaigne's empire, the realm in which he lived and wrote.
We ought not to be surprised that Pascal had such difficulty
disposing of Montaigne. The problem Montaigne poses
is not one of philosophy but that of nature itself, of the
individual self: he poses a philosophical problem only in
the sense that he represents nature in all its purity.

Pascal inveighed against Montaigne, studying him
closely so as to condemn him more sternly—and with a
vehemence such as only the true believer may permit
himself (and then only on the condition that the end
justifies such means). And yet, in order to gain full understanding of Montaigne and of the "indulgence of so many
intelligent persons" who "have failed to realize how dangerous he is" (as Arnauld complains in his *Art de penser*),
we must consider Montaigne's thought in its original, informal, loose expression. The tidiness of Pascal's indictment is a barrier to grasping Montaigne as a whole.[1] The

[1] The variety of Montaigne's thought comes through most
clearly in the oldest editions of the *Essais*—the first (in two
books, 1580) and even the fifth (in three books, 1588) which
contains no fewer than 600 additions. More modern editions
read very differently, and do not convey so good an idea of
Montaigne's original plan. (It is the same with editions of La
Bruyère and La Rochefoucauld.)

fact is, all things considered, three-quarters of Montaigne does not essentially differ from what we find in a number of other writers: but those others do not arouse criticism, because they speak without malicious intent. Had M. de Saci read Montaigne before talking to Pascal about him— M. de Saci who made it his rule to follow the will of God at every moment (*in lege Dominis fuit voluntas ejus die ac nocte*)—he would have said something like this to Pascal:

"This author to whom you ascribe so much intelligence and whose ideas you erect into a system, does not rely upon arguments to all that extent. What appeals to the reader is present in most men, including those who call themselves Christians, but who live as if the Cross had never been. When I am walking in the countryside—when, perhaps, I have retired there in my old age, taking my ease, free of responsibility, with nobody to think of but myself—where then is my Christianity? When I look at a lovely flower, admire a shaft of sunlight, or lie down on a patch of greensward to take a little nap, there to dream of who knows what fantastic things, wholly caught up in concerns of this world, forgetting all else—where then is my Christianity? When I read, as I like to do, of unusual manners and customs in books of travel, and meet the Devil in a hundred guises, now as a naked cannibal, now as an Italian fop, not caring so much that he is the Devil but only whether he is interesting—where then is my Christianity? And when I sit down to Montaigne in moments of leisure, with nothing more in my mind than reading Montaigne—where then is my Christianity?"

That is enough about what I call "three-quarters of Montaigne." Now we must address ourselves to the rest, his attitude toward religion, which Pascal and the recluses of Port-Royal condemned so harshly. They did not misrepresent him. Montaigne is, indeed, naïve, and we do not underestimate the naïve, casual, easygoing aspect of his thought. However, there is also in him a background of conscious intention, which gives a special sense to the whole. The hostility and fear which Montaigne has aroused in religious men comes from their realization that his portrayal of nature conceals a consistent paganism. He almost always treats religion as a thing apart, as something much too respectable to be discussed—but this does not prevent him from discussing it constantly. He is against translating and reading the Scriptures—a point on which, as on many others, he prefers the Catholic Church to the Reformers. Politically, such an attitude was not unwise, but there is more to it. He also says that the use of the "sacred and divine songs" (i.e., the Psalms) ought to be restricted to the priesthood. Being himself but a layman, a mere writer of imagination, he would not presume so far as to recite the Psalms. For him, a simple Lord's Prayer is quite enough, he tells us. Such is his way of inspiring respect for religion! Where Voltaire said, "These things are sacred, *because* no one will touch them"—he was speaking of canticles by Lefranc de Pompignan—Montaigne in effect says, "These things are sacred, *therefore* no one should touch them." The higher the portals of the Temple, the less risk we run of knocking our heads against them as we go in or out. He knows very well that so extreme a point of view was out of date in his own day. That he would have been perfectly happy in certain countries where, apart from the obligatory observances, one does as one likes, where you can be a cardinal and a man of the world at the same time—this is clear from the general tenor of his book. I know that he made a proper Christian death—Gassendi and La Rochefoucauld also received the sacraments. It is not for me to judge his sincerity at such an awesome moment, but his book is there for all to read, and my judgment is of it.

Many a chapter—that on Prayers and Orisons, and that on Repenting, for example—would be as revelatory, on close analysis, as the Apology of Raymond Sebond. In such chapters, we find sentences that are moderate and unobjectionable from the religious point of view, but they are not enough to modify the general tone.[2] In fact, we

---

[2] For instance the chapter on Prayers and Orisons ends with a pious, sensible remark, as if the author were afraid that he

never know quite where we are with men of this ilk—
with Bayle any more than with Montaigne. We might say
of them what Pascal said of Opinion, that it is the more
fraudulent for not being consistently so.

Pascal also said: "One saying of David, or of Moses, for
instance that 'God will circumcise the heart,' enables us to
judge of their spirit. If all their other expression were
ambiguous, and left us in doubt whether they were philosophers or Christians, one saying of this kind would in fact
determine all the rest. From that point on, ambiguity no
longer exists." The very opposite is true of Montaigne: if
some passages state his thought, others conceal it. He is
betrayed by random remarks that are like flashes of lightning illuminating a whole landscape. Montaigne's "dirty"
passages are especially revealing, when he addresses him
self to the most intimate aspects of human life. He really
enjoys tearing away the poor rags with which we cover our
baser nature—and it is then that we glimpse him as he
truly is under the high spirits, the eloquence, and the
gentility. He sets out to humiliate us in such passages (try
listening to them read aloud). Unlike Pascal's, his tone
is never one of grief at our natural condition, but one of
malicious delight: he fairly rubs his hands with self-satis-
faction.

Montaigne's longest, most vigorous, and most important chapter is the one titled "An Apology of Raymond
Sebond." This is the heart of the *Essais;* everything about
it is purposeful, and the calculated tortuous sentences
which say the opposite of what the author really thinks
nonetheless convey it. Studying it closely, we find that his
so-called Pyrrhonism rings hollow: for all his restless
rambling Montaigne knows where he is going. Out of this
"Apology" I can imagine assembling a chapter that might
be headed "Montaigne's Dogmatism." Where Spinoza's

had gone a little too far. The later additions Montaigne made
to the *Essais* contain many such sentences, as well as sentences
intensifying his disrespect.

form is geometrical, Montaigne's is skeptical, but the essence of his doctrine seems to me unmistakable.[3]

The Apology was apparently written for Marguerite (the wife of Henri IV), in her way as delightful a writer as Montaigne. She, too, was fond of learning, no prude, and intellectually uninhibited. In the end, however, she became devout; her chaplain for a time was the still unknown Vincent de Paul who went on to become tutor of the future Cardinal de Retz. What a trio they would have made—Montaigne, Queen Marguerite, and the Cardinal de Retz!

To humor his father (who was more of an enthusiast for the new learning than himself learned) the youthful Montaigne had translated a Latin book by the fifteenth-century Spanish author, Raymond de Sebond. Titled *Theologia naturalis,* it demonstrated the existence of God and the truth of the Christian religion on the basis of rational arguments, drawn as far as possible from observation of nature. In some respects, this work anticipated Fénelon's *Existence de Dieu* and deistic works by Clarke and Paley. It often leaned on St. Thomas Aquinas, and represented an attempt to provide natural explanations for such mysteries as the Trinity, Original Sin, and the Incarnation.

Montaigne's French version of *Theologia naturalis* was published in 1569, in compliance with a wish expressed by his father on his deathbed—the older Montaigne had been charmed and consoled by this book. It was criticized on two counts. Some (the Catholic party) said that the at-

[3] The fact that this self-styled skeptic was actually quite set in his ideas may be clearly seen in the following passage: "What I doe, is ordinarily full and compleate, and I march (as wee say) all in one piece: I have not many motions that hide themselves and slinke away from my reason, or which very neare are not guided by the consent of all my partes, without division or intestine sedicion: my judgement hath the whole blame, or commendation; and the blame it hath once, it hath ever: for, almost from its birth, it hath beene one of the same inclination, course and force. And in matters of generall opinions, even from my infancy, I ranged my selfe to the point I was to hold." (*Essays,* III, 2)

tempt to give revelation and faith a foundation in reason was opening a door that should remain closed. Others maintained that Sebond's arguments were weak and failed to make their point. It was ostensibly to answer both types of objection that Montaigne wrote this chapter of the *Essais*.

He addresses himself first to his religious critics, treating them with conspicuous respect. He says that he cannot blame those who, because of their "zeal of piety," are afraid to let reason be used in support of religion. But while he is well aware that the knowledge of God can be attained only by extraordinary supernatural means, he "fears" that we could not "enjoy" it unless we had access to it "not only by discourse, but also by humane means." For, he says, if we could grasp Godhead "through the interposition of a lively faith," surely we would not find so many contradictions and inconsistencies between Christian words and Christian deeds. Citing one instance after another, he goes on maliciously to demonstrate the inadequacy of precisely these "humane means," that is, without the intervention of divine grace. What is he driving at? It is obvious that from this point on he is no longer concerned with Raymond de Sebond. He had translated the latter's book to please his father; now, on the pretext of defending that author, he is pursuing another aim altogether. If he is not actually refuting Sebond, he is using him as a pretext for carrying on a very broad and "probing" discussion of religion. His tone of respect for all who would place faith above reason makes him seem to be on their side. With the greatest humility he confines his defense of Sebond to the observation that the latter's method, though very crude and limited, might have a certain practical value for bringing certain persons back to the faith. And he cites one such instance: he knew a man who had actually been influenced by Sebond's arguments. As he puts it, "Faith, giving as it were a tincture and lustre unto Sebond's arguments makes them the more firme and solid."

However, when he addresses himself to those of his critics who were not inspired by "zeal of piety" and who

found Sebond's arguments weak and inconclusive, his tone
changes. Now he is as outspoken as one could wish. "Such
fellowes must somewhat more roughly be handled," he
says, "for they are more dangerous and more malicious
than the first." In fact, it is he who becomes more dangerous and more malicious at this point. For what does he do?
To refute the second type of objectors, he proceeds to
outdo them at their own game on a tone of high indignation. What he says, in effect, is: Of course, I am well
aware that poor Sebond's arguments are weak and don't
prove much. Yet, madmen that you are, proud wretches
(he is taking up the cudgels in defense of the Godhead
they would defame)—tell me, how can there be any arguments capable of proving anything in such matters? Cannot every one of them be countered with an argument
equally—that is to say, just as little—convincing? There-
upon, as though carried away by his own self-righteous-
ness, he embarks on a long discussion, in the course of
which he enumerates ad infinitum every possible cause
of errors and ineffectuality to which the human reason
is prone when unsupported by religious beliefs. Once this
chapter has been properly understood, we realize that
Montaigne is from beginning to end playing a part. Only a
reader determined to be deceived could be taken in by it.
For Montaigne, Sebond serves the same function the Mani-
chaeans were to serve for Bayle.

To begin with, Montaigne tries to show that man "alone
without other help," without the grace and knowledge of
God, is but a miserable and wretched creature. "Who hath
perswaded him that this admirable moving of heavens
vaults; that the eternal light of these lamps so fiercely
rowling over his head; that the horror-moving and con-
tinuall motion of this infinite vaste Ocean, were established,
and continue for so many ages for his commoditie and
service?" In such connections, Montaigne does not seem to
notice that he is actually refuting the same Raymond de
Sebond whose apology he claims to be undertaking. The
latter had argued in favor of final causes, and had de-

fended the idea that the universe is made for man.[4] To chastise such human presumptuousness, he studies each animal in turn—the swallow, the dog, the falcon, the elephant, the ox, the magpie, the spider—each of whom has his own instincts, his own language, his own way of life, his own talents, his own reasoning power, his own capacity of loyalty, even his own (in the case of the elephant) kind of religious worship. Consequently, they are all our "fellow bretheren and compeers." This is the opposite pole from Descartes, who viewed animals as automatons, and whose ideas on that score influenced Pascal and Port-Royal. Pascal, the inventor of the adding machine, had no difficulty thinking of animals as pure automatons. In this connection, there is a much-quoted passage: "Touching strength, there is no Creature in the world open to so many wrongs and injuries as a man: He need not a Whale, an Elephant, nor a Crocodile, nor any such other wilde beast, of which one alone is of power to defeat a great number of men: seely lice are able to make Sulla give over his Dictatorship; The heart and life of a mighty and triumphant Emperor, is but the breakfast of a seely little worme."

Pascal imitated and rediscovered Montaigne's words when he attributed the death of Cromwell, the modern Sulla, to "one little grain of sand." He was also indebted to Montaigne when he said: "Man is but a reed, the most feeble thing in nature; but he is a thinking reed. The entire universe need not arm itself to crush him. A vapor, a drop of water suffices to kill him. But if the universe were to

---

[4] This is what Sebond says: "Man, cast boldly thy glance far around thee, and reflect whether among so many parts, so many diverse pieces of this great machine, there is any that does not serve thee. This sky, this earth, this air, this sea, and everything that is in them are continually laboring in your service. These diverse movements of the sun, this constant variety of the year's seasons, are concerned only with thy needs. Listen to the voice of the things created which speaks loudly to thee; the sky says: 'I am supplying thee with the light of day that thou mayest be awake; with the shadows of night that thou mayest sleep.'" Clearly, Montaigne turns his Apology into a palinode.

crush him, man would still be more noble than that which killed him, because he knows that he dies and the advantage which the universe has over him; the universe knows nothing of this."

It has been said that Montaigne's thought has been incorporated and completed in Pascal. When the latter employs coarse language calling attention to man's baser nature, we feel that he speaks in all sincerity, and that his purpose is to lift man above the mire in which he finds himself; when he speaks of the miseries of the human condition, we are sure that he really wants to put an end to them. Montaigne, for his part, seems always to be gloating. Nonetheless, there are several passages in the Apology where Montaigne rises to real heights of sincerity and eloquence: "This manyheaded, divers-armed, and furiously raging monster [an army] is man; wretched weake and miserable man: whom if you consider well, what is he, but a crawling, and ever-moving Ants-neast? *It nigrum campis agmen.* A gust of contrarie winds, the croking of a flight of Ravens, the false pase of a Horse, the casual flight of an Eagle, a dreame, a sodaine voyce, a false signe, a mornings mist, an evening fogge, are enough to overthrow, sufficient to overwhelme and able to pull him to the ground. Let the Sunne but shine hot on his face, he faints and swelters with heat: Cast but a little dust in his eyes, as do the Bees mentioned by our Poet, all our ensignes, all our legions, yea great Pompey himselfe in the forefront of them is overthrown and put to rout."

When Pascal treated this subject, he could at best equal, not surpass, such passages.

After this humbling comparison between mankind and the animals, Montaigne addresses himself to each of the philosophical schools in turn, beginning with Thales. Making the most of their disagreements, he puts himself to great trouble, summoning up every resource of learning, to pit the arguments of each school against those of the other schools, so as to confute them all. Having accomplished this, he is at pains not to be misunderstood, and he warns Queen Marguerite and his other readers that the tactic he has employed, rejecting reason so as to deprive his adversary of its aid, is a "desperate" tactic, and one to be resorted to but rarely.

At the very moment he utters his warning, however, and we might think he will not go on in this vein, he abandons the philosophers' changing systems and attacks all human faculties in so far as they might be supposed to be means of getting at the truth. Having doubted of reason, now he doubts of the senses, and we read: "It is not onely fevers, drinkes and great accidents, that overwhelme our judgement: The least thing in the world will turne it topsieturvie." This and the passage that follows directly anticipate Pascal's saying: "The mind of this sovereign judge of the world is not so independent that it is not liable to be disturbed by the first din about it."

As we trace the development of Montaigne's thought in this part of the *Essais,* we are continually reminded of Pascal. The latter's *Pensées* could be described as a profounder version or revision of the apology of Sebond. Pascal repeats many of Montaigne's sayings on the vanity, weakness, and contradictoriness of mankind. In doing so, however, he makes the sign of the Cross over Montaigne's words, and what is more striking than their obvious similarities (which Pascal would certainly have acknowledged in publication) is their difference in tone. Where Montaigne was simply employing a novel intellectual tactic, Pascal has a serious purpose. Where the former abandons himself to every passing current, the latter knows where he is going and works hard with the oars. The one is distracted, even entranced with his own shipwreck, while the other clings to the bit of driftwood with whose help he still can, by indomitable effort, reach the distant shore, his homeland in eternity. The feebleness, the wretchedness, the nullity of human life: this is their common refrain. But while Montaigne finds amusement in the spectacle, and sneers at man's kinship with the animals, Pascal counsels courage and prayer. To him, man, however wretched, is an exiled monarch, of the noblest lineage, and it behooves him to regain his rightful place.

We have said enough about this Apology, which is very
long, and which concludes with a pompous quotation from
Plutarch. God alone *IS*, we are suddenly told, and aside
from God, who is eternal, necessary, and immutable, all
things are transitory and in flux. Montaigne's intention in
quoting this religious passage from Plutarch is highly sus-
picious. If we scrutinize it carefully, taking into account
where Montaigne inserts it, and in the light of the chapter
as a whole, we must conclude that the ideas it expresses
are Spinozist and pantheistic. By elevating God above
created things, including mankind, Montaigne denies the
notion of a provident and personal God. We are now in
possession of a key that enables us to pass from conjecture
to certainty, to assess Montaigne's intentions both stated
and unstated.

His playfulness and casualness are purely superficial.
Montaigne, in the Apology as well as throughout the
Essais, is a kind of sorcerer, an evil genius who takes us by
the hand, and who, guiding us through the labyrinth of
opinion, tells us at every step, just when we think we know
where we stand, "All this is false or at least dubious; don't
give your trust so readily; don't pay too much attention to
this or that in the hope it can serve as a landmark. All
you can trust is the light I go by; nothing else matters.
This light is enough." And after he has led you far afield,
got you thoroughly disoriented and exhausted from being
led down so many garden paths—just then he blows out
the light and leaves you utterly in the dark. You may
hear a little snicker from your guide.

To what conclusion does Montaigne lead? Universal
doubt? But if so—if this is his final conclusion, what a vastly
significant conclusion it is! When we stand there, finally
having lost our way in utter darkness, it is Spinoza whom
we are to call upon. The world is to be grasped as a great,
gloomy, endless universe moving silent and unknown under
skies perpetually gray. A bit of life appears now and again
for a brief span, only to flicker out and die like an insect in
a swamp. Such is the supreme answer a number of men
have given, sometimes in the form of mathematical demon-

stration, sometimes in the form of Pyrrhonian argument. Montaigne's charm and good humor serve merely to screen off the spectacle of the abyss or, as he would put it, to prettify the tomb.

One of the great reasons for Montaigne's popularity—indeed, the one and only explanation for it—is his magical style. Style, in the exalted degree to which Montaigne possessed it, suffices to absolve any writer in the eyes of posterity. The disorderliness of his argument, his inconsistencies, licentiousness, and lapses of taste—all are covered over most attractively, plausibly, and pleasantly. We can never admire him enough. Style is the golden scepter which, in the last analysis, holds sway over the kingdom of this world.

Perhaps more than any other man, Montaigne had the gift of pleasing expression; his style is one continuous metaphor, sustained and renewed at every step. He always presents ideas in the form of images, varying them and yet keeping them clear and striking. Only the slightest interval separates one from another—the reader is given but a moment to prepare for the transition. Any one of his pages is a luxuriant, untamed field bursting with rustling plants and fragrant flowers, buzzing insects, and gurgling brooks. His is no integral conception, no ordered large-scale structure. He did not put himself to so much trouble. To him, inventiveness in detail and unflagging brilliance of expression sufficed. He understood this very well: "I have no other Sergeant of band to marshall my rapsodies, than fortune."

In Montaigne, idea and image are one and the same thing: *junctura callidus acri*. There is no real link between image and image; one merely succeeds the other: like a sure-footed Basque, he jumps from rock to rock. Here is one example, chosen almost at random, of how his metaphors escape the rhetoricians' rules. The passage refers to writers who insert long classical quotations in their works and thereby risk invidious comparisons:

"It was my fortune not long since to light upon such a place: I had languishingly traced after some French words, so naked and shallow, and so void either of sence or matter, that at last I found them to be nought but meere French words; and after a tedious and wearisome travell, I chanced to stumble upon an high, rich, and even to the clouds-raised piece, the descent whereof had it been somewhat more pleasant or easie, or the ascent reaching a little further, it had been excusable, and to be borne-withall; but it was such a steepie downe-fall, and by meere strength hewen out of the maine rocke, that by reading of the first six words, me thought I was carried into another world: whereby I perceived the bottome whence I came to be so low and deep, as I durst never more adventure to go through it; for if I did stuffe any one of my discourses with those rich spoiles, it would manifestly cause the sottishnesse of others to appeare."

He "languishingly traces" after "naked and shallow" words, as if "traveling," then drops this figure and a "to the clouds-raised" piece will become a "rich spoil" which he would not use to "stuff his discourses" with, and so on.

In respect of style, Montaigne is like Ovid and Ariosto. The rhapsodic felicity of the successive images, however varied, is an unbroken stream. The thread of his thought is never lost amid the continual metamorphoses.

Shakespeare and Molière, geniuses with the gift of creating unified wholes, could with ease endow characters with life. Montaigne's imagination, on the other hand, operates within individual sentences and in the articulations of the ideas. The result is just as alive, and, viewed closely, just as marvelously poetic. Every detail, every stage in the development of the thought, takes shape and wakes to life as though of itself, and is sufficient unto itself. The result is a whole new world most agreeable to dwell in. This very personal style—I shall not weary of repeating—is an important characteristic of Montaigne. Pascal, who takes little joy in his own style and keeps firm control of it, did not make enough of this characteristic of Montaigne's. Montaigne uses the expression "*Avoir le boutehors aisé,*" meaning to have what we would call "the gift of the gab"; actually, with him language is the *boute-en-train*—the life and soul of the party.

From Chapters Two and Three of Book Three of *Port-Royal* (published in Vol. II of that work, 1842).

These pages form the most brilliant, concentrated, and sustained of Sainte-Beuve's many writings on Montaigne. They are part of a long and fascinating series of chapters on Pascal, and follow a discussion of the *Entretien sur Epictète et sur Montaigne,* a dialogue between Pascal and Monsieur de Saci, one of the spiritual directors of Port-Royal, immediatcly following Pascal's arrival to take up temporary residence at the monastery. It is hoped that this selection will suggest some of the qualities of Sainte-Beuve's great *Port-Royal.*

Other notable digressions in *Port-Royal* are sections on Guez de Balzac (one of the original French academicians), on Corneille, on Molière, on Racine.

The English translations of portions of Montaigne's essays in the text are those of Florio (1603), slightly modified.

CORNEILLE (*Le Cid*)

PART I

1

WE SHALL begin our analysis by noting—it will save a great deal of repetition later—that for all his efforts to follow the classical rules of time, place, and unity of action, Corneille was unable to do so consistently. He did keep strictly within the twenty-four hours prescribed (so that the play which opens, presumably, at noon or one o'clock, ends the following day at about the same hour), nor did he violate the rule of unity of action. However, he could not observe the rule of unity of place with equal exactness. We stay within the same city (Seville), but we are taken now to Chimène's house, now to Don Diègue's, now to the king's palace, now to the street. The first act contains three changes of scene, the second three, the third two, the fourth two, and the fifth four. These were not represented by scene changes: the viewer lent himself to them readily enough. Moreover, Corneille called as little attention as possible to these changes, and his dialogue refrains from direct reference to them. His characters act and tell us their thoughts, but they never take advantage of small details such as would localize and specify the place of action. Thus Corneille's backgrounds do not supply added emphasis, never serve as support to his dramas. For this reason his characters have a more abstract quality than they have in the Spanish version of *Le Cid*, where changes of scene are strongly stressed. In real life a thousand particularities of speech continually remind us of the exact spot at which we are. The great disadvantage of the classical system was that it could not rely on such realistic effects.

The first scenes take place in the Count's house and are pure exposition. The marriage between Rodrigue and Chimène seems to have been agreed upon in advance, despite the rivalry of Don Sanche who serves merely as a foil. The Count gives his assent, speaking to Elvire, Chimène's lady in waiting, just as he is leaving for a meeting of the Council. At the meeting, the King is to appoint a tutor for the young Prince, and the Count is sure that the choice will fall upon himself. In the following scene, Chimène expresses the fear and deep sense of foreboding that becloud her happiness in her father's consent to her marriage.

The Infanta (for the third scene takes us to the Infanta's apartment) confides to her governess that she is in love with Rodrigue. She is personally to give him away in marriage to Chimène, and yet she is in love with him, though she is the King's daughter and Chimène's friend. But she is determined, even were she to die because of it, to sacrifice her passion to her sense of duty and honor, to the dignity of her position.

The character of the Infanta in Corneille's play is often looked upon as an insipid part that can be cut out in production. In the Spanish author's play it is much more of a part. Whereas in the French play the first scenes consist in pure exposition of offstage events, in the Spanish drama everything takes place on the stage. The curtain goes up on an arresting spectacle. Rodrigue has just completed the vigil of arms, and the King is about to knight him and give him a suit of royal armor—a gesture intended to honor and reward Rodrigue's father. Then Rodrigue is presented with his sword and admitted ceremoniously to the knightly ranks in front of the altar of St. James, in the presence of the Queen and before the eyes of the Infanta and Chimène, both of whom fall in love with him at the same moment. By the King's order the Infanta affixes Rodrigue's spurs—spurs which cut into Chimène's heart as she watches. The Infanta, meanwhile, cannot help thinking that Rodrigue is really a very handsome man. We witness the visible birth of their love, and the future rivalry of these two young women will be associated in our minds during the rest of the play with this very vivid opening scene. The French theater in Corneille's day was less picturesque: moral analysis took precedence over action. Corneille everywhere rationalized or intellectualized the varied, amusing, loosely constructed but colorful Spanish play. He depicted only the conflict of feelings.

Napoleon, a great critic when he found time to be one, attended a performance of *Le Cid* under the Consulate. Noticing that the part of the Infanta had been cut, he asked why this was done. Told that the part was judged pointless and ridiculous, he said: "Not at all, the part is very well conceived. Corneille wanted to give us the highest idea of his hero's merit, and it is a great honor for the Cid to be loved both by the King's daughter and by Chimène. Nothing elevates this young man more than the circumstance that these two women are rivals for his heart."

The observation is sound, and yet it is not surprising that the Infanta seems dispensable in performances of Corneille's version. In the play as he conceived it, everything tends to move rapidly, and its effectiveness depends upon our not being distracted from the essential.

In the Spanish drama, the Infanta, who in the very first scene presented Rodrigue with the spurs of knighthood, receives many evidences of his respect and admiration. She would prefer a little less respect, however, and a little more tenderness. As a character, she has a well-defined life of her own, experiencing striking and interesting changes of fortune. It is she who rescues Rodrigue and protects him when he is pursued after the Count's death. She is filled with new hope when, standing on the balcony of her country house, she recognizes him as he leaves at the head of his 500 friends to fight the Moors. He salutes her smartly as he rides past. He shows himself chivalrous and more than courteous on this occasion, and sets out only after she has given him her blessings and good wishes. In the Spanish play, the part of the Infanta—who toward the end loses her mother, who is disliked by her brother, and who wishes she had a tiny kingdom all her own—has a solidity completely lacking in Corneille's analytic adaptation. It is thus understandable that the French stage, which seeks to avoid long developments at all costs, has occasionally—perhaps wrongly—succumbed to the temptation of cutting out the part altogether.

Because she is not given sufficient room to move in the French play, the Infanta is not a living, flesh-and-blood character, if I may say so. She is merely a vehicle for two or three feelings expressed in dialogue—the feeling of pure love in conflict with the feeling of duty or social dignity.

This is, moreover, the way Corneille always worked, and through him it has become the way of French tragedy in general. Everything visible or otherwise sensuously powerful—whatever speaks distinctly to the eyes and vividly or even oddly portrays the physical world as it is—he absorbs within himself and transforms into abstraction, as it were, distilling it into pure feeling expressed through rational, analytical dialogue. He transposes the visual plane to the plane of the intellect, an intellect that is open and clear, never cloudy or misty, and that resembles the somewhat austere mind of Descartes, who was *Le Cid's* great contemporary.

Le Cid is less abstract than Corneille's subsequent plays. If we care more for the brilliant Rodrigue than for Corneille's other heroes, it is because there is more life in him, more fire and flash.

The scene between the Count and Don Diègue, the insult scene, takes place in the street or in some antechamber or vestibule, after the two men have left the Council chamber where Don Diègue has been victorious over the Count. In the Spanish drama, this scene takes place in the palace and in the king's presence: Guillén de Castro here merely followed the old romances. In France, the breach of etiquette would have seemed too great, no French king ever witnessed anything like it. Moreover, in the French conception of dramatic effect, the verbal duel of the dialogue is more emphasized; the quarrel is outlined more clearly;

it works up to extreme insult by slow degrees. The Count
bursts out at the opening, but at first it is only an outburst
of resentment and boasting:

> Enfin vous l'emportez, et la faveur du roi
> Vous élève en un rang qui n'était dû qu'à moi . . .

Enfin vous l'emportez! . . . The opening is magnificent.
All the opening lines in the set speeches of *Le Cid* are effective: *Rodrigue, as-tu du coeur?* . . . *A moi, comte,
deux mots!* . . . *Sire, Sire, justice!* . . . What follows does
not always come up to the same level, but the impetus, the
initial impulse is there. *Le Cid* is entirely made up of such
spontaneous surges of feeling; the whole play pulsates with
a generous lyricism. There is no time to think; we are
swept off our feet. Malherbe has such fiery opening lines
in his odes, sonnets, and songs: Corneille has them in
drama.

The Count and Don Diègue are at first concerned only
with praising themselves, and Don Diègue even begins
quite gently, asking the Count to accept his son as his son-
in-law. But both men's pride has been aroused and grows
more and more unrestrained. One says in every possible
variation, "I am," and the other, "I have been." In the
Count's proud enumeration of his many claims, one line
stands out:

> Grenade et l'Aragon tremblent quand ce fer brille!

Corneille's later plays, although they abound in lines con-
veying characters' thoughts, have all too few of such im-
aged lines, which are one of the charms of *Le Cid*. Finally,
by dint of boasting, the two rivals become heated and the
irreparable happens. Slapped in the face, Don Diègue
draws his sword, but the Count knocks it out of his hand,
and to cap the insult, gives it back to him.

Left alone, Don Diègue gives vent to his despair,
deplores the humiliation which is in such contrast with his
past fame, and repudiates his own sword now useless to
him. His apostrophe to the sword is well-known:

Et toi, de mes exploits glorieux instrument,
Mais d'un corps tout de glace inutile ornement,
Fer jadis tant à craindre . . .

In the Spanish play, Don Diego returns to his own
house, where his sons notice his grief without knowing its
cause. Only after he has bid them leave him alone, does he
test his hand with his old sword. In the scene with the
Count he wore no sword, but carried a stick and broke it in
anger. It is at home, in the room where his weapons hang,
that he takes down one of the mighty swords which remind him of his former exploits. He tries to hold it and
fence with it, but the heavy sword drags him down with
every lunge and parry. It must be granted that the scene is
more natural and more evocative visually; Corneille gives
us the *idea* of the thing rather than the thing itself.

In the Spanish original the exhausted Don Diego immediately embarks on another course of action. He sum-
mons his three sons to him, one after another, presses their
hands (just as in the old romances), and when the first
two groan with pain like women, he orders them to leave.
"Oh, shame!" he says to his second son, "do you mistake
my weak hands for the claws of a lion? And even if they
were strong, should you utter such unworthy complaints?
Out with you, disgrace to my blood!" But when Rodrigue's
turn comes, Don Diego not only squeezes his hands, but
also bites one of his fingers. Rodrigue reddens and expresses
his pain with threats and anger. Don Diego calls him his
own "soul's son" and asks him to avenge him. At the same
time he thinks it his duty to explain to him, by way of an
apology, why he had addressed himself to his younger
brothers first: "The reason I did not summon you before
them, is that I love you best. I had rather the others exposed themselves to danger, so that I might keep in you
the illustrious future of my race." A bit of fatherly affection
survives along with wounded pride.

Corneille could not so much as refer to any such "testing"
of the sons. It is more a practical demonstration than a
true moral testing, and French audiences, being unfamiliar

with the legend of the Cid, would have found it excessive. Therefore he begins *in medias res*, in the French manner. There is but one son; Rodrigue is Don Diègue's only son. The father opens the scene with the crucial question: *Rodrigue, as-tu du coeur?* He uses the formula of chivalry, omitting the purely physical action of the original, rather too reminiscent of medieval crudities.

For many centuries the Cid had been an epic figure in Spain, and so Guillén de Castro, the dramatic poet, could draw freely upon the elements of a familiar legend. The situation was very different in France; the legend of the Cid was completely unknown until Corneille. The poet and father of the French theater had the task of revealing him to the French public, and he had to arouse admiration for him from the outset by supplying a clear unambiguous portrait as speedily as possible.

However, the scene in which Don Diègue entrusts Rodrigue with his sword and swears him to revenge is as vigorous and even as crude in tone as French manners of Corneille's day would allow:

> Ce n'est que dans le sang qu'on lave un tel affront:
> Meurs ou tue . . .

The harshness of the words is elegant enough—only so could they be bearable to the French ear. The name of the offender, the redoubtable father of Chimène, is launched like an arrow at the end, and Don Diègue rushes out crying, *Va, cours, vole, et nous venge!* These words call for no reply: we are swept off our feet.

Rodrigue, left alone on the stage, expresses his inner struggle in the "Stanzas" (translated or imitated from the Spanish), which are always pleasing, in spite of a liberal use of conceits:

> Percé jusqu'au fond du coeur
> D'une atteinte imprévue aussi bien que mortelle . . .

Although the words are subtle and flowing, they are inadequate. Music alone could render the heart-rending con-

flict in Rodrigue's breast. If only because the name of
Chimène is mentioned at the end of each strophe, the
"Stanzas" give the over-all fundamental tone of feeling.
While the play of antitheses makes us smile, we cannot
help being moved when we read the lines aloud. One day,
the critic Vinet was reading *Le Cid* to his family. When he
came to the "Stanzas," he walked out of the parlor and
went up to his room. As he did not come back, someone
went in search of him and found him reciting the melodious lines aloud, tears streaming down his face. Like
Joseph, he had slipped away to weep—the mark of a beautiful soul that has stayed young!

2

The first scene of Act II takes place between the Count
and Don Arias, an emissary from the King ordering him to
present his humble apologies to Don Diègue. Where the
scene occurs is not clear—in the vicinity of the royal palace,
perhaps. The Count admits he was wrong, but refuses to
make amends:

> Je l'avoue entre nous, quand je lui fis l'affront,
> J'eus le sang un peu chaud et le bras un peu prompt.
> Mais puisque c'en est fait, le coup est sans remède.

Corneille excels in such semitragic, yet highly informal
lines, which we miss a great deal in later writers. In the
course of the dialogue, the Count persists stubbornly in his
refusal, imprudently confident in his high rank and the
eminence of his past services. Don Arias speaks to him
firmly and threatens him in the name of the all-powerful
King, who expects to be obeyed. Their scene fits in well
with the subject and at the same time with the feelings
and dispositions of the French audience, many of whom
found in it what they had observed or experienced themselves. When the Count, sure of his importance, exclaims:

> Un jour seul ne perd pas un homme tel que moi,

the spectators were reminded of Montmorency, of Les-
diguières, and of Rohan—that was how the last great independent lords of France had spoken only a few years
earlier. The echo of feudal pride and arrogance, which
Richelieu had barely managed to outlaw, must have been
thrilling in the theater.

The next scene, in which Rodrigue challenges the
Count, was no less effective to Corneille's contemporaries.
The question of the duel had aroused great interest under
Richelieu, and it was still a burning topic. Ten years earlier
Bouteville and Des Chapelles had both paid with their
heads for similarly refusing to follow the king's orders.
Every courtier and nobleman took sides in the quarrel rep-
resented on the stage. I imagine that during these two
scenes a shudder ran through the theater, and many of the
young nobles must have exchanged meaningful glances.
Being timely, these scenes redoubled interest in the play.
At this moment more than one sword must have felt restless in its scabbard.

A moi, comte, deux mots! . . . Corneille, as I noted
above, always leads off with his most striking line: he introduces a situation at its most dramatic pitch. In the
Spanish play, the scene is longer and more diffuse. Rodrigue, under his father's eyes in the presence of the Infanta, Chimène, and other witnesses, clearly has a hard
time making up his mind. He challenges the Count in
front of all these people—Don Diego prodding his son on
with looks and words. The boy's hand is practically forced,
and the duel begins right away, in front of the palace, and
is finished only a few steps away. This is more natural,
but then, the proprieties are not observed, not even the
proprieties governing dueling. In Corneille's version, we
must assume that Rodrigue beckons to the Count and gets
him somewhat apart from the group as it passes by. Rodrigue's words, *parlons bas, écoute,* imply clearly enough
that the men of the Count's retinue might hear them.

The dialogue is impetuous, progressing by leaps and
bounds. It is a sequence of ripostes, very like fencing: the
words cross and clash as will the swords just a bit later.

The Count says that Rodrigue deserves to be his son-in-law, seeing that he is giving up the title so soon, and pities his youth. How old can Rodrigue be? In the very earliest chronicles, he is not yet thirteen. In the tragedy, he is hardly more than sixteen or seventeen. He is still a mere stripling, a slender lad.

This scene presents us with the perfect example of "split" lines of verse, essential to all tragedy, but especially characteristic of Corneille's:

> Es-tu las de vivre?
>   —As-tu peur de mourir?

This is the very model of the form.

The next scene is laid in the Infanta's apartment. She is comforting Chimène. Every time Corneille introduces the Infanta, his play turns dull and cold. In this scene, however, Chimène sustains the dialogue; she says beautiful things, yet which are consistent with her passion. The princess tries to give her reasons for hope, but Chimène does not for a moment believe in the possibility of a reconciliation between her father and Rodrigue. She too is an adherent of the cult of honor:

> Les accommodements ne font rien en ce point:
> Les affronts à l'honneur ne se réparent point . . .

Chimène is truly feminine in her love for men who fight fiercely and kill one another, who are more generous than wise, who are heroes rather than philosophers. She expects Rodrigue not to back down, even if this means hurting her. She will be furious at him for killing her father—and will not hide her fury—but in secret she is proud of Rodrigue and, if I may say so, she is grateful to him. The Spanish author knew this well when he made the Infanta say, "Chimène and Rodrigue used to love each other, but since the death of the Count they adore each other."

In the following scenes, in the French version, there is decidedly too much of the Infanta. The moment Chimène leaves, the good princess begins to hope again: this is really too soon. She tells her governess that if Rodrigue should by chance be victorious over the Count (for a page has just informed her that a duel is probably being fought), she will be able to marry him honorably and to raise him to her own exalted status. She sees him on the throne, master of the lands of Spain, conqueror of the Moors, of Africa, etc. Such is the Infanta's daydream; but her fantasies are lost on us and cannot possibly hold our interest.

We are next in the throne room, presumably. The King, surrounded by his gentlemen in waiting, is perplexed. He has been told that the Count disobeyed his order to apologize to Don Diègue, and sends one of his courtiers to bring him in—a little too late. Don Sanche, a young nobleman, tries to justify Chimène's father, for he himself is in love with Chimène. Poor Don Sanche and the Infanta make a perfect pair: he too keeps trying to edge his way into the dramatic action throughout the play. He speaks in favor of the duel, the settling of wrongs by recourse to arms as the sole means worthy of a warrior. In this he expresses the opinion of the majority of French noblemen who attended the first performances of *Le Cid*. The King scolds him, refutes him, and advances reasons of state against such a disastrous prejudice:

> Vous parlez en soldat, je dois agir en roi.

Then, without transition, the good King proceeds to discuss the danger which the Moors currently present to his kingdom. There is fear of a surprise attack—their ships have been seen at the mouth of the river . . . All this, one feels, is to prepare us for Rodrigue's future exploit, which is to take place the same night. But we are left wondering why the King, who has been forewarned, takes no preventive measures himself. He puts off everything till the next day: the monarch is decidedly easygoing and slightly ridiculous. Corneille was unaware—and always remained unaware—of the ridiculous sides of certain of his noble characters.

Now several events occur in rapid succession. The death of the Count is announced, and at the same moment Chimène enters crying, *Sire, Sire, justice!* This is a very ef-

fective scene, apart from some details in poor taste, all of
which have long since been sufficiently regretted: at this
distance of time, they seem merely piquant touches of local
color. Don Diègue rushes in directly after Chimène and
throws himself down at one of the King's knees, while she
clutches the other. We are shown two solemn feelings at
odds with each other: the daughter who wants to avenge
her father, and the father who has been avenged by his
son.

> Il a tué mon père.
>   —Il a vengé le sien.

The two feelings touch off sparks and clash again and
again: one flash of lightning echoes the other.

The King is torn between two opposite courses, and he
would seem a little comical if we had the time to notice
him. In the Spanish theater, kings are peaceful, careful,
lovers of justice, rather resembling Louis XII at the end of
his reign.

Chimène pleads eloquently, but she speaks for appearance's sake: we feel that she is declaiming, and there is no
harm in the fact that we feel it.

Don Diègue's reply is magnificent, both in respect of
tone and feeling; it is superb in its bitterness. Old and
useless, but avenged and satisfied, he offers himself as
victim to appease the lust for revenge that speaks through
Chimène's mouth. If his son is allowed to live so as to
perpetuate the honor of his name and to serve his king
and country, Don Diègue will die content. But how proud
and virile are the words he uses to say this! His language is
Corneille's at its greatest. What is so remarkable about *Le
Cid* is that the tide of feeling keeps steadily rising. In
vain does common sense object, in vain does good taste
protest here and there. We are swept up entire, not masters
of our own emotions when we read *Le Cid*. Even when
the play is poorly performed, the character of Don Diègue
is likely to enchant the audience. At one performance of
the play after the death of Rachel, the only actor ap-

plauded was the one who played the part of Don Diègue (Maubant); he had made the strongest impression.

In the Spanish version, Diego relates (in the corresponding scene) that seeing his enemy lifeless on the ground, he had dipped his hand in the wound and literally bathed his cheeks with the other's blood. He appears on the stage with blood on his face, a barbaric touch.

We must realize, however, that every nation endows its theater with just that degree of harshness or sensitivity which reflects its characteristic temperament, and which can be seen in its favorite games. The English would have to be a people fond of boxing in order to accept all of Shakespeare; Spain has its bullfights; France, in the years before *Le Cid*, had only its duels in the Place Royale.

The act concludes with the King deciding that the matter must be deliberated upon at greater length. In the meantime, Don Sanche will escort Chimène back to her house (a singular choice for the task), Don Diègue stays in the palace, a prisoner on his own recognizance. Orders are given to find Rodrigue.

3

They look everywhere for Rodrigue, but he is in the one house where no one would think to look: at the home of the man he has just killed, in Chimène's apartment. We are coming to a beautiful scene, Rodrigue's meeting with the woman he loves, who is at once very angry and very tender. The Cid will twice call on Chimène. This first meeting is borrowed from the Spanish author, but the second meeting in Act V is entirely Corneille's. These were the most criticized scenes of the play when it was still new, and aroused the strongest emotions. Spectators took such a lively interest in the situation that almost all of them wanted the meetings to take place; they were looked forward to either as a peril for the two lovers to overcome, or as a triumph for their love. In his *Examen du Cid*, Corneille writes: "I noticed at the first performances that when the unfortunate lover appeared before her, a kind of thrill ran through the audience, signaling enormous interest and a renewal of attention. What would they have to say to each other in such a pitiful situation?"

When Rodrigue arrives and enters Chimène's apartment, she has not yet come back from the palace. He finds only Elvire, the lady in waiting, who is frightened to see him here and who the moment she sees her mistress coming, forces him to hide.

Don Sanche accompanies Chimène. He attempts to press his suit, offering her his services and sword against Rodrigue:

> Souffrez qu'un cavalier vous venge par les armes.

This is a surer and quicker way than the king's justice. He hopes to earn a claim to her gratitude. She neither accepts nor refuses the offer, and dismisses him politely.

Alone with Elvire—or believing herself alone—Chimène opens her heart and gives vent to her sorrow:

> La moitié de ma vie a mis l'autre au tombeau!

We are approaching the beautiful pathetic scene, though we are not spared the apparently indispensable "points" and bad taste. There is a deep moral conflict going on in Chimène's heart, a duel unlike the other one, which she describes to us:

> Rodrigue dans mon coeur attaque encor mon père,
> Il l'attaque, il le presse, il cède, il se défend . . .

Elvire acts as would any good maid or attendant: she urges the most common, the easiest course. When this is rejected, she asks, *Après tout, que pensez-vous donc faire?* And Chimène exclaims:

> Le poursuivre, le perdre et mourir après lui!

All of the French *Cid's* unity and perfection are in this line.

It is at this point that Rodrigue suddenly emerges from the place where he has been listening, and gives himself up to her anger. From the first words, he cannot keep the *vous* and uses the more familiar form of address, both heroic and affectionate, which she accepts at once:

> Hélas!—Ecoute-Moi.—Je me meurs.—Un moment.
> —Va, laisse-moi mourir . . .

It is by suddenly using this familiar form of address and by no more complex means, that Rodrigue indicates he has heard her pouring out her heart to Elvire. He takes her up at the point she has already reached and does not rush her. He offers her his sword that she may strike him down. We note the hint of a play on words in the clash of thoughts evoked by the sword and by the blood with which it is stained, a stain which only another "stain" can obliterate. But our heart is not in it. We are swept off our feet by the tide of feeling that keeps surging on and on to the final curtain. After a number of refined lines, there comes suddenly one of perfect simplicity:

> Tu sais comme un soufflet touche un homme de coeur!

By explaining his conduct and his motives for it, in which Chimène and his desire to be respected by her played a great part, Rodrigue chooses the surest means of making her listen to him. Listening to him, seeing that she was so much in his mind even while he was committing his crime, she is radiant, though her fury does not abate.

She accepts the debate: this is already a favor. When he has finished, she endeavors in a long speech to convince him that he is wrong:

> Je ne t'accuse point, je pleurs mes malheurs . . .
> Je me dois, par ta mort, montrer digne de toi . . .

He accepts his condemnation, falls on his knees, and offers her his head. Then it is her turn to refuse:

> Si tu m'offres ta tête, est-ce à moi de la prendre?
> Je la dois attaquer, mais tu dois la défendre.

Involuntarily, she is betraying a very faint hope, she is pointing to a way out of her dilemma. Chimène's anger is a product of reflection; her natural impulse is to affection. Finally we come to the crucial word, which is wrested from her, and which she was burning to utter: *Va, je ne te hais point!* And when, a moment later, she says, "You must go," we feel that she means, "Stay." He stays; the two come close to each other and begin to dream as did Romeo and Juliet:

Que de maux et de pleurs nous coûteront nos pères!

And this delightful evocation of the past:

Rodrigue, qui l'eût cru?
                                —Chimène, qui l'eût dit?

This is tender affection. They hold hands. They are together again. They have forgotten. She is obliged to keep saying, "You must go," and to pretend to be brusque, for otherwise she could never be parted from him again.

This is a beautiful scene, which is surpassed only by a second one of the same kind. It is not uniformly sustained throughout, but what a beautiful subject and what beautiful music, even though the words fail occasionally! Moreover, Corneille is here at his best. He will never be better in his subsequent plays; he cannot learn anything, he cannot develop, unlike Racine who did learn and develop and achieved complete perfection. Racine's talent is one that allows him to accomplish all he sets out to accomplish —and besides, he had leisure and the habit of reflection. Corneille, on the other hand, owed everything to inspiration. What he could not do right off, he could not learn to do later. Racine's gift was that of art: he always gives us pure pleasure, even in his moments of weakness. Corneille's is the gift of spontaneous sublimity of thought and feeling—a firm grasp of his theme and of his language— but he also has lapses. In this scene, how strongly we are aware that the lovers are longing to put away all thought of the dead father! Chimène's love for Rodrigue is the greater not *despite* the fact that he killed her father but *because* he did. And he, feeling that what he did was his duty, is aware of her secret approval, and so he desires all the more to be forgiven, still dares to hope. Shakespeare would never have invented such a situation; it is too unnatural; there are too many barriers to be overcome, too many subtle contradictions. But *Le Cid* is beautiful, of a beauty that takes chivalry and the medieval cult of honor for granted. And there is also the eternal human element —love. These two young and generous beings are in love— that is the whole point of their maneuvering—and their love steadily increases and becomes more intense.

Part II

1

Act III is not finished. After killing the Count, Rodrigue's first thought was to rush to Chimène, but he still has to see his father. Don Diègue, for his part, after throwing himself at the King's feet to ward off Chimène's demand for revenge and to implore his son's pardon, now is searching everywhere for his son. Night has fallen; worried about Rodrigue, Don Diègue wanders through the dark streets; by a lucky coincidence he runs into Rodrigue. In the Spanish play the meeting is handled better: the father has made an appointment with his son at an isolated spot, which is very natural under the circumstances. The father gets there first and waits anxiously, listening intently to the distant galloping of a horse. . . . His monologue is most effective. But Corneille would never have ventured to introduce the sound of a galloping horse, for this would have made the change of scene to a remote spot too clear. Therefore he chose to make the father search the streets for his son, well-nigh groping for him blindly. The beauty of the language makes us opportunely forget the slightly unusual, even comical side of the old man's predicament:

Tout cassé que je suis, je cours toute la ville . . .

The moment Don Diègue and Rodrigue meet, Corneille

finds himself again and translates his model admirably,
which in this passage is especially fine:

> Touche ces cheveux blancs à qui tu rends l'honneur;
> Viens baiser cette joue, et reconnais la place
> Où fut jadis l'affront que ton courage efface.

"Splendid, splendid!" youthful admirers of our stage exclaim, and rightly so. Yes, it is splendid; but it is only fair
to add that these lines are no more than a fine translation
of Guillén de Castro, just as are so many passages and
felicitous expressions, which have been circulating and
resounding in the French language for two centuries.
France possesses the singular ability and privilege of being able to mint freshly even in other people's coinage.

Rodrigue, the moment he sees his father, embarks on a
lament for his love, describing the loss of his happiness.
Don Diègue gives him heart and steers him around again
until he is in his more customary generous mood. This is
no time to complain or die of love; new dangers lie in wait.
Now the old man tells of the Moors who must be driven
back. The sudden shift of subject is beautifully developed
—here entirely Corneillian and original:

> Il n'est pas temps encor de chercher le trépas;
> Ton prince et ton pays ont besoin de ton bras.
> La flotte qu'on craignait, dans le grand fleuve entrée,
> Vient surprendre la ville et piller la contrée.
> Les Maures vont descendre, et le flux et la nuit
> Dans une heure, à nos murs les amènent sans bruit.
> La Cour est en désordre, et le peuple en alarmes. . . .

At this point Corneille was obliged to depart radically
from the Spanish play. So to depart could scarcely shock a
public ignorant of the history of Spain, but Corneille's
changes clearly illustrate the strange constraints to which
he was subjected and the embarrassing rules he had to
observe. At the same time, his departures illustrate the
prodigious and ingenious resources of his talent—I insist on
the word "ingenious." In the Spanish drama, Don Diego
speaks of a raid on the Moors, who are pulling back to the

border with their prisoners and with rich booty. There is
an opportunity to distinguish oneself by cutting off their
retreat; Rodrigue should as quickly as possible put himself at the head of 500 friends and kinsmen, who have
already been gathered or summoned to this end. The expedition, however prompt, takes several days. Corneille,
on the other hand, bound by the iron rules of the French
stage, had to strain his ingenuity to get around the difficulty, and to take certain liberties at the same time. He
imagined a river near its mouth, because he needed a
tide to help preserve the twenty-four-hour rule. Once he
had imagined the river, he went on to assume that the
King of Castile ruled at Seville on the Guadalquivir two
hundred years before that city had been reconquered from
the Moors. He upset the topography of the Spanish play
by mentally transporting himself to the time of the Norman pirate invasions around the mouth of the Seine. In the
Spanish play it is an expedition overland, and we witness
Rodrigue's brilliant departure, and his courteous, chivalric
conversation with the Infanta who watches him from the
balcony of her summer palace. There are many pretty
scenes and pretty motifs. There is even one somewhat
grotesque character, a shepherd who on catching sight of
the Moors ravaging the plain flees to the mountains, to the
highest rock, and who, after the battle is over, having witnessed Rodrigue's victory and seen how he cleaved the
infidels with broad sweeps of his sword, exclaims: "For-
sooth! 'Tis a pleasure to see them like this from the outside. Spectacles of this sort should be seen from high up!"
Sancho Panza was to speak like this shepherd.

We must not expect such naïve and varied scenes of
Corneille. He was a prisoner of the heroic style. The entire action had to take place during a single night, because of the imperious unity of time. His difficulties became still more apparent in the next act, Act IV. It opens
in the morning; we are at Chimène's house. She is being
told about the victory Rodrigue had won that night over
the Moors. Their ships had scarcely put in before they
were routed and put to flight:

Leur abord fut bien prompt, leur fuite encore plus
   prompte,
Trois heures de combat laissent à nos guerriers
Une victoire entière et deux rois prisonniers.

A three-hour battle . . . The clock is never lost sight of.
The hours have to be measured carefully, lest the total
exceed twenty-four. "I am afraid that no matter how hard
they tried," an acquaintance of mine said facetiously, "it
must all have taken an extra hour, at least." The most
serious moral inconvenience, which leaps to the eye, is
that Chimène is forced to undergo implausible changes of
feeling over a very short period. In quick succession she
ceases to be angry, becomes angry again, and then ceases
to be angry again, all without pausing for breath.

I shall speak my mind on this score, putting myself in
the spirit of the old French system, which was inaugurated
by Corneille, and which held sway over the French theater
down to Voltaire and his disciples. Under the conditions
of that day, it was not a bad thing in a French tragedy
that the characters should not have time to catch their
breath. When you have the audience in the palm of your
hand, it is safer to get things over with then and there. It
is wise not to give it time to reflect and consider. The
Frenchman is very susceptible to being carried away and
at the same time very prone to be critical. While the curtain is up, don't give the spirit of criticism time to be
aroused; don't let the spectators have long intermissions,
cooling off their enthusiasm in the theater lobby. It is
preferable to dispense with intermissions, and to keep your
audience winded by a breathless succession of scenes. I
am speaking of the old French public, of course, whose
habits were such that it deemed two hours quite long
enough for a serious play.

Chimène learns of Rodrigue's victory, and though she is
happy knowing him to have won the battle, she reminds
herself that her filial piety obliges her to be angry again,
and so she sets out at once to ask the King again for his
head. There are no circumstances under which this would

be a sensible thing to do, nor a plausible one. She should have waited at least until the next day. The Infanta calls on Chimène: her purpose is to explore the ground, to see whether there is anything to be done. She urges Chimène to desist from her undertaking and says some very sensible things to her: what was right yesterday is no longer right today, Rodrigue has now become indispensable to the state. She makes a suggestion which, if followed, would turn to her advantage: "Deprive him of your love," she says to Chimène, "but grant him his life." The good Infanta would not mind fishing for the Cid in these troubled waters and catching him for herself. A bit of comedy is now and then added to the play, were it only to justify its designation as a tragicomedy.

The King's palace rings with joy at Rodrigue's victory. The King thanks and congratulates him; he confers upon him the title of Cid by which the two Moorish kings had addressed him. We have the magnificent description of the nocturnal expedition and the battle:

Nous partîmes cinq cents, mais, par un prompt renfort,
Nous nous vîmes trois mille en arrivant au port . . .

This marvelous epic narrative, which is entirely Corneille's, makes up abundantly for all its improbabilities. We like this narrative far more than Théramène's [in the last act of Racine's *Phèdre*]: it is less rhetorical, indeed, it is not rhetorical at all, and it contains more genuine beauties. It is the noblest of all battle descriptions, the most chivalrous of all war stories. Condé could scarcely have described Rocroi differently. A strong yet coolheaded imagination takes us to the battle and makes us see it with our own eyes. Only the essential details are given:

Cette obscure clarté qui tombe des étoiles,
Enfin, avec le flux, nous fit voir trente voiles;
L'onde s'enflait dessous, et d'un commun effort
Les Maures et la mer entrèrent dans le port.
On les laisse passer, tout leur paraît tranquille:
Point de soldats au port, point aux murs de la ville.

Notre profond silence abusant leurs espirits,
Ils n'osent pas douter de nous avoir surpris:
Ils abordent sans peur, ils ancrent, ils descendent
Et courent se livrer aux mains qui les attendent.
Nous nous levons alors, et tous en même temps
Poussons jusques au ciel mille cris éclatants. . . .

Nous nous levons alors . . . We may say of the movement
of these verses, their splendid impetuosity, what Cicero
said of similar war narratives in Thucydides: *Canit bel-
licum.* This is the very sound of the bugle. We also recall
the line of the poet:

Aere ciere viros martemque accendere canta.

Whatever you may dream up, combine, or imagine,
style alone makes it live. As a very vigorous Spanish phrase
has it, it is when you are in "the straits of style" that the
real difficulty begins. Now, it is precisely in these straits
that Corneille is triumphant: he emerges victorious, colors
flying, so to speak.

Chimène, who arrives at the end of the narrative to ask
for justice, leaves us no time for reflection. The good-
natured King, when she is announced, makes a face and
an impatient gesture: it is obvious that he is a little fed up
with Chimène's importunings. Surely, she is in such a hurry
to return to the charge only in order to catch a glimpse of
Rodrigue again. The good King suspects this—he has been
informed of their love—and at once imagines a dodge
which seems just a bit too clever for him. He puts Rodrigue in another room, and everyone is to pretend that he
was mortally wounded in the course of his victory and has
expired. In the Spanish play, it is Don Arias who suggests
the idea of thus testing Chimène's real feelings, and a
servant is brought in to announce the death of Rodrigue.
There is an excellent natural touch when old Don Diego,
hearing this false report, says to himself in an aside: "This
report, though I know it is false, brings tears to my eyes."

Suddenly given the news of Rodrigue's death, Chimène
betrays herself: she turns pale and is about to faint. The

good King hastily undeceives her to revive her. But he
spoke too soon. Chimène takes it all back in a single line:

> Sire, on pâme de joie ainsi que de tristesse.

This is taken from the Spanish. But in the original drama
the situation is handled more effectively. Above all, the
intervals between her scenes are longer, so that Chimène's
conduct and contradictory emotions are more plausible.
Several months had passed since her first appeal to the
King; to motivate her second intervention, she complains
that in the interval Rodrigue, less courteous than is proper,
has not ceased to provoke her, to insult her. And she says
it in a very picturesque way, which recalls the old romances:

"I see the man who killed my father pass by every day,
and there is no way of stopping him, his sword at his side,
dressed in rich clothes, a falcon on his fist, mounted on his
fine horse. Under the pretext of hunting near the country
house where I have retired, he comes and goes, watches
and listens, as much indiscreet as bold, and to spite me lets
his arrows fly at my dovecote; these arrows are aimed at
my heart: the blood of my young doves has reddened my
apron. . . ."

These are remnants of old folksongs, which have been
incorporated in the drama. No Spanish author would have
dared omit them. But what would Mme. de Rambouillet
and her friends have said, had Corneille so much as alluded to such things? By now, all Frenchmen were more
or less won over to the convictions of the Hôtel de Rambouillet in such matters. They looked for neither realism
nor colorfulness in tragedy. They were more or less of the
school of Descartes: "I think, therefore I am; I think, therefore I feel." The whole of drama is confined to and takes
place in the "inner substance . . . whose entire essence or
nature consists in thought, and which needs no place in
order to exist and depends on no material thing." Those
are Descartes' words, and Corneille followed them out
pretty much to the letter.

Denied the justice she seeks in the form of Rodrigue's

punishment, Chimène does not insist too much and falls
back upon asking for a duel, the ordeal by arms:

A tous vos cavaliers je demande sa tête;
Oui, qu'un d'eux me l'apporte et je suis sa conquête . . .
J'épouse le vainqueur . . .

All this is play-acting: in her heart she knows very well
that she will never marry anyone else, and that Rodrigue
will prove the winner in any duel. The King at first resists
the idea of a duel, again for reasons of state, and also because he no longer looks upon Rodrigue as guilty of anything since his latest exploit:

Les Maures, en fuyant, ont emporté son crime.

This admirable line says everything, makes up for much
of the King's previous complacency. After having spoken
for so long like a fatherly judge, he suddenly speaks like a
king.

The old Don Diègue, however, is for the duel—as noblemen had so often been in similar circumstances—and he
asks that Rodrigue should be treated without any special
consideration:

Sire, ôtez ces faveurs qui terniraient sa gloire . . .
Le comte eut de l'audace, il l'en a su punir:
Il l'a fait en brave homme et le doit soutenir.

Every time Don Diègue speaks, he utters Corneille's
simplest, noblest language. In this youthful play, the old
man comes off best.

The King consents to the duel, on condition that after it
Chimène make no new demands. But who will be Chimène's champion, the bold man who dares meet the proud,
invincible warrior? Don Sanche comes forward:

Faites ouvrir le camp; vous voyez l'assaillant.
Je suis ce téméraire ou plutôt ce vaillant . . .

Even the vapid Don Sanche is granted a sudden flash of
spirit in Corneille's drama. Chimène accepts him. "Tomor-

row," says the King, very sensibly. But the rule of twenty-four hours prevents such a postponement. There is just time for the fight, if the play is to end before the clock strikes the same hour as it did yesterday when the action began. Strange, absurd—utterly absurd—but that's the way it has to be. The King objects as anyone would: Rodrigue is tired, he has been up all night fighting the Moors:

> Sortir d'une bataille et combattre à l'instant!

But Don Diègue replies:

> Rodrigue a pris haleine en vous la racontant.

—this is one of the boasts that are always applauded and that may be forgiven such a father. The King shifts ground and tries a compromise:

> Du moins une heure ou deux, je veux qu'il se délasse.

We can't help smiling. The good King has found a way to reconcile Rodrigue's legitimate need for rest with the twenty-four-hour rule! No doubt with one eye on the clock, he ventures to suggest an hour or two of respite for the hero. I suppose it is about nine or ten in the morning; Rodrigue can rest for a couple of hours, and the singular combat can take place around noon, thus getting under the sacrosanct deadline. As one last condition, the King demands that the winner, whoever he may be, be given Chimène's hand in marriage. She puts on the air of someone who accepts with great reluctance. Inside herself she wallows in bliss.

2

As Act V opens, the duel has not yet taken place. We are back in Chimène's house. Rodrigue does what he has already done once before. He walks straight to the center of greatest danger and greatest attraction. He is alone with Chimène, and this time he has not sneaked in, but come with his head held high and in broad daylight. This

scene is the only great scene in *Le Cid* which owes nothing
whatever to Guillén de Castro. It is entirely Corneille's.
Corneille had every right to say of this original scene:

> Je ne dois qu'à moi seul toute ma renommée.

The idea, which reflects the subtlest refinement of passion,
is this. Under pretext of saying farewell to her, Rodrigue
has come to tell Chimène that he will not defend himself
against Don Sanche, that he is determined to let himself
be vanquished and killed. By this means he hopes to wrest
from her the order to live and to win. But he wants her to
tell him this herself, in the most formal terms, and he will
be satisfied with nothing less. These characters observe the
cult of honor in all things—in matters of vengeance, of filial
piety, of love. They are not content merely to feel the right
thing nor even merely to do the right thing: they demand
as well the ultimate refinements, all the punctilious flour-
ishes of honor. Rodrigue would not feel happy or satisfied
enough to defeat Don Sanche and to win Chimène,
whether she approved the bargain or not. By a kind of
added refinement of sensibility, he wants her to consent in
advance to it all, to will it so, to ask that he make it happen so. Only on this condition will he be able to enjoy all
the gratifications and refined pleasures of pure passion.

> Je vais mourir, Madame, et vous viens en ce lieu,
> Avant le coup mortel, dire un dernier adieu . . .

Tu vas mourir! she exclaims horrified, thus betraying the
fact that she hopes for the opposite. She certainly hopes
that he will win the duel, and she wants him to share this
hope. She will make her love clear enough, but only bit by
bit, as though under moral compulsion. And he, who suspects, more than suspects, her real wishes, he has come to
see her—I repeat—not so much to make sure (for at bottom he is sure) as to enjoy his certainty and be proud of it.
He is resolved that she shall make her wishes plain.

Chimène, in order to encourage him to win, begins by
playing on his courage and vanity. Poor Don Sanche, who
is devoted to her and who has offered to fight for her, she
belittles, making it clear that she has less respect for him

than for Rodrigue. Love has neither consideration nor pity for whatever may stand in its way:

> Tu vas mourir? Don Sanche est-il si redoutable
> Qu'il donne l'épouvante à ce coeur indomptable?
> Qui t'a rendu si faible, ou qui le rend si fort? . . .
> Celui qui n'a pas craint les Maures ni mon père
> Va combattre don Sanche, et déjà désespère?

But she cannot arouse him by appealing to so unequal a rivalry. Rodrigue puts up no remonstrance, and her irony slides over him without leaving a trace. He persists in the notion that he must let himself be punished and sacrificed: he wants to be given a different and better reason for living than this one.

Chimène then finds other arguments and side issues, while still pressing him on the score of honor. If he is not eager to live, believing himself condemned by her, then let him consider what people would think of him should he be killed. His glory—his very dignity—is at stake:

> Quand on le saura mort, on le croira vaincu.

Passion has its sophisms: it is in the name of her dead father, of the Count who was so feared, that she tries to persuade Rodrigue that he is obliged to defend himself valiantly against someone less valorous than that famous warrior. Otherwise people will believe that the Count was even less valorous than Don Sanche! What an argument!

Don Rodrigue is pitiless; he won't be deceived. He has become deaf on the score of honor; if she wants to move him, she must touch another chord, that of love. The moments are numbered, it is late in the day: with her back to the wall, Chimène has no choice but to do what is expected of her, to spell it all out:

> Puisque, pour t'empêcher de courir au trépas,
> Ta vie et ton honneur sont faibles appas,
> Si jamais je t'aimai, cher Rodrigue, en revanche
> Défends-toi maintenant pour m'ôter à Don Sanche.
> . . . .
> Sors vainqueur d'un combat dont Chimène est le prix!

Well, now she has said the very thing he has wanted
her to say to his face. He had wanted to be told to live and
to be victorious. He had wanted to drive her into a corner,
as the saying goes, and to see with his own eyes passion
take wing and soar. He has been successful. Chimène's
pride is hurt—she has been sorely tried—but her fear that
he might let himself be killed has won the upper hand.
Carried away, she has held nothing back. It is the very
acme of tenderness. On hearing these intoxicating words
Rodrigue once more becomes the fire-breathing hero, the
young lion:

> Est-il quelque ennemi qu'à présent je ne dompte?
> Paraissez, Navarrais, Maures et Castillans,
> Et tout ce que l'Espagne a nourri de vaillants! . . .

Nothing can be exaggerated at such a moment: it is full of
grandeur. Whatever objections may be raised against it,
the form of tragedy which inspired Corneille to compose
such a scene, with such heroic outbursts, is a beautiful and
noble form of the human spirit.

Once the development has been carried to its ultimate
explosion, interest can only weaken. At the opera, after
the great passages, we need a rest, and there are whole
scenes we do not listen to. Here, the Infanta is in her
apartment and delivers one of her monologues. It would
no doubt seem pretty and full of wit, if only we could pay
some attention to it. Sorrowful, she wonders candidly
whether, with respect to Rodrigue, she is to follow the
sense of her dignity or the attraction of her love. At this
point her governess enters and advises her to take the
proudest course, whereupon the Infanta tells her that she
will once more give Rodrigue to Chimène—as if the latter
had need of her permission. The overgenerous Infanta
spends a good deal of time giving away what has never
belonged to her.

Although everything happens very quickly, Act V contains some tedious passages. We are taken back to Chimène's apartment for no good reason. There she has a
conversation with her confidante Elvire. She goes back

over what has already been said, and she either pretends or sincerely believes that her heart is more divided than it really is. She implores Heaven that the duel, now being fought, may end without a decision:

> Sans faire aucun des deux ni vaincu ni vainqueur.

For her own benefit she plays the part of a neutral. Whatever may happen, and despite all the promises made, she persuades herself that she will never belong to Rodrigue. If need be, she will expose him to a thousand armed combats. Such superfluous rehashings and recapitulations are quite customary in the last acts of French tragedies.

But then, what happens right after? Don Sanche comes in, kneels down, and suddenly presents her with his sword. Giving him no chance to explain himself, Chimène interrupts him and insults him, calling him a traitor and a murderer:

> Va, tu l'as pris en traître; un guerrier si vaillant
> N'eût jamais succombé sous un tel assaillant.

Farewell to dignity! She is an infuriated, frenzied woman in love, unable to understand anything, who has forgotten everything she ever knew or believed. Not only does she fail to recognize the champion she had selected to defend her honor, she throws in his face almost the same words that Hermione flings at Orestes [in Racine's *Andromaque*] after the death of Pyrrhus: *Qui te l'a dit?* In order to make Chimène do what she wants in the time allotted him, Corneille thought it necessary to commit her in this way, to compromise her by an involuntary outburst. Such beauties are not of the kind I admire.

Frantic with grief (she is like a madwoman), she runs to the royal palace and implores the King not to force her to go through with an odious marriage to Don Sanche. To escape such a fate, she will give up everything, strip herself of her possessions, and enter a convent. Finally she is silenced with great effort and told what really happened. Rodrigue is not dead; far from it, he has won the duel. He disarmed his adversary and was satisfied with sending him

to present his vain and useless sword to Chimène. Now all
present crowd around Chimène—the King, Don Diègue,
Don Sanche himself, and the Infanta, who renews her
habitual offer to give Rodrigue away in marriage. Rodrigue now repeats himself, once again laying his head at
the feet of his mistress—a pure formality which cannot possibly be meant seriously—and concludes with some beautiful lines. Chimène raises him to his feet; she has gone too
far already to put up much more resistance. To her it is
now only a matter of propriety and time. She makes the
sensible objection against the twenty-four-hour rule:

> Sire, quelle apparence a ce triste hyménée,
> Qu'un même jour commence et finisse mon deuil,
> Mette en mon lit Rodrigue, et mon père au cercueil!

Only too true! The King arranges everything by postponing
the conclusion until a period of mourning has been observed:

> Prends un an, si tu veux, pour essuyer tes larmes.

And addressing himself to Rodrigue he closes the play with
these words:

> Pour vaincre un point d'honneur qui combat contre toi,
> Laisse faire le temps, ta vaillance et ton roi.

All's well that ends well.

3

Such is this marvelous play, a singular mixture of beautiful things and strange things, which ushered in a great
period of dramatic literature. It was the first great literary
exploit of seventeenth-century France. Whatever its faults,
and I have not concealed them, the over-all impression
cannot be gainsaid: from one end to the other it is swept
by a single creative surge. Corneille's genius is essentially
uneven and intermittent, but we feel these faults less in
Le Cid than in his other plays. Corneille was thirty when
he wrote it—a fine age, when, as Molière said, "a man has

all his roguery and all his divine inspiration." Had he written it earlier, the play would have abounded in oversweet
pairs of artificial lovers; later it would have been affected
by his stiff, dry, Corneillian manner. Never before or after
was he in such full possession of his genius. *Le Cid* has all
the defects, but also all the qualities of its age. If it seems
so beautiful still today, despite the many masterpieces
that have come after it, how effective it must have been
when there was nothing else in French theater! *Le Cid*
and *Polyeucte,* even if we admire *Horace* and *Cinna,* are
today the two plays by Corneille which in rereading keep
all the promises they arouse, perpetually renewed by his
immortal renown.

My few references to the Spanish play may have suggested differences in point of view, in inspiration, in detail.
Even when Corneille imitates Guillén de Castro, we have
seen how much he differs from him. This would have been
more striking, had I pushed the comparison further. The
Cid of the Spanish drama is not only the most courageous
of all knights, he is also the most devoutly religious; at one
point he is the most fervent of pilgrims. There is a whole
scene which stresses this trait. At the time of Chimène's
second petition to the King, when the latter decides to
publish the challenge she proposes—awarding her hand and
her possessions to the man who brings her the head of
Rodrigue, on the sole condition that he be a noble, her
equal—Rodrigue goes on a pilgrimage to St. James of Com-
postela, accompanied only by two squires. He is the hero
of a very moving incident, the legacy of an old tradition,
seemingly unconnected with the main action. In a moun-
tainous forest, groans are heard; Rodrigue is first to perceive them, for his companions say that they hear nothing.
When they sit down in the shade to eat, the groans start
again. They are uttered by a leper who has fallen into a
sort of ditch and who implores passers-by in the name of
Christ to help him. The two squires and a shepherd who is
also with Rodrigue are afraid to go near the unfortunate
man. Rodrigue walks up to him alone, covers him with his
cloak, makes him eat from his dish, gives him to drink

from his flask, and has him sleep next to him where he can protect him. The leper is profuse in his gratitude, calling Rodrigue the most humane and most pious of all knights. He addresses him as "the good Rodrigue," a name which is certainly as precious as that of the Cid (which means "Lord") given him by the Moors he vanquished. But after sleeping, the leper is suddenly transfigured and addresses him as "the Great Cid, the Great Rodrigue." He infuses Rodrigue with his breath, gives him back his cloak which is now permeated with a divine fragrance, and disappears among the rocks only to reappear dressed in white in a cloud. The leper turns out to be none but Lazarus himself, and as a reward for Rodrigue's good deed, he promises the latter victory over all adversaries and invincibility even after death. It is an admirable scene, but very Spanish in character. It would have been impossible even to refer to it in France in Corneille's day. Mysteries and "miracles" had been banished from the French stage for more than a century. All that Corneille could take from the Spanish original was a model of love and honor, a Cid capable of misting the eyes of a young d'Enghien and others of his generation. From a play that is certainly very interesting and rich, but very loosely constructed, and more of a biography than a drama, he carved out a very French Cid, a Cid suitable to Parisian taste.

On this score, I cannot help recalling a lecture the scholar Fauriel gave at the Faculté des lettres thirty years ago. Fauriel excelled in comparative studies of this sort, and for all his impartiality he was by taste only rarely inclined to favor French literature. In pointing out differences between the Spanish and French versions of the drama, he noted that Corneille practically always shortened the original scenes, making cuts and simplifications of every kind. He would add with a gently ironic smile: "It is as though Corneille's characters were paid by the hour, so ruthlessly does he drive them to do as much as possible in the shortest possible time!" The fact is, Corneille knew his public—his hurried, impatient French public—and he knew he had to engage its interest quickly and never let it flag. Only thus can the flighty French goddess of success be conquered.

The most respectable scholars are concerned with something else entirely—with the whole truth; and I commend and admire them for it. Their method is not that of art, but that of pure science. This method was Fauriel's, and today it is that of M. Viguier. In scales no less precise and scrupulous, he has once again weighed the two versions, and for once finds the French play not altogether wanting. The learned M. Viguier must not suppose that just because I take a different kind of approach in the face of a public which is our master and whom we must satisfy, I have not read his excellent work and profited from it. In these pages I had to confine myself to *Le Cid* which is familiar to all of us, the magnificent fruit of the branch grafted by Corneille on the Castilian tree. M. Viguier has done more: in a comparative analysis of exquisite thoroughness, which presupposes the most sensitive familiarity with the two languages, he has tried to initiate us into the mystery of this grafting process. He has tracked everything down to its origins, studying the tiniest capillary vessels. We scarcely think of the great Corneille as a busy, methodical bee, and yet M. Viguier has caught him out in just this posture, showing him to us in a new light. Every student of literature will read him with interest and profit.

My own criticism necessarily keeps closer to the surface: we note only what is obvious to everyone. The French *Cid* was a great event in the history of literature. It has been justly said that any work that receives recognition in France quickly achieves general fame and influence. It was clear even in Corneille's time that so far as things of the mind were concerned, Paris was becoming a sort of eyes and ears for all Europe. In transforming the Spanish Cid into a French Cid, Corneille by the same token secularized it and popularized it. Nothing less was required if it was to travel outside the Iberian Peninsula. It has been observed that Don Juan had to be treated by Molière before Mozart could put it to music and before its hero could become the well-known universal type. The same is true of *Le Cid;*

thanks to Corneille it reached the whole of Europe within
a few years. According to Fontenelle, Corneille's library
contained translations of this play into all the European
languages. It was even retranslated into Spanish, or at least
imitated, by Diamante (whom Voltaire was too quick to
identify as a predecessor of Corneille). More than any
other play *Le Cid* determined the nature of the theater on
all continental stages for more than a century. In Germany,
where it was translated first by Clauss (1655) and then by
Gressinger (1656), it began a vogue of imitations from the
French which prevailed down to Lessing. Never before had
a literary success been both so prompt and so universal.

4

I have done my best to indicate the triumphant career
of *Le Cid*, but to complete our impression I should also
show the sequel to this career. As we all know, the Frenchman is quick to become enthusiastic, especially for something beautiful, but he is also quick to resent having been
carried away. He loses no time getting even. The other
fellow's opinion counts for a great deal. In France you can
never prove convincingly that you have a perfect right to
be amused or moved. Vanity plays a part in this: the scoffer
prides himself on discovering defects in celebrated works.
"You saw one defect in this masterpiece? Well, I can find
two . . . a hundred!" Before long there is a hue and cry
against the work. There come cruel days when fine talents
are made to pay for their initial success. Béranger put it
very well in a verse of no great quality:

> De tout laurier un poison est l'essence.

Corneille's rivals—the Scudérys, the Mairets, and even,
alas, the great Cardinal himself—rose up in arms after the
success of *Le Cid*. When one peruses, as I have had the
sad satisfaction of doing, all the pamphlets to which the
triumph of *Le Cid* gave rise, one has a feeling of disgust
and almost nausea, perhaps something like what Corneille

himself experienced. How many ugly insults, stupid remarks, and absurdities inevitably follow in the train of
beautiful works! In a way insults are the normal accompaniment of fame. For having created *Le Cid,* Corneille was subjected to almost as many inept criticisms
and effronteries as was M. Etienne (I apologize for bringing the two names together) for his *Les Deux Gendres.*

And what about the Academy's famous criticism of *Le
Cid?* From this quarter at least there were no insults, the
only shocking thing being the indictment itself. Richelieu,
as jealous as a rival author, and as imperious as a great
one, demanded that the Academy draw up a report criticizing *Le Cid.* It was to be at Corneille's expense that the
members of the newly created body should earn their hon-
orariums. In all fairness, we must recall that the Academicians, trapped between a cardinal with the power to grant
or withhold pensions and a public which alone could make
a work successful, solved the problem decently enough.
Chapelain, the official censor, wrote the text and was sensible in his ponderousness; some of his observations are
after all judicious. Confronted with this extraordinary play,
consisting of one emotional outburst after another, he drew
up a list of implausibilities and inaccuracies. He would
have preferred evasiveness and compromise, as though the
beauty of *Le Cid* were not precisely its simplicity and
vividness. Perhaps it is hardly surprising that a work so
impregnated with love and divine madness should have
been little understood by our erudite body. You don't club
together to perceive a passion, nor can you justify passion
in the eyes of reason. Chimène's femininity, which
makes her at once forever dear and forever sympathetic to
young hearts, would seem even more unmistakable if we
paid attention to the pettish cross-examination she was subjected to by this headquarters of the Literary Union, this
committee of the tried-and-true.

But this subject would take us far afield, and we have
already strayed from our purpose. We must leave this chapter to the historians of literature.

From a four-part article, 29 February, 7, 14, and 21 March 1864 (*Nouveaux lundis*).

A major study by the mature Sainte-Beuve. Parts One and Two of the article are largely devoted to a discussion of the Spanish play, *Las Mocedades del Cid,* by Guillén de Castro, and its sources in legend and romance. As is well known, Corneille's play, the first great French tragedy, was a brilliant adaptation from de Castro. The pages translated here, which come from Parts Three and Four, constitute a "close reading," or *explication de texte,* of Corneille's great drama. Sainte-Beuve constantly refers to the Spanish original in order to underline the nature of Corneille's genius.

RACINE

I

THE GREAT poets, the poets of genius, independent of the genre they practice, regardless of whether their temperament is lyric, epic, or dramatic, fall into two glorious families, which for many centuries have alternately intermingled and vied for pre-eminence in fame. According to period, the admiration of men has been unequally divided between the two.

The primitive poets, the founders, the pure archetypes, born of themselves and sons of their own works—Homer, Pindar, Aeschylus, Dante, and Shakespeare—though occasionally neglected are most often placed above the others. At all times they have been contrasted with studious, polished, docile writers whose talents were developed by hard work. Horace, Virgil, Tasso are the most brilliant leaders of this secondary family, justly reputed inferior to its elder, but as a rule more understood by all, more accessible, and more cherished. In France, Corneille and Molière stand apart from it in many respects; Boileau and Racine belong to it entirely and adorn it, especially Racine, the most marvelous, the most accomplished of this family, the most venerated of our poets. It is characteristic for writers of this order to command almost unanimous acceptance, whereas their illustrious adversaries, though surpassing them in merit and towering above them in fame, are in each century challenged by a certain class of critics.

This difference in popularity is an inevitable consequence of the difference in talents. The writers of the first group,

truly predestined and divine, are born with their allotted
share. They do not seek to increase it grain by grain in this
life, but dispense it profusely, by the handful as it were, in
their works, for their inner riches are inexhaustible. They
create without undue concern for their means, without even
being aware of them. They do not reflect upon their work
at all waking hours; they never cast glances backward to
measure the road they have covered and to figure out the
distance they still have to cover; they advance by forced
marches, never tired, never content. Secret changes take
place within them, in the recesses of their genius, and
sometimes transform it. These changes are like a law of
nature, they proceed without outside interference or aid—
any more than men hasten the moment when their hair
turns gray, the birds that of molting, or trees the changes
of color in their foliage at the various seasons. Thus pro-
ceeding from great inner laws and a potent primordial
source, they succeed in leaving an imprint of their force in
sublime, monumental works which, like nature, disclose
true order and stability under their seeming irregularity—
works which are often uneven, bristling with peaks and
opening into depths. So much for the first group.

The writers of the other group need to be born under
propitious circumstances, their talents need to be cultivated, to ripen in the sun. They develop slowly, consciously,
fertilized by study, and they create themselves like works
of art. They advance by degrees; they never skip a stage,
they never attain to their goal at a bound. Their genius increases with time and rises like a palace to which each
year a new story is added; they spend long hours in silent
reflection, when they pause to revise their plans. Thus the
edifice, if it is ever completed, is skillfully conceived, noble,
lucid, admirable, of a harmony that strikes the eye from the
outset, and of perfect execution. The viewer's mind easily
discovers the consecutive steps climbed by the artist and
follows him with a kind of serene pride.

Now, according to a very subtle and very just remark
of Père Tournemine, we admire in a writer only those
qualities whose seeds and roots we have within ourselves.

It follows that in the works of superior minds there is a relative degree to which a lesser mind can attain, but above which he cannot rise, and from which he judges the whole as best he can. It is almost like the various families of plants thriving at different levels in the Cordilleras—each of them is never found above a given altitude; or, better, it is like families of birds whose capacity to rise in the air has a certain limit. Now, if at the relative height to which a given family of minds can rise in grasping a poem it encounters no element to provide support, no platform opening a view on the whole landscape—if, instead, it encounters nothing but sheer cliffs, torrents, precipices, as it were—what will happen then? Minds that have found no place to rest from their flight will return like the dove to the ark, but without even an olive leaf.

I am at Versailles, on the garden side, and I mount the grand staircase, breath fails me halfway, but at least I can see in front of me the lines of the palace, its wings, and I can appreciate its regularity. Whereas, if I walk up a winding path on the banks of the Rhine to some Gothic turret, and I stop exhausted halfway up, it may happen that an accident of the terrain, a tree, or a bush will completely hide the view. That is a true image of the two types of poetry. Racine's is so constructed that at every level weaklings find footholds and platforms with views. The path leading to Shakespeare's art is more arduous, the eye does not encompass it at every point. We know some very able persons who worked hard to climb it, and after finding their view obstructed by some hillock or bush, came back swearing in good faith that there was nothing up there; but the moment they were down in the plain, that cursed enchanted tower reappeared to them in the distance. But today we shall leave the tower of Shakespeare and try to climb some of the steps, slippery from having been trodden by so many previous worshipers, that lead to the marble temple of Racine.

Racine, born at La Ferté-Milon in 1639, became an orphan at a very early age. His father, who was a tax official at La Ferté-Milon, died a few months after his

mother, daughter of a *procureur du roi des eaux et forêts*
at Villars-Cotterets. He was four when he was given in
charge of his maternal grandfather, who sent him while
yet very young to school in Beauvais. After his grandfather
died, the boy was taken to Port-Royal des Champs, where
his grandmother and one of his aunts had retired. The
first interesting details concerning the poet's childhood date
from that time. The famous recluse Antoine Le Maître developed a special affection for him. A letter he wrote him
during one of the persecutions has come down to us; in it
he urges Racine to be obedient and to take good care during his absence of his eleven volumes of St. Chrysostom.

"Le petit Racine," as they called him at Port-Royal,
quickly learned to read the Greek authors in the original.
He made excerpts, annotated them, and memorized them.
He did this successively with Plutarch, Plato's *Sympo-
sium*, St. Basil, Pindar, and, at moments of leisure, Heliodorus' romance *Aethiopica, or Theagenes and Chariclea.*
Even at this early age Racine revealed his discreet, innocent, and dreamy nature by taking long walks, book in
hand (which he did not always read), in that beautiful
lonely region whose charm often moved him to tears. He
exercised his nascent talent by translating the stirring
hymns of the Breviary into French verse (he later revised
these translations); but above all he took pleasure in cele-
brating Port-Royal, the landscape, the pond, the gardens,
and the meadows. The youthful works that have come
down to us show genuine feeling under obvious inexperi-
ence and weakness of expression and color, and in some
passages we can discern a groping anticipation of the
melodious choruses of *Esther.*

He stayed three years at Port-Royal, and then entered
the class of logic at the Collège d'Harcourt in Paris. The
austere religiosity that his first teachers had inculcated into
him grew gradually weaker in his new world. His amiable
and dissipated young friends, the Abbé Le Vasseur and La
Fontaine, whom he met at that time, encouraged his in-
born taste for poetry, romances, and the theater. He composed love sonnets, and concealed this fact from Port-Royal

and the Jansenists, who were writing him letter after letter and threatening to anathematize him. As early as 1660 he had dealings with the actors of the Marais concerning a play that has not come down to us. His ode *La Nymphe de la Seine,* composed on the occasion of the king's marriage, was submitted to Chapelain, who received it "with the utmost kindness," and "though he was ill, kept it three days, annotating the manuscript in his own hand." The most important of these notes informed the author that Tritons never lived in rivers but only in the sea. The ode earned Racine the protection of Chapelain and a bounty from Colbert. His cousin Vitart, *intendant* of the château of Chevreuse, on one occasion sent him there to supervise masons, glaziers, and carpenters. The poet had by now become so accustomed to the bustle of Paris that he felt an exile at Chevreuse and dated his letters "from Babylon." In one of these, he relates that he goes to the tavern two or three times a day, treating the workmen to drinks, and that a lady has mistaken him for a bailiff; and he goes on to say, "I read verses, and I am trying to compose some; I am reading the adventures of Ariosto, and having some adventures myself."

All his friends at Port-Royal, his aunt, his teachers, seeing him bound straight for perdition, united to rescue him. They remonstrated with him on the necessity of a profession and induced him to go to Uzès in Languedoc, to stay with one of his maternal uncles, canon of Sainte-Geneviève, in the hope of obtaining a benefice. He stayed at Uzès through the winter of 1661 and the spring and summer of 1662, clothed in black from top to toe, reading St. Thomas Aquinas to please the good-natured canon, and Ariosto or Euripides to comfort himself. Because the canon was his uncle, the schoolmasters and priests of the neighborhood treated him with special consideration; and because of his minor reputation in Paris and his famous ode, all the local poets and lovers consulted him about their verses. However, he rarely went into society: the town greatly bored him; all its inhabitants seemed to him hard and self-seeking, "like bailiffs." He compared himself to Ovid on the

shores of the Euxine, and his greatest worry was that
the patois of the south might adulterate and spoil his excellent, authentic French, pure French as it was spoken at
La Ferté-Milon, Château-Thierry, and Reims. Nor did he
think very highly of the landscape: "If the country had a
little refinement, and if the rocks were a little less frequent,
it might be taken for a real Cythera." But the rocks an-
noy him, the heat stifles him, and the grasshoppers spoil
the nightingales for him. He finds the passions of southern
France violent and excessive; as for himself, he likes reflection and silence; he stays in his room, reads a great
deal, and does not even feel the urge to compose. His
letters to the Abbé Le Vasseur are cold, refined, correct,
flowery, mythological, and slightly bantering; the sentimental delicate wit that was to come to bloom in *Bérénice*
breaks through everywhere; there is a profusion of Italian
quotations and gallant allusions, but never a crude expression of the kind young men indulge in among themselves,
not a single ignoble detail; a tone of the most exquisite
elegance is maintained even though the addressee is a
close friend. The local women at first dazzled him; a few
days after his arrival he wrote to La Fontaine: "All the
women here are brilliant, and . . . as for their persons,
Color verus, corpus solidum et succi plenum. But since
this is the first thing I was told to be on guard against, I
will say no more about it; indeed to go into details on this
matter would be to desecrate the house of a beneficed
priest, like the one I am living in: *Domus mea, domus
orationis.* This is why you must expect me to say no more
on this subject. I was told: be blind. Since I cannot be
that entirely, I must at least be mute; for, you see, one
must be a monk with monks, just as I was a 'wolf' with you
and the other 'wolves,' your cronies." But now that he
was no longer with his companions in pleasure, his naturally reserved character reasserted itself. A few months
later, in answer to a facetious insinuation of the Abbé Le
Vasseur, he wrote very seriously that, thank God, he still
was free, and that when he left that place, he should bring
back his heart sound and intact. And he went on to relate

a recent danger from which his weakness had happily escaped.

The passage is little known and is sufficiently revealing to be quoted at length: "There is a very lovely young lady here, with a most attractive figure. I had never seen her except from five or six paces, and I had always found her very beautiful; her complexion seemed to me fresh and dazzling, her eyes large and of a magnificent black, her throat and everything else that women in this place show rather freely, very white. I had always thought of her with some tenderness, which came close to an inclination. But I was seeing her only in church; for, as I wrote you, I keep to myself here, even more than my cousin advised. In the end I wanted to see whether my ideas about her were not mistaken, and I found a very respectable opportunity. I approached her and spoke to her. This happened less than a month ago, and my sole intention was to see how she would respond to my advances. I spoke to her about indifferent matters; but the moment I opened my mouth and looked at her, I was taken aback. I discovered blotches on her face, as if she were recovering from an illness, and this certainly changed my ideas. Nevertheless I did not stop talking, and she answered very gently and civilly; and to tell you the truth, I must have come upon one of her bad days, for she passes as a great beauty in the town, and I know many young men who sigh for her. She is even thought to be one of the most modest and sprightly girls here. However, I am glad of this encounter, which has at least helped me to rid myself of something that might have disturbed me; for now I am trying to live a little more sensibly, and not let myself be carried away by all kinds of things. I am beginning my noviciate." Racine was then twenty-three. The naïveté of his impressions and the youthfulness of his heart so evident in his account mark a starting point from which he progressed gradually, by dint of experience and study, to the utmost depths of the same passion in *Phèdre*. However, he did not complete his noviciate. He wearied of waiting for the benefice he had been promised, and deserting the canon and the province, he went back to Paris where his new ode, *La Renommée aux Muses*, brought him another "gratification," admission to Court, and the acquaintance of Boileau and Molière. *La Thébaïde* came soon after. Up until then Racine had encountered only protectors and friends on his path; his first dramatic success aroused envy, and from that moment his career abounded in vexations and humiliations, which more than once threatened to sour or discourage our oversensitive poet.

The tragedy *Alexandre* set him at loggerheads with Molière and Corneille—with Molière, because he withdrew the play from him to give it to the Hôtel de Bourgogne; with Corneille, because the famous old man told the younger after listening to his play that it disclosed a great talent for poetry, but not for the stage. The partisans of Corneille tried to interfere with its success at the performances. Some said that Taxile was not a real gentleman; others that he did not deserve to die; some that Alexander did not behave as a real lover should, others that he appeared on the stage only to talk of love. When *Andromaque* was staged, Pyrrhus was criticized for a residue of ferocity—he should have been more polished, more gallant, more consistent. This reflected the influence of Corneille, whose heroes were all of a piece, good or bad from top to toe. Racine replied very judiciously that "Aristotle, far from asking for perfect heroes, believes on the contrary that tragic characters, that is to say, those whose misfortune makes the catastrophe of the tragedy, must be neither entirely good nor entirely wicked. He does not want them to be extremely good, because the punishment of an upright man would arouse more indignation than pity in the audience, nor does he want them to be extremely wicked, because no one pities a criminal. For this reason they should be only moderately good, that is to say, their virtue should be capable of weakness, and their misfortunes should be caused by some failing, which would arouse pity rather than detestation."

I insist on this point, because Racine's great innovation and his most incontestable dramatic originality consist in this very reduction of heroic characters to more human, more natural proportions, and in a subtle analysis of the most secret nuances of feeling and passion. What above all distinguishes Racine's method of composition, both in his style and in his dramas, is logical sequence, the uninterrupted connection of ideas and emotions. He fills up and motivates everything, leaving no gaps; he never surprises us by those sudden changes, those abrupt reversals, those *volte-faces* of which Corneille makes frequent abuse in the play of his characters and the development of his dramas. This is not to imply that, even on this score, Racine is always superior to Corneille; but when he appeared, he had the advantage of novelty, a novelty perfectly adapted to the taste of a Court which abounded in weaknesses, which appreciated nuances, and which opened its amorous chronicle with a La Valière and closed it with a Maintenon. It still remains to be seen whether Racine's careful and analytic method, employed to the exclusion of every other, is dramatic in the absolute sense of the term. For my part, I do not think so. But we must grant that it met the requirements of the society of that time, which in its polished idleness did not demand a drama more stirring, more stormy, more "transporting," to use Mme. de Sévigné's term, and which contented itself with *Bérénice*, while waiting for *Phèdre*, the masterpiece of this genre.

Bérénice was commissioned by Madame, the Duchesse d'Orléans, who championed the new poets at Court, and who on this occasion played a nasty trick on Corneille by making him compete in single combat against his young rival. At the same time, Boileau, a sincere and faithful friend, defended Racine against the pack of envious authors, helped him get over his temporary discouragements, and by his severity stimulated him to progress continually. Boileau's daily supervision would surely have been disastrous to a free, impetuous, or effortlessly graceful genius, for example, to a writer like Molière or La Fontaine; it could only benefit Racine, who even before meeting Boileau had unswervingly followed, save for some indulgence in Italian conceits, the path of correctness and

sustained elegance. Boileau kept him to it and strength-
ened his determination to follow it. For this reason I think
that Boileau was right when he boasted of having taught
Racine to "write easy verses with difficulty," though he
went a bit too far if, as we are told, he advised him "to
compose, as a rule, the second line before the first."

Andromaque was produced in 1667, and *Phèdre* in
1677; we know how Racine filled the ten years between the
two tragedies. Prompted by youth and ambition, spurred
on by admirers as well as by the envious, he gave himself entirely to the development of his genius. He broke
openly with Port-Royal, and in answer to an attack by
Nicole on dramatic poets, he came out with a stinging
letter, which created a stir and made him the target of
reprisals. By dint of waiting and soliciting, he finally obtained a benefice, and the license for the first edition of
Andromaque was granted to Sieur Racine, Prior of Epinay.
A monk contested his claim to the priory; a lawsuit followed, which no one understood; in the end Racine out of
sheer weariness desisted, taking revenge on the judges by
his comedy *Les Plaideurs,* which might have been written
by Molière. This admirable farce reveals a little known
aspect of Racine and reminds us that he read Rabelais,
Marot, and even Scarron, and that he sat in taverns between Chapelle and La Fontaine. Thus for ten years Racine
led a full life marked by pleasures, disappointments, and
fame against a background of serious studies; in addition
there were literary quarrels, visits to Court, the Academy
(from 1673), and perhaps, as we suspected, several love
affairs with actresses. In 1677, at the age of thirty-eight,
he broke off his dramatic work, married, and became a devout Christian.

There can be little doubt that his last two plays, *Iphigénie* and *Phèdre,* had redoubled the violence of the
attacks on him. All the hissed playwrights, the Jansenist
pamphleteers, the die-hard nobles, and the remnants of
the *précieuses,* Boyer, Leclerc, Coras, Perrin, Pradon—I
was going to add Fontenelle and Barbier-d'Aucourt—and
above all, in this case, the Duc de Nevers, Mme. De-

shoulières, and the Hôtel de Bouillon set upon him shamelessly like a pack of hounds, and the unworthy maneuvers of that cabal might have deeply disturbed the poet. But after all, his plays had triumphed; the public applauded them and was moved to tears by them; Boileau, who never flattered, even in friendship, dedicated a magnificent epistle to the conqueror, "blessing" and proclaiming "fortunate" the century that saw the birth of these "stately marvels." This was less than ever the moment for Racine to leave the stage which resounded with his name; he had many more reasons for intoxication than for literary disappointment, and we must conclude that his decision to give up the theater had nothing to do with petty sulkiness, as has been claimed.

Some time before that, the first youthful ardors of the spirit and the senses having been spent, the memory of his childhood, of his teachers, of his aunt, the nun at Port-Royal, had regained a hold on his heart. He could not help comparing his peaceful contentment in former days with his present fame, so troubled and frustrating, and inevitably came to long for a settled life. The secret thoughts that had been preying on his mind are discernible in the preface to *Phèdre*, and must have inspired him more than is generally realized in his profound analysis of the "*douleur vertueuse*" [Boileau] of a soul that curses evil and yet surrenders to it. His own heart made him understand that of Phèdre; and if we assume—which is plausible enough—that he kept on at the theater against his will because of some amorous attachment which he could not easily shake off, the similarity becomes closer, and suggests that in his poignant portrayal of Phèdre, who is more individualized than his other characters, he drew upon his own experiences and inner struggles. However that may be, the moral intention of *Phèdre* is beyond a doubt; the great Arnauld himself was forced to recognize it, almost fulfilling the author's hope "by means of this play to reconcile to tragedy a number of persons famous for their piety and their doctrine." However, as the idea of reforming his life took deeper hold on him, Racine judged it more pru-

dent and more consistent to renounce the theater, and he
left it with courage, but without too much effort. He married, made his peace with Port-Royal, and made ready to
assume his duties as a father. When the king appointed
him historiographer (with Boileau), he did not neglect his
duties as a historian either: with this in mind, he made a
kind of résumé of Lucian's treatise *On the Manner of Writing History,* and read the works of Mézeray, Vittorio Siri,
and others.

On the basis of the foregoing brief remarks on Racine's
character, way of life, and intellectual habits, it is easy to
infer the essential qualities and defects of his work—to
foresee, as it were, both his strong and weak points. Great
art in organizing and arranging his material, ability to
build slowly and gradually, rather than the simple and
direct power to build a play around a number of strikingly
dramatic situations, which characterizes a natural dramatic talent; alertness to every detail, even the smallest;
singular dexterity in following up only one thread of plot
at a time; skill in pruning rather than in multiplying
powerful effects; ingenuity in getting his characters on and
off the stage; occasional scanting of obligatory scenes either by a grandiloquent narrative or by the motivated
absence of the most embarrassing witness; similarly, nothing aberrant or eccentric about his characters; all subordinate elements, all superfluous backgrounds omitted, and
yet nothing too bare or too monotonous, only two or three
well-chosen colors against a simple background; then,
amid all this, a passion whose beginning is not shown
comes to us already in full flood, gently swirling, and
sweeps us up like the irresistible current of a mighty
river: such is Racine's drama. And if we were to go into
his style and the harmony of his versification, we would
discover in them beauties of the same order held down
within the same limitations, and tonal variations which are
no doubt melodious, but within the scale of a single octave. A few observations on *Britannicus* will clarify my
thought and justify it, if the foregoing general statement
seems somewhat overbold.

The play deals with Nero's first crime, the one by which he shakes off the authority of his mother and his tutors. Tacitus shows Britannicus as a fourteen- or fifteen-year-old boy, gentle, intelligent, and sad. He relates how one day, during a feast, Nero got drunk and told Britannicus to sing, hoping to make him ridiculous. Britannicus began to recite verses in which he alluded to his own precarious fate and to his expulsion from his father's house and from supreme power. Instead of laughing and jeering at him, the other companions, less dissembling than usual because they were drunk, openly expressed their pity for the youth. As for Nero, though his hands were still pure of blood, his native ferocity had long been smoldering in his heart waiting only for an opportunity to break loose. He had already tried to get rid of Britannicus by slow poison; he was already given to debauch, suspected of having defiled the young manhood of his future victim, and he had been neglecting his wife Octavia for the courtesan Acte. Seneca lent his ministry to this disgraceful intrigue. Agrippina was at first indignant, but in the end she embraced her son and offered him her house for the trysts. Agrippina, mother, granddaughter, sister, and widow of emperors, homicidal, incestuous, prostituted to freedmen, has only one fear—to see her son escape her, taking with him the power she wields. Such is the situation of the three principal characters at the moment Racine's play opens. What does he do? To begin with, he simplifies: he reduces the number of the protagonists—keeping Burrhus and Narcissus and eliminating Seneca and Pallas. Otho and Senecio, the young voluptuaries who cause the prince's fall, are scarcely mentioned. In his preface Racine quotes Tacitus' ferocious reference to Agrippina: *Quae, cunctis malae dominationis cupidinibus flagrans, habebat in partibus Pallantem* ["Who, inflamed with the passions of an evil ascendency, had Pallas on her side"] and adds: "I quote only these words on Agrippina, for there are too many things to say of her. She is the character I have tried to portray most completely, and my tragedy is not less the disgrace of Agrippina than the death of Britannicus." Yet, despite the author's explicit intention, Agrippina's character is imperfectly expressed. Because interest had to be focused on her disgrace, her most odious vices are glossed over, and as a result she is unreal, vague, unexplained, no more than a loving and jealous mother. Her adulteries and murders are only hinted at, for the benefit of those who read Tacitus. Finally, Acte has been replaced by the romantic Junia. Nero in love is no more than the passionate rival of Britannicus, and the hideous features of the tiger disappear or are only faintly outlined when they manifest themselves. And what shall we say of the denouement? Of Junia taking refuge with the Vestals and placed under the protection of the people—as though the people ever protected anyone under Nero! But what Racine may be most justifiably criticized for is having omitted the scene of the banquet. Britannicus is at table, he is served a drink; one of his servants tastes it, as is customary, so indispensable was it to guard against a crime. But Nero has foreseen everything. The drink is too hot, cold water must be added, and it is the cold water which has been poisoned. The effect is sudden; the poison kills instantaneously; Locusta had been ordered to prepare it under threat of death. Either because Racine scorned these details or because it was impossible to express them in verse, he omits them in Burrhus' narrative. He confines himself to relating the moral effect of the poisoning on those present, and in this he is successful; but it must be granted that even on that score he did not equal the incisive brevity, the brilliant conciseness of Tacitus. When Racine translates Tacitus— just as when he translates the Bible—he too often follows a path between the extreme qualities of the original, and carefully keeps to the middle of the road, avoiding the precipitous sides.

I shall show this in greater detail below, in so far as the Bible is in question; I shall quote only one example of his treatment of Tacitus.

In her beautiful invective against Nero, Agrippina at one moment exclaims that the words of "the daughter of Germanicus" will have to be compared with those of the "son of Aënobarbus,"

> Appuyé de Sénèque et du tribun Burrhus
> Qui tous deux rappelés de l'exil par moi-même
> Partagent à mes yeux le pouvoir suprême.

Now, in the language of Tacitus, this portion of the invective reads: *Audiretur hinc Germanici filia, inde debilis rursus Burrhus et exsul Seneca, trunca scilicet manu et professoria lingua generis humani regimen expostulantes.* ["On one side the daughter of Germanicus will be heard, on the other the crippled Burrhus and the exile Seneca, claiming with disfigured hand and a pedant's tongue the government of the world."] Clearly Racine shrank from the energetic insult of "pedant" addressed to Seneca and of "cripple" addressed to Burrhus, nor does Agrippina accuse these pedagogues of seeking the government of the world. In general, all the defects of Racine's style are rooted in this fondness of his for understatement. For it he has been excessively praised; sometimes it makes him fall short of the good, of the best.

Britannicus, Phèdre, Athalie—the first a Roman tragedy, the second Greek, and the third biblical—these are Racine's greatest dramatic works, superior to his other masterpieces. I have stated the reasons for my admiration for *Phèdre* on a previous occasion; however, it seems clear today that the portrayal of Greek ways of life in this tragedy is even less exact than that of Roman ways in *Britannicus*. Hippolyte the lover resembles Hippolytus the hunter and favorite of Diana even less than Nero the lover resembles the Nero of Tacitus; and Phèdre, queen mother and regent for her son after the presumed death of her husband, is even more implausible than Junia protected by the people and given refuge by the Vestals. Euripides himself no doubt leaves much to be desired in respect of truth; he has lost the higher sense for mythological traditions, which Aeschylus and Sophocles possessed so profoundly. But he at least shows us a whole order of things—landscape, religious rites, family memories—a background of reality which provides the reader with a foothold. In Racine, everything that is not Phèdre and her passion escapes and evaporates: the sad Aricie, the Pallantides, the various adventures of Theseus leave scarcely a trace in our memory. Closer examination shows that Racine ingeniously attempts to reconcile contradictory traditions, but the result is not too enlightening. On the one hand, he accepts Plutarch's version, according to which Theseus, instead of descending to the underworld, was merely held captive by a king of Epirus whose wife he had attempted to abduct for his friend Pirithous, and on the other he makes his Phèdre say, on the basis of the mythical story, *"Je l'aime, non point tel que l'ont vu les Enfers. . . ."*

In Euripides, Venus appears in person to take her revenge; in Racine, *Vénus tout entière à sa proie attachée* is no more than an admirable metaphor. In some places, Racine omits details descriptive of the background, which are also expressive of his heroine's passion. His Phèdre says:

> Dieux que ne suis-je assise à l'ombre des forêts!
> Quand pourrais-je, au travers d'une noble poussière,
> Suivre de l'oeil un char fuyant dans la carrière?

In Euripides, this passage is much longer. Phaedra first wishes she could quench her thirst with pure spring water and rest in the shade of poplars; then she asks to be taken up the mountain, to the pinewoods, where deer are hunted by hounds, and says that she wants to throw the Thessalian javelin; finally she asks for the sacred precincts of Limna where swift horses are trained. The nurse who has interrupted her at each wish, tells her: "What is this new fancy? You have just been on the mountain hunting deer, and now you are yearning for the gymnasium and horses! Someone should be sent to consult the oracle . . ." In the third act, when the supposedly dead Theseus appears, Phèdre can think of nothing better than to run away crying,

> Je ne dois désormais songer qu'à me cacher.

If we were daring enough, this might lead us to conclude with Corneille that Racine had a far greater talent for poetry than for the theater, and to suspect that if his contemporaries saw in him a dramatist, it was because his age was not above this level of the dramatic, but that if he were living in our day, his genius would have preferred another outlet. The secluded life he led during the twelve years of his full maturity, when he devoted himself to his family and his studies, would seem to confirm our hypothesis. Corneille, too, tried for a few years to give up the theater; but though his powers were declining, he could not go through with it, and soon re-entered the lists. Racine's silence does not seem to have been disturbed by any such impatience and inability to contain himself. He wrote the history of Port-Royal and that of the king's campaigns, he made two or three speeches at the Academy, and translated several church hymns. Around 1688 Mme. de Maintenon roused him from his literary slumber by asking him to compose a play for Saint-Cyr. Thus, at the age of forty-eight, Racine suddenly reawakened to a new and prodigious career, marked by two plays *Esther*, his first attempt at religious drama, and *Athalie*, a masterpiece.

Do not these two plays, so sudden, so unexpected, so different from the others, refute my opinion of Racine? Do they not escape the general criticisms I have ventured? Let us see.

In his treatment of Hebrew subjects, Racine is far more at ease than with his Greeks or his Romans. Steeped in the sacred books, sharing the beliefs of the people of God, he keeps closely to the biblical narrative and does not feel obliged to lean on Aristotle in the action, nor, above all, to center his drama around an amorous intrigue (and love is of all things human the one which, resting upon an eternal foundation, varies most in its forms according to the epochs, and hence is most apt to mislead the poet). However, for all the kinship of the two religions, and the identity of certain beliefs, there is in Judaism an element apart, intimate, primitive, oriental, which must be grasped and stressed; otherwise the result is colorless and unfaithful, even if an appearance of accuracy is preserved; and this essential element, so well understood by Bossuet in his *Politique sacrée*, was virtually inaccessible to the gentle and tender poet who saw the Old Testament only through the New, and whose only guide to Samuel was St. Paul.

Take, for instance, the architecture of the Temple in *Athalie*. For the Hebrews, everything was metaphorical, symbolical, and the importance of forms was reflected in the spirit of the Law. But in Racine I look in vain for the marvelous temple built by Solomon, in marble, in cedar, overlaid with gold, gleaming with cherubim and palms. I am in the vestibule, but I do not see the two famous pillars of brass, each eighteen cubits high, called Jachin and Boaz; I see neither the molten sea, nor the twelve brazen oxen, nor the lions; within the oracle, I miss the cherubim of olivewood, each ten cubits high, their wings stretching from wall to wall within the inner house. In Racine, the scene in the temple takes place under a somewhat bare Greek peristyle, and I feel less disposed to accept "the blood sacrifice" and the immolation by the sacred knife than if the poet had transposed me to the colossal temple where Solomon on the first day slaughtered 22,000 oxen and 120,000 sheep as a peace offering. Similar criticisms can be made of the characters and their speeches. *Athalie* is an impressive work as a whole, and magnificent in many passages, but not as complete and poignant as has been thought. In it Racine does not penetrate into the very heart of oriental Hebrew poetry.

Shall I confess it? *Esther*, with its charming sweetness and its lovely pictures, though less dramatic than *Athalie*, and though less lofty in intention seems to me more complete in itself, leaving nothing to be desired. It is true that in the Bible this graceful episode takes place between two strange events, which Racine is careful not to mention, namely, between the sumptuous feast of Ahasuerus, which lasted 180 days, and the slaughter of their enemies by the Jews, which lasted two whole days and was carried out at the formal request of the Jewess Esther. Except for or perhaps because of that omission, this delightful poem, so perfectly constructed, so filled with modesty, with sighs and pious unction, seems to me the most natural fruit borne by Racine's genius. It is the purest effusion, the most enchanting plaint of this tender soul, who could not witness the ceremony of a novice taking the veil without bursting into tears.

At about the same time he composed for Saint-Cyr four spiritual canticles, which are among his finest works. Two are after St. Paul, whom Racine treats as he previously treated Tacitus and the Bible, i.e., enveloping him in suavity and rhythm, but sometimes weakening him. It is to be regretted that he did not go further in this type of religious composition, and that in the eight years which followed *Athalie,* he did not give original expression to some of the personal, tender, passionate and fervent feelings which he harbored in his heart. Certain passages in the letters he wrote to his oldest son, then serving in the embassy in Holland, suggest that he was capable of a stirring spiritual poetry, which was ready to overflow but which he contained within himself for years, pouring it out only in prayer at the foot of God. The poetry of that age was so "literary," so completely divorced from life, that there was no way leading from one to the other, that even the idea of joining the two occurred to no one. However, since no deep feeling remains barren within us, this "repressed" poetry without normal outlet occasionally added a secret fragrance to life, flavoring the slightest actions and words, penetrating into them by imperceptible channels and impregnating them with the good odor of merit and virtue. That was the case with Racine, and that is how we are affected today when we read his letters to his son, already a grown man launched on his career. They are simple paternal letters he wrote by the fireplace, sitting beside his wife and their six other children. Every line bears the imprint of grave tenderness and austere gentleness. Critical remarks on his son's style, advice to avoid "repetitions of words" and "the locutions of the *Gazette de Hollande*" are naïvely mingled with precepts of conduct and Christian admonitions. "You are justified to some extent in ascribing the happy outcome of your trip in such bad weather to the prayers made on your behalf. I count mine for nothing; but your mother and your little sisters prayed God every day to preserve you from accidents, and the same was done at Port-Royal." And farther on: "M. de Torcy tells me that you were in the *Gazette de Hollande;* had I known, I should have bought it to read it to your little sisters, who would have thought that you had become a man of consequence."

We learn that Mme. Racine was always remembering her absent son, and that each time something *"d'un peu bon"* was served, she could not stop herself from saying, "Racine would have liked to eat that." A friend returning from Holland, M. de Bonnac, brought the family news of the beloved son; he was showered with questions, and his answers were quite satisfactory. "But I did not dare to ask him whether you gave some thought to God," the excellent father writes, "I was afraid that his answer might not be such as I would have wished."

The most important family event of Racine's last years was his youngest daughter's taking of the vows at Melun at the age of eighteen. He reports the ceremony to his son, and relates the details to his old aunt, still living at Port-Royal, of which she had recently become abbess. He sobbed throughout the service; treasures of love, inexpressible effusions flowed from the broken heart in these sobs; it was like the oil poured from Mary's vase. Fénelon wrote to him for the sole purpose of comforting him.

This excessive susceptibility to emotion, and this sensibility that grew sharper, more vulnerable from day to day, are adduced to account for the fatal effect Louis XIV's remark* had on Racine; he died a few months after it was made. But before that he had long been ill, afflicted with the sickness of poetry; only toward the end did this unknown predisposition degenerate into a kind of insidious

---

* Expressing displeasure that Racine had written a report on the wretched condition of the poor, Louis XIV is supposed to have said: "Just because he is a fine playwright does he think he is one of my ministers?"—*Eds.*

dropsy which dissolved his humors and made him defenseless against the slightest shock. He died in 1699 in his sixtieth year, revered and lamented by all, at the peak of his fame, but leaving—it must, after all, be said—a not too virile literary posterity, writers well-intentioned rather than talented—men like Rollin and d'Olivet in criticism, Duché and Campistron in drama, Jean-Baptiste [Rousseau] and his own son Louis Racine in odes and poems.

Since then down to our day and through all variations of taste, Racine's fame has remained intact, and has been the object of unanimous tributes, essentially fair and well-deserved, though sometimes not too intelligent in their motives. Unimportant critics have abused the right to cite him as a model and have too often held up for imitation his least valuable qualities. But for those able to understand him, his work and his life contain enough to ensure that he will be admired forever as a great poet and cherished as a dear friend.

II

Racine was a playwright—there is no doubt about that; but he was writing in an age when drama had little scope. In an epoch like ours when the range of drama is far vaster, what would he have done? Would he still have written for the theater? Would his genius, meditative and serene by nature, have been equal to that intensity of action which our blasé curiosity clamors for? Would he have been capable of that realism in portrayal of character and mores, which always prevails in post-revolutionary periods? Could he have risen above plots that are no more than glorified intrigues? Could he have aimed at profound philosophical truths in interpreting historical episodes? Did he possess the strength and temperament to take all these elements into account, to harmonize them, to join and link them into an indissoluble and living form, to fuse them all in the fire of passions? Would he not have thought it simpler and more in tune with his nature to deal with passion free from all foreign alloys, and to treat it in the noble elegiac style of which *Esther* and *Bérénice* are the most accomplished examples? These are delicate questions, which can be answered only by hypotheses. I have ventured my own; it implies no disrespect for the genius of Racine. Nor am I disrespectful of Racine when I say that I prefer his poetic to his dramatic qualities, and that I am tempted to classify him as a lyrical genius, one of the elegiac and religious bards whose mission in this world is to celebrate love (taking love in the same sense as Dante and Plato).

Apart from direct scrutiny of his works, I find confirmation of my opinion in Racine's behavior during the long years of his silence as a playwright. Normally, a man who at the peak of his career ceases abruptly to exercise his innate talents, enjoys his rest for only a brief period; then comes a reawakening, a desire to resume his customary activity. At first, he perceives this reawakening only as a muffled, distant, vague longing, whose effects resemble those of boredom. Soon his restlessness assumes a more definite form. His faculties, deprived of nourishment, become famished, as it were; they loudly assert their demands, like a thoroughbred that neighs in its stable, clamoring for the race track; the desire cannot be held back any longer, and all resolutions of retreat are forgotten. Imagine, for instance, one of the incontestably dramatic geniuses—Shakespeare, Molière, Beaumarchais, or Scott— in the same situation as Racine after he resolved to withdraw from the theater. How many ideas will assail him, how many characters will be spontaneously generated by his effervescent brain, how many unfinished beings, hovering in midair, will haunt his dreams and daydreams and beckon to him! How many plaintive voices will speak to him, as they speak to Tancred in the enchanted forest! Queen Mab in her chariot, Ariel or Puck, Scapin or Dorine, Cherubino or Fenella, marvelous elves, malicious and eager messengers, will press upon the slumbering genius, will pester him in a thousand ways, demanding that he attend to their absent lovers, their princesses in distress. They will conjure up the souls of heroes who had never lived, just as the seer Tiresias or rather the old Anchises conjured them up in the Elysian fields. There will be a procession of shadows, laughing or weeping, clamoring for life, waiting to be taken out of the limbo of the poet's mind, to be brought to the light of day. Diana Vernon on horseback, Juliet on her balcony, the ingénue Agnès exchanging sweet words with her lover, the mocking Suzanne and the beautiful countess dressing up Cherubino, and so many other enchanting figures will smile at the poet and summon him. He will not resist them long, but will plunge headlong into this world eddying around him. Each will go back to his former pursuits: Beaumarchais to his extravagant intrigues, Walter Scott to his adventures, Molière to his profound and comical portrayals of human failings, Shakespeare to his graceful fancies and tragic terrors; and finally the great Corneille (for he too is of this family) will once again be at the head of his old Spanish warriors, leading them to battle.

So much for the dramatic poets. I shall not go so far as to say that Racine was never like them after he retired, that he lost all interest in his former life, that in his daydreams he never had the charming visions that used to stir his heart. But his feminine creations, his noble women in love—Monime, Phèdre, Bérénice with her long veil—all of whom must have occasionally haunted him, taking on the features of La Champmeslé, could not have done so for long. He promptly forgot them; his heart was elsewhere, with Port-Royal so sorely persecuted, and he indulged in sweet childhood memories. "Indeed, no religious house had a better reputation than Port-Royal," he wrote (*Abrégé de l'histoire de Port-Royal*). "Everything you saw of it outwardly inspired reverence; one admired the grave and touching manner in which God was praised there, the simplicity and cleanliness of the church, the modesty of the servants, the solitude of the visiting rooms, the reluctance of the nuns to prolong conversations there, their lack of curiosity for the things of the world and even the affairs of their families; in a word, total indifference to-

ward everything unrelated to God. But how many new
subjects of edification were found by those who knew the
inside of this monastery! What peace! What silence! What
charity! What love of poverty and mortification! Work
without respite, continual prayer, no ambition save to perform the lowliest, most humiliating tasks, no complaining
among the sisters, nothing overbearing in the mothers, invariably prompt obedience and invariably reasonable orders."

At about the same time he wrote to his son: "I heard
from M. de Rost that La Champmeslé is at death's door,
which seems to distress him a great deal; but what is most
distressing is something he apparently is not concerned
with at all, namely, the obstinacy with which the unfortunate woman refuses to renounce the theater; I have been
told that she considered it very honorable to die as an
actress. Let us hope that when she sees death more closely
she will sing a different tune, as most people do who are
so self-assured when they are in good health. It was Mme.
de Caylus who informed me of this detail, which she found
frightening, and which she had learned, I believe, from
M. le curé de Saint-Sulpice." And in another letter he
said: "Poor M. Boyer died a very Christian death; on this
occasion I must add, incidentally, that I owe amends to
the memory of La Champmeslé, who died a Christian
after renouncing the theater and greatly repenting her past
life, though what distressed her most was the thought of
death itself; at least this is what M. Boileau told me, having learned it from the curé d'Auteuil who saw her die.
For she died at Auteuil, in the house of a dancing master,
whither she had moved for a change of air."

To excuse this dry tone we must assume that Racine
intended indirectly to give a lesson to his son and to condemn his own sin of lechery in the person of the woman
who had been its object. But even taking this intention
into account, we may safely conclude after reading and
comparing these passages, that the poet had become estranged from the theater, and that the figure of La Champmeslé had long been erased from his memory. Port-Royal

was in full possession of his soul; in it he found peace, to it went his prayers; he was full of the groans of this house of affliction when he wrote the stirring melodies of the choruses of *Esther*. In other words, the poet's lyrical disposition had clearly gained dominance. . . .

If it were argued that my hypothesis might be admissible if Racine had not written *Athalie,* and that *Athalie* alone is enough to refute it, since it reveals that the poet's genius was essentially dramatic, I should reply that while having great admiration for *Athalie* I do not grant it that much importance; that the amount of elevation, energy, and sublimity it contains does not seem to me to go beyond what is needed to be successful in great religious poetry, and that in my view this magnificent tragedy is merely evidence of Racine's strong and powerful qualities, which were the culmination of his usual tender style.

A closer scrutiny of Racine's style will compel the same conclusion. What is a dramatic style? It is something simple, familiar, lively. It flows on and breaks off, rises and falls, changes effortlessly as it shifts from one character to another, and varies in one and the same character, according to the emotion he expresses. There are meetings, conversations, jokes; then there is irony, anger swells, and the dialogue is like the interlacings of a pair of serpents in combat. Gestures, inflections of the voice, and meanderings of speech are in perfect harmony; the natural accidents, the everyday particularities of a lively conversation are reproduced at the proper places. Augustus is seated in his study with Cinna and speaks to him at length; each time Cinna is about to interrupt him, the emperor stops him authoritatively, holds out his hand, bids him resume his place, and continues. Talma's acting was a translation into visual terms of the entire dramatic style.

The characters of the drama, since they are actually alive like everybody else, must continually evoke the details and habits of everyday life. "Yesterday," "today," "tomorrow" are very significant words for them. They never miss an opportunity to evoke vivid memories on which their favorite passion feeds. They often let escape phrases

such as "on that day," "at such a moment," "in such a
place." The love which fills a soul and which looks for
words seizes hold of everything within reach, draws images from it, countless comparisons, and taps unexpected
sources of emotion. Juliet on the balcony imagines that she
is hearing the song of the lark, and urges her young husband to leave; but Romeo, in order to stay, insists that it is
the nightingale. [*Sic:* Sainte-Beuve partially misremem-
bers the scene. (*Eds.*)]

Grief is superstitious; the soul in its moments of extrem-
ity experiences singular reversals; before leaving this life, it
seems to cling to it by the thinnest, most fragile threads.
Desdemona, shaken by the vague premonition of her
death, continually recalls, without knowing why, an old
willow song which one of her mother's maids used to sing
to her as a child. Thus even lyrical elements, thanks to
artless details that record and embody them, are not mere
additions, but contribute directly to the dramatic effect.

Epic picturesqueness, pompous descriptions do not go
well with the style of drama; but a seemingly chance remark in a dialogue, without deliberate descriptive intention, can convey local color and define in advance the
scene of passionate action. Duncan arrives with his retinue
at Macbeth's castle; he finds the site pleasant, Banquo
points out to him that there are nests of martlets in every
frieze and buttress of the wall; this is proof, he says, that
"the air is delicate." Shakespeare abounds in such traits;
they are also found in the Greek tragic authors. Never in
Racine.

From the outset Racine's style appears to us as almost
uniformly elegant and poetic; nothing in it stands out
specially. It usually proceeds by analysis and abstraction.
Every main protagonist, instead of externalizing his passion
and being no more than its vehicle, most often contem-
plates it within himself, and relates it in his words as he
sees it in his inner world, in his I, as philosophers put it.
Hence a general method of exposition and narration which
presupposes in every hero or heroine a certain leisure for
preliminary self-examination; hence also a whole order of

subtle images, and a different, subdued light, borrowed from an intricate metaphysics of the heart, but little or no reality, and none of those details that take us back to the human aspects of life. Racine's poetry eludes details, scorns them, and when it tries to render them, it seems powerless to grasp them.

In *Mithridate*, Monime tries to strangle herself with her headband, or, as Racine puts it, *faire un affreux lien d'un sacré diadème.* She apostrophizes this diadem in enchanting lines which it is far from me to criticize. I shall merely note that for all the anger and contempt she heaps upon this *fatal tissu*, she ventures to name it only in general terms and with exquisite insults. Because the poet imposes upon himself a perpetual nobility and elegance, his verse inevitably weakens when he comes to a transition that cannot be ennobled or enhanced, and that may seem prosaic by contrast with the tone of the whole. (Chamfort found lines in *Esther* which he thought were rather banal.) Moreover, Racine sought to avert this kind of criticism to such a point that at the risk of violating dramatic convention he made his most subordinate characters use a language as stately and flowery as that of his most accomplished heroes. He treats his confidantes on the same footing as his queens, Arcas expresses himself as majestically as Agamemnon.

Racine's analytical method, which he employs continuously, the marvelous elegance with which he presents his ideas, the solemnity and smoothness of his sentences, the rhythmic melody of his verse, all contribute to making his style very different from most direct and pure dramatic styles. Talma, who in his last years acted with a striking and sublime simplicity, particularly the heroes of Corneille, could never have achieved these qualities with Racine's heroes. Is this to imply that Racine's style is completely devoid of dramatic quality? Such a blasphemy is far from my thought. Racine's style fits perfectly the kind of drama it expresses, providing us with a perfect combination of the same felicitous qualities. Everything in it is skillfully harmonized, there is nothing jarring or dissonant; in this complete ideal of gracefulness and delicacy, Monime would indeed be wrong to speak otherwise. It is a gentle and exquisite conversation, of ever increasing charm, a penetrating confidence full of emotion, as might have been suggested to the poet by the peaceful conversation of a society where a woman could write *La Princesse de Clèves*. It is an intimate, unique, outgoing feeling which mingles with everything, seeps in everywhere, is found in every sigh, every tear, and is breathed with the very air itself.

If we shift suddenly from the paintings of Rubens, while we are still under the impression of the great Flemish master's brilliant richness, to those of M. Ingres, we see in the French artist at first only a fairly uniform tone, a diffuse hue of pale and gentle light. But move closer and look more carefully, and a thousand subtle nuances will come to bloom before our eyes, a thousand intricate intentions will emerge from this deep and tightly knit fabric, and we will be unable to tear our eyes away from it. This is how Racine appears to us when we approach him after leaving Molière or Shakespeare: then he more than ever requires a long close look; only in this way can the secrets of his style be discovered. Then, in the atmosphere of the dominant emotion that is the essence of every tragedy, we shall see the various characters and their individual features being drawn and coming to life. The differences of emphasis, fleeting and tenuous, will become tangible and lend a kind of relative truth to the language of each, and we shall know to what exact extent Racine is dramatic and in what sense he is not.

Racine wrote *Les Plaideurs*, and in this admirable farce he at once achieved the true style of comedy so completely that we may be surprised that he confined himself to this first attempt. Why did he not sense, the questioning critics of our day cannot help wondering, that the use of this genuinely dramatic style which he had borrowed from Molière was not limited to comedy, and that the most serious passion could resort to it and elevate it to its own level? Why did he not recall that the style of Corneille, in many pathetic passages, does not differ essentially from that of Molière? All that was needed was to fuse both; the task of the dramatic reform that is being carried out today before our eyes would have been carried out then. The answer to these questions is no doubt that in tragedy as he conceived in Racine had no need for this open and free language; that *Les Plaideurs* was never more than an accident in his literary career, and that invincible prejudices always stand in the way of the simple "fusions" that the critic imagines so easily after two centuries.

In Racine's lifetime, Fénelon, his friend and admirer, whose genius seems most closely related to his, wrote about Molière: "Although he thinks well, he often expresses himself badly. He uses the most forced, the least natural language. Terence says in four words with the most elegant simplicity what Molière says only with a multitude of metaphors that come close to gibberish. I like his prose far more than his verse. For instance, *L'Avare* is written less badly than his plays in verse. It is true that he was embarrassed by French versification; it is also true that he was more successful in *Amphitryon*, where he took the liberty of using irregular verse. But all in all, it seems to me that even in his prose he does not speak simply enough to express all the passions." . . . Racine would probably have agreed with Fénelon in many of his criticisms of Molière's diction.

His own is scrupulous, irreproachable, and all the praise usually showered on Racine's style applies unreservedly to his diction. No one knew the value of words better than he, the power of their positions and combinations, the art of transition, "that most difficult achievement of poetry," as Boileau would tell him (this is confirmed by their correspondence). Keeping to a slightly restricted vocabulary, Racine multiplied the combinations and resources of our language. It will be noted that he occasionally shows light traces of a French older than his own, and for my part I find infinite charm in those all too few idioms, for which he occasionally was chided by eighteenth-century critics.

All in all, it seems to me that it would be unfair to treat

Racine differently from all true poets of genius, to ask of
him what he has not, and not to accept in judging him the
conditions of his nature. His style is self-sufficient, as self-
sufficient as his drama. It is the product of a rare and
flexible temperament, modified by experience and train-
ing, and a number of social circumstances which have
vanished forever. It is, as much as any other, marked with
the imprint of a distinct individuality, and almost everywhere evokes the noble, gentle, melancholy profile of the
man and his time. This also implies that to erect his style
as a model of style, to profess it on every occasion, to compare all other styles with it as an invariable type, is to
understand him very little and to admire him very superficially, to confine him entirely to his qualities of grammar
and diction. I believe we are closer to the truth when we
say that the style of Racine, like that of La Fontaine or
Bossuet, deserves to be studied forever, but cannot and
should not be imitated. Above all, it can scarcely be used
in the new drama, precisely because it is so perfectly attuned to a type of tragedy that is a thing of the past.

> From *Portraits littéraires*. Reprinted there from
> three separate essays originally published in
> 1829, 1830, and 1844.
>
> In addition to this long early study of Racine and
> his plays, Sainte-Beuve wrote later articles (col-
> lected in *Nouveaux lundis*) about Racine's letters
> and about the last five months of his life, as well
> as considering him at length in the last book of
> *Port-Royal*—for Racine's changing relations with
> that religious community were of great interest
> from both a biographical and a literary point of
> view.
>
> In *Port-Royal* Sainte-Beuve revised his opinion
> of *Athalie*. He speaks of it there as Racine's
> greatest achievement, one of "the three loftiest
> monuments of Christian art in the seventeenth
> century," along with Bossuet's *Discours sur
> l'histoire universelle* and Corneille's *Polyeucte*.

In particular, he retracts his earlier objections to Racine's treatment of the temple in *Athalie;* he recognizes that "a more elaborate setting would have been harmful to the idea, excessive descriptions would have obscured the true subject—the one and only God, who is all spirit and pervades everything."

MOLIÈRE

THERE IS a class of writers who stand out even among the greatest, a very small class comprising no more than five or six names in all. Their hallmark is universality, a sense of eternal human values which pervades their portrayal of an age's customs and passions. Spontaneous creators, forceful and prolific, they are characterized first of all by this mixture of fertility, firmness, and freedom; by deep knowledge and richness of resources; by true indifference to conventional genres and techniques—any framework, any point of departure serves their purpose. They produce copiously, spurred on by obstacles, and they often achieve perfection without working less rapidly, and without resorting to artifice.

After the great figure of Homer, who gloriously inaugurated this supreme class of writers by incarnating the primitive genius of the noblest portion of mankind, it is difficult to decide which other men of ancient Greece should be included. Sophocles, however productive he may seem to have been, however human he showed himself in the harmonious expression of feelings and sufferings, Sophocles remains so perfect a figure, so sacred, as it were, in form and attitude, that we can scarcely imagine him removed from his purely Greek pedestal. The works of the famous comic authors have been lost; all we have is the name of Menander, who was perhaps the most accomplished in the group of geniuses we are speaking about. Aristophanes' marvelous imagination, so Athenian and so

charming, nonetheless detracts from his universality. In
Rome I can see only Plautus belonging here, a writer
whose merits have not yet been fully appreciated. He was
a profound and versatile portrayer of human nature, head
of his own company, like Shakespeare and like Molière, at
once an actor and an author. We must see him as one of
Molière's most legitimate forebears. But Latin literature
was too much of a Greek import, too artificial from the
outset, to provide sufficient scope for many of these free
creators to develop. Ovid and Cicero, the most prolific
among the great writers of this literature, are also the
most "literary" and at bottom the most rhetorical. However, ancient Rome must be credited with having contributed two admirable poets to the literature of imitation,
learning, and taste—those polished, accomplished artists,
Virgil and Horace.

We have to come down to the modern era, to the Renaissance, to find the other men we are looking for—Shakespeare, Cervantes, Rabelais, Molière—these, with two or
three more uneven talents of a later date, complete the
classification. They all have a great deal in common. Their
lives were eventful, beset with difficulties; they suffered,
struggled, and loved. As soldiers, as physicians, as actors,
as prisoners, they knew the hardships of poverty, they
knew passion, and they were harassed by all sorts of
worries, including financial ones. But their genius over-
came all limitations, and none the worse for having had to
struggle, they worked hard and continuously to give full
scope to their gifts. We have all seen how true and natural
beauty can blossom even in the poorest, most unhealthy,
and most unpropitious surroundings. Very occasionally we
come across a young woman of the common people who
is accomplished and enlightened (though we cannot imagine how she became so), and elegant to her fingertips.
Such persons keep alive our notion of the nobility of the
human race, our belief that it was formed in the likeness
of the gods. These rare geniuses who give us great beauty
effortlessly—beauty native to them, "genuine" in the ety-
mological sense of the word—represent similar triumphs

over the most adverse conditions. They seem to have grown and developed that way almost as though they could not help it. There seems nothing accidental about their careers, nor do they seem ever to have been at the mercy of circumstances. They are not merely prolific or merely facile, in the manner of secondary geniuses like Ovid, Dryden, and the Abbé Prévost. Although their works were as quickly turned out and are as numerous as those of merely facile writers, they are also composed to last, are sturdily constructed as well as highly accomplished and sublime. Unlike the poets of the studious, polished school such as Gray, Pope, and Boileau, they never arrive at their great effects by means of sometimes overcareful calculation and continual self-correction. I admire those poets and enjoy their works as much as anyone, and I recognize that scrupulous correction gives their poetry an indispensable quality, a specific charm such as was defined by Vauvenargues in his excellent aphorism, *La netteté est le vernis des maîtres*—"Precision is the classic writer's varnish."

In the perfection of the other, superior poets there is something freer and more daring, which turns up less predictably, has a wider range of appeal, and is less dependent upon strict observance of elaborate rules. It seems to arise of its own accord, effortlessly, in a way that surprises and baffles some of their most distinguished contemporaries. Their resources of invention, down to the most minor details of their crafts, are astonishing.

Molière belongs among these most illustrious names, although he fully encompassed only the comic aspect of mankind: our vices, weaknesses, and follies. When he touched on the pathetic side of life, he did so quickly, incidentally. And yet he is second to none among the most complete geniuses, so greatly did he excel in his domain and explore every conceivable vein from the freest fantasy to the most serious observation. He was sovereign in every corner of reality he chose to treat in his works—and if that was only half of life, it is the half we encounter most often and that society is most concerned with.

Molière is of the century in which he lived, in that he

portrays certain of its failings and his characters wear its costumes. But he is even more the portrayer of human nature in every time and place. To take the measure of his genius, it suffices to notice that though it is easy to link him to his century, yet he is not entirely determined by it; he attuned himself to it, but he is no less great transplanted to other times and places. His illustrious contemporaries Boileau, Racine, Bossuet, and Pascal are far more bound up with the age, the age of Louis XIV, than was Molière. Their genius (and this goes for the greatest among them) bears the unmistakable imprint of their times; it would probably have been very different had they been born in another age. What would Bossuet be today? What would Pascal write? Racine and Boileau make a marvelous accompaniment to the reign of Louis XIV in all its youthful gaiety and brilliance, when it was still victorious and had not yet become insensitive. Bossuet dominates the reign at its apogee, when it had already become highly religious, but was not as yet hopelessly bigoted. Molière, who, I think, would have been oppressed by the increasing dominance of religious authority, and who died just in time to escape it—Molière belongs like Boileau and Racine (he was older than they) to the earlier period. And although he portrayed its life more truly than anyone else, he remained somehow independent of it. He added to the brilliance and majesty of the Great Monarch's reign, but he is not marked, particularized, or narrowed by it. He adopted its forms but he did not make himself their prisoner.

Today, when we judge things from a distance and by their results, Molière seems far more radically aggressive with respect to the society of his time than he himself supposed he was. We must guard against such distortion of perspective in judging him. Among the illustrious contemporaries just mentioned, only one—the one whom we would be least tempted to liken to our poet—questioned the very foundations of French society in that age even more than Molière, and analyzed birth, status, and property without preconceived ideas. This bold thinker was Pascal. However, the only consequence Pascal drew from his insights—rather, from his destructive analysis of everything around him—was to cling more desperately to the pillars of the temple, to embrace the Cross in his agony.

Pascal and Molière seem to us today the best observers of the society of their epoch. Molière ranged over an immense territory which extended as far as the wall of the Church; he and his troupe peeked and probed into every corner of the old society, and held up to ridicule indiscriminately the conceit of the nobles, the inequality of matrimonial rights, the speciousness of religious hypocrisy. At the same time—more frighteningly—they showed the effects of these abuses upon true piety and the marriage sacrament. Pascal, meanwhile, though he remained within the central orthodoxy of the age, in his own way shook the vault of the edifice with his cries and anguish, and there was something Samson-like about the way he clasped the sacred pillars. However, in my opinion Molière did not deliberately set out to overturn the existing order —any more than Pascal did. He was probably unaware of the ultimate implications of his attitude. Similarly, it is hardly likely that Plautus had some systematic idea at the back of his mind when he made jokes about usury, prostitution, and slavery—those vices and mainsprings of ancient society.

In short, like Shakespeare and Cervantes, like three or four superior geniuses who have appeared over the ages, Molière was essentially a portrayer of human nature as he found it—without concern for organized religion, fixed dogma, or philosophical interpretation. In treating the society of his time, he portrayed the life that is everywhere that of the majority, and in castigating certain ways of life, he happened to write for all mankind.

Jean-Baptiste Poquelin was born in Paris, January 15, 1622—not, as was for a long time supposed, in a market stall, but (according to the findings of M. Beffara) in a house in the Rue Saint-Honoré, at the corner of the Rue des Vieilles-Etuves. On both sides, his family was engaged in the upholstery trade. His father, who in addition to his profession held the appointment of *valet-de-chambre-tapis-*

sier to the royal household, intended his son to follow him in his footsteps, and the young Poquelin at an early date began to serve his apprenticeship in the family shop. By the age of fourteen he had learned only to read, write, and count—as much instruction as the family business required. His maternal grandfather, however, was very fond of the theater and occasionally took him to see the plays given at the Hôtel de Bourgogne, where Bellerose acted in high comedy parts, and Gaultier-Garguille, Gros-Guillaume, and Turlupin appeared in farces. Every day that followed an evening of theater, the young Poquelin was dejected, inattentive to his work in the shop, and sick at heart at the prospect of a life of trade. We may imagine what daydreams filled the morning-after thoughts of the adolescent genius, before whom human life must already have been shaping itself into a series of scenes upon a stage. Finally he opened his heart to his father and, supported by his grandfather who "spoiled" him, was allowed to continue his studies. It seems that he moved into a boarding house and attended classes at the Collège de Clermont (later the lycée Louis-le-Grand) at this time run by the Jesuits.

After completing his courses, Poquelin replaced his aged father in the appointment as *valet-de-chambre-tapissier* to the king (the office was reversionary). In this connection, he followed Louis XIII to Narbonne in 1641 and witnessed the execution of Cinq-Mars and de Thou the next year—a bitter mockery of human justice. It seems that in the following years, instead of continuing to exercise the office, he studied law in Orléans and was admitted to the bar. But his love for the theater carried the day. Back in Paris, he is said to have frequented the stage of the Pont Neuf and closely followed the Italians and Scaramouche, before heading an incorporated troupe of actors, which soon became a regular professional company. The two Béjart brothers, their sister Madeleine, and Duparc (popularly known as Gros-René) were members of this traveling company which called itself "L'Illustre Théâtre." Then our poet broke with his family and took the name of Molière.

With his company he played in various quarters of Paris and in the provinces as well. It is said that in Bordeaux he staged a *Thébaïde,* an attempt at a serious drama, which was a failure. But he was not sparing with farces, skits in the *commedia dell'arte* tradition, and impromptus such as *Le Médecin volant* and *La Jalousie du Barbouillé,* these last the earliest surviving sketches for *Le Médecin malgré lui* and *George Dandin.* Other early works, only the titles of which have come down to us, were *Les Docteurs rivaux, Le Maître d'Ecole,* and *Le Docteur amoureux,* which Boileau condescended to deplore. The life of the company touring the provinces was a haphazard one. Molière was well received by the Duc d'Epernon at Bordeaux and by the Prince de Conti [with whom he had been at school] whenever they met; d'Assouci praised him, and Molière in turn treated him as a prince. He was hospitable, generous, a good companion, often in love, discovering and experiencing all the passions, driving his youthful company at a furious pace all around France like some spirited artistic Fronde, his mind gradually acquiring a rich store of original observations of character. It was in the course of this wandering player's life that in 1655, at Lyon, he staged *L'Etourdi,* his first true play. He was then thirty-three.

Clearly, Molière had considerable experience of life and the passions before setting out to portray them. This is not to say that his biography falls into two successive parts, like that of many eminent moralists and satirists—first a more or less fervent life of action, and then, as a result of excess or encroaching old age, a jaundiced recollection dissecting and disapproving of all that had gone before. This was not at all the case with Molière nor with the other great men endowed with supreme creative genius. Distinguished minds who do develop in this way and promptly reach the second stage may acquire a keen, subtle talent for criticism, as did M. de la Rochefoucauld, but no life-giving movement or creative power. Dramatic genius, and especially that of Molière, is marvelous in that its development is entirely different, much more complex. Even as a passionate young man, no less given to rash and credulous enthusiasms than most people of his age, Molière possessed to a high degree the gift of observing and repro- ducing, the ability to probe and grasp human motivations —a gift and an ability which in his plays would subse- quently give great delight to all. Later in life, as a man who had acquired a fuller, sadder knowledge of the hu- man heart and human motivations, we shall see that he nonetheless preserved the freshness of his youthful impres- sions and a faculty for still experiencing all the passions, including love with its jealousies. A sublime contradiction, which one can only admire in the life of the great poet! These contradictory features are inherent in what is most mysterious in the dramatist's gift, his ability to portray bitter reality by means of animated, graceful, pleasing characters who possess all the features of nature; the pro- foundest dissection of the heart is made visible through active, original beings who need only be themselves!

The story goes that while staying at Lyon, Molière, who had already become intimate with Madeleine Béjart, fell in love with both Mlle.[1] Duparc (or with the woman who became Mlle. Duparc when she married the actor of that name) and Mlle. de Brie, actresses in another company. According to the story, despite Madeleine Béjart's objec- tions, Molière succeeded in getting both actresses to join his company, and when rebuffed by the haughty Duparc, he found in Mlle. de Brie at this time the consolation he was later to seek again from her during his stormy mar- riage. Some have even gone so far as to see in the first act of Les Femmes savantes, in the scene between Clitandre, Armande, and Henriette, a reminiscence of this situation which antedated the play by twenty years. There is no doubt that between Molière and the young actresses he directed, shifting and intricate bonds of affection grew up, bonds which were more than once broken and renewed. However, I think it would be rash to seek specific traces of them in his works; certainly the particular attempt cited

---

[1] At the time of Molière, a married woman of the common people was called "Mademoiselle." "Madame" was reserved for the wives of titled nobles.—Eds.

above, which failed to note a twenty-year lapse of time, seems farfetched.

At Pézenas in Languedoc a chair has been preserved, in which Molière is said to have sat every Saturday at the local barber's, counting the week's box office receipts and at the same time observing the physiognomies and the speech habits of the customers. It may be recalled that Machiavelli, who was also a great comic writer, did not scorn conversing with butchers, bakers, and such. But Molière, in his long sessions at the barber-surgeon's, probably pursued an aim more directly relevant to his art than the Florentine ex-secretary, who—as he tells us himself— was principally whiling away his time in the provinces, waiting for the day when his exile from Florence would be ended. Molière's habit of watching people for hours on end while keeping quiet himself increased with age, experience, and the sorrows of life. Boileau was particularly struck by this and nicknamed Molière "The Contemplator." And there is the following speech by Elise in *La Critique de l'Ecole des femmes:* "You know him, and how lazy he is about keeping the conversation going. Célimène had invited him because he was supposed to be so clever, and he just sat there like a stick, among the half dozen or so people she had been praising him to. . . . He disappointed them greatly by keeping still." On one occasion Molière was seen sitting for hours at Auxerre waiting for a stagecoach to leave. He was observing what went on around him, but so seriously that he seemed like a mathematician pondering an abstract problem or a writer of romances composing a new tale.

The Prince de Conti, before he became a Jansenist, had Molière and his company give performances at his house in Paris, and when he went to Languedoc he again summoned his old schoolmate to him. Molière joined him at Béziers or Montpellier, coming from Pézenas. There the poet presented his most varied repertory, including sketches in the Italian manner, his recent play, *L'Etourdi,* and the charming comedy *Le Dépit amoureux.* The prince was enchanted and attempted to persuade Molière to be-

come his secretary, successor to the poet Sarrasin who
had died shortly before. Molière refused because he was
attached to his company, loved the profession, and appreciated the independent life. After several more years
spent wandering in the south, where he made friends with
the painter Mignard at Avignon, Molière moved closer to
the capital. He stayed at Rouen for some time, where he
finally obtained permission to perform in Paris under the
eyes of the king. His patron was no longer the Prince de
Conti (as was long believed), for the latter had turned to
religion in 1655 under the guidance of the bishop of Alet.
His new patron was Monsieur, the Duc d'Orléans, brother
of Louis XIV.

It was on October 24, 1658, in the guards' hall of the
old Louvre, in the presence of the court and the acting
company of the Hôtel de Bourgogne—a rather severe audience—that Molière and his company ventured to stage
Nicomède. After the applause that rewarded their performance of this tragicomedy, Molière, who was accustomed to speak for the company, and who on this crucial
occasion could not yield the role to anyone else, came to
the front of the stage, and, after having "thanked His
Majesty in very modest terms for having so kindly forgiven
his faults and those of the company, which was overawed
at appearing before so august an assembly, he said that
their desire to have the honor of amusing the greatest king
in the world had made them forget that His Majesty had
at his service excellent originals of whom they were no
more than pale copies; but that since His Majesty had
been good enough to bear with their unpolished way, he
implored him very humbly to be allowed to stage for him
one of the short *divertimenti* which had earned him some
reputation, and to which he had been treating the provinces." He chose *Le Docteur amoureux*.

The king was satisfied with the spectacle and gave permission to Molière's company to settle in Paris under the
name of *La Troupe de Monsieur*, and to perform on the
stage of the Petit-Bourbon, alternating with an Italian
company. In 1660, when the colonnade of the Louvre

began to be erected on the site of the Petit-Bourbon, the *Troupe de Monsieur* was moved to the theater of the Palais-Royal. It became *La Troupe du Roi* in 1665, and later, on Molière's death, it was first merged with the Troupe du Marais, and seven years later (1680) with that of the Hôtel de Bourgogne to become the Théâtre Français.

Now installed in Paris with a theater of his own, Molière staged *L'Etourdi* and *Le Dépit amoureux* for the first time there, and was no less successful than in the provinces. Even though *L'Etourdi* is still no more than a comedy of intrigue imitated from the Italian, what verve Molière already displays—what warmth, what life! How imaginative, indeed stunning, are the frantic goings on of Mascarille—a name never before heard in the theater! To be sure, Mascarille, in his first appearance, is a direct descendant of the valets of the *commedia dell'arte* and ancient comedy and the valet of Marot. Mascarille is a true son of Villon, who also lived on free meals, one of the many hundred ancestors of Figaro. In *Les Précieuses*, however, he will become individualized, Mascarille the marquis, a wholly modern valet who wears no other livery but Molière's own. *Le Dépit amoureux*, behind the implausibility and conventionality of the disguises and mistaken identities, provides in the scene between Lucile and Eraste an eternally fresh love situation, eternally young since the dialogue between Horace and Lydia. Molière was to go back to the situation in *Le Tartufe* and in *Le Bourgeois gentilhomme*, always felicitously yet never surpassing this first portrayal. The author who best knows how to castigate and ridicule shows as early as this that he also understands love.

Les Précieuses ridicules, staged in 1659, attacked contemporary manners observed from life. Here Molière departed from Italian farce and theatrical tradition generally and shows us what he saw with his own eyes, speaking his mind loudly and firmly against the most trying enemies of every great dramatic poet when he is beginning: enemies such as the inability to call things by their right names, a prudishness masquerading as wit, a parochial taste which is essentially hostile to art. With his frankness and naturalness, Molière had to sweep away all such petty harassments before he could give free rein to his genius. There is a story that when *Les Précieuses* was performed for the first time, an old man in the audience, thrilled by this new frankness—doubtless seventeen years earlier the same gentleman had applauded Corneille's *Menteur*—could not keep from calling out to Molière, who was playing the part of Mascarille: "Courage, courage, Molière! This is good comedy!" On hearing these words, which he divined were those of his true public, the one which would bring him the warmest universal applause, Molière felt, Segrais tells us, enheartened. Shortly afterward, he let slip this remark, showing his noble pride and announcing his coming of age as an artist: "No more studying of Plautus or Terence or Menander. Now I study people." And indeed, the whole world was now opening to Molière; he was discovering it and making it his own. From now on, all he had to do was to decide what to portray. When occasionally he still imitated, it was of his own choice and for his own reasons. He continued to take what he liked where he liked, no longer out of lack of self-confidence, but like a sovereign enlarging his kingdom by conquest. His borrowings honored their source and improved upon it.

During the fourteen years that followed his definitive return to Paris, down to his death in 1673, Molière never stopped producing. For the king and the Court he executed specially commissioned entertainments, while for the pleasure of the public at large, in the interests of his company, and for his own fame in the eyes of posterity, Molière exerted himself to his utmost and coped with everything. There is nothing pedantic about him, nothing that smells of the lamp. A true dramatic poet, his works are made to be played on the stage; they are not so much written down as performed by the author. His preparation as an actor-manager in the provinces gave him experience akin to that of primitive popular poets, the bards, the jongleurs, or the anonymous creators of the miracle plays who wandered from town to town, borrowing subjects from one another, occasionally adding a thing or two, leaving behind no written records of their performances. Thus most of Molière's sketches and impromptus in the *commedia dell'arte* style (we have the titles for about ten of them) have been lost, except for *Le Médecin volant* and *La Jalousie du Barbouillé,* and it is doubtful whether the texts we possess are Molière's own.

Also like the primitive poets who often combined several separate works, Molière later readapted these early sketches and incorporated them in his "regular" plays. He shifted whole tirades from *Don Garcie de Navarre* (which was a failure) to *Le Misanthrope* and other plays. *L'Etourdi* and *Le Dépit amoureux,* the first full-fledged plays by our poet, were not printed until ten years after their first production (1653–63); *Les Précieuses* was published shortly after its successful presentation, but against the author's will, as can be seen from the preface. Here we are not dealing with sham modesty, as has been the case with many writers since. That Molière was genuinely embarrassed at being published for the first time, and really reluctant, is clear from that preface. *Le Cocu imaginaire,* though it had nearly fifty performances, was never intended to be printed. A lover of comedy, however—his name was M. de Neufvillenaine—one day realized that he had memorized the entire play. He wrote it down and published it, dedicating it to Molière. M. de Neufvillenaine obviously knew what he was about. Molière cared so little that he never prepared an edition of *Le Cocu imaginaire,* although Neufvillenaine admits that his copy made from memory may well have altered a number of words. What would Racine or Boileau have said if someone had maltreated his careful productions, in which every word is worth its weight in gold? Here is where we glimpse just what it was that essentially separated Molière from the tidy, economical, painstaking type of writer—from the Boileaus and the La Bruyères of his day. In

Neufvillenaine's edition, which because of Molière's silence must be regarded as the authoritative one, the play is in one act, although the edition of 1734 has it in three acts. There are reasons to believe that for Molière, as for ancient writers of tragedy and comedy alike, division into acts is a purely artificial, post-facto convention.

In his early plays Molière no more kept to this regular division than did Plautus. He often leaves the stage empty, and we cannot be sure whether the act ends there or not. True, he soon enough fell in with the "regularity" so highly prized at the time, but it is clear (though this is not the point I wish to make) to what extent habits from his earlier period had become ingrained. To obviate such pilferings as Neufvillenaine's, Molière had to consider undertaking book publication of his plays himself, especially as he became more and more successful. *L'Ecole des maris*, dedicated to his patron the Duc d'Orléans, was the first of his works to be published under his own supervision, and from then on (1661) he was in steady communication with the reading public. However, he repeatedly displays diffidence in this connection. He fears competition from the bookstalls in the gallery of the Palais-Royal; he would rather be judged "by candlelight," that is, by spectators in the theater.

One passage in the preface to *Les Fâcheux* has given rise to a notion that he had once entertained the idea of publishing his own comments—even a sort of poetics—with each play. Closer scrutiny of the passage, however, shows that such a notion (in any case hardly compatible with the bent of his genius) is not to be taken seriously. Rather, he was making fun of the great theoreticians of the drama in his own day, successors to Aristotle and Horace. Moreover, his poetics—both as author and as actor—was set down very fully in *La Critique de l'Ecole des femmes* and in *L'Impromptu de Versailles*. We have it all there in terms of dramatic action, in terms of comedy. In Scene 7 of the *Critique*, is it not Molière speaking, through the mouth of Dorante, when the character says: "You and those rules of yours, that you impose on ignorant people and din into our ears everyday! To hear you talk, one might think that the rules of art are the greatest mysteries in the world, whereas actually they come down to a few common-sense observations on what should be avoided if we are to enjoy poems of this kind; and the same good sense that formerly made these observations can easily make them again without the help of Aristotle and Horace. . . . So let us enjoy in good faith the things that touch us to the quick, and let us not seek out arguments to prevent enjoyment." As a final touch in this demonstration of Molière's carelessness as a man of letters, which contrasts so strongly with his rich prodigality as a poet and his painstaking zeal as actor and director, we may add that no complete edition of his works was published in his lifetime. It was La Grange, an actor in his own company, who first collected and published one in 1682, nine years after Molière's death.

Every one of Molière's plays, if we follow them in the order of their appearance, can supply material for an extensive and interesting historical article. This has already been done, and well done, by others; to attempt it again would simply be to copy them. There was a battle when *L'Ecole des femmes* was presented in 1662, and another on the occasion of *Tartufe*, just as earlier there had been a battle over *Le Cid*, and another over *Phèdre*. Those were glorious days for the art of the drama. *La Critique de l'Ecole des femmes* and *L'Impromptu de Versailles* give us enough information about the first of Molière's battles: above all, it was a dispute over aesthetics and good taste, although religion played a part in connection with the advice on marriage given to Agnès. The "humble petitions" to the king and the preface to *Tartufe* sufficiently stress the wholly moral and philosophical character of the second battle, which has since that time been renewed often and passionately. All I should like to recall here is the fact that Molière held his own very ably through it all—the attack by the devout, the envy of other authors, the lionizing by the great. Not to mention his duties as *valet-de-chambre* to the king, his indispensable aid at all celebrations, the

marital jealousy he suffered, his frequent chest illnesses
and his racking cough, his responsibilities as director of
the company and tireless actor (though often on a diet of
bread and milk). For fifteen years Molière was equal to all
these demands upon his time. Every time the need arose,
his genius coped with it, and in addition he found time for
inspired creations undertaken wholly on his own. Between
hastily discharged duties in connection with court entertainments at Versailles or Chambord and productions intended to amuse the bourgeoisie, Molière found time to
create the most carefully composed, the most immortal of
his works.

He never failed Louis XIV, his benefactor and protector,
or kept him waiting. *L'Amour médecin* was composed,
memorized, and staged in five days. Only the first act of
La Princesse d'Elide is in verse; the rest is in prose. A contemporary observed wittily that this time the company had
only managed to get one buskin on, and that the other
was down around their ankles when the curtain went up
—all the same, it went up on time. Of all the plays only
Mélicerte is unfinished, but *Les Fâcheux* was completed in
two weeks; the *Mariage forcé*, the *Sicilien, George Dandin,
Pourceaugnac,* and *Le Bourgeois gentilhomme*, these spirited comedies with intermezzos and ballets, were ready on
time without a detail missing. In the interests of his company he often had to force his pace as a writer, as in the
instance of *Don Juan*—the players of the Hôtel de Bourgogne and La Troupe de Mademoiselle already had their
Don Juans. It seems the public could never get enough of
the walking statue. But Molière's concern for popular entertainment did not prevent him from writing for such
difficult judges as Boileau, himself, and the whole human race in *Le Misanthrope, Tartufe,* and *Les Femmes
savantes*. The year *Le Misanthrope* was produced was the
most memorable, the most significant in Molière's life. Immediately after completing this serious work—it is a little
too serious for the bulk of the public—he turned out the
hearty *Médecin malgré lui* for his bourgeois public, and
then from the theater in the Rue Saint-Denis rushed di-

rectly out to Saint-Germain to put on a bill consisting of *Mélicerte* and *La Pastorale comique*. Molière never disappointed any of his publics.

Boileau, reproach him though we may for his reservations in *L'Art poétique* and for his naïve and understandable surprise at Molière's rhymes, was supremely equitable in all things pertaining to the poet and friend whom he called "The Contemplator." He understood and admired the aspects most alien to himself; he took pleasure in helping with the macaronic Latin of Molière's maddest comedies; he supplied the malicious Greek etymologies in *L'Amour médecin*. He knew Molière's true value. When Louis XIV once asked him who was the rarest of the great writers who had honored France during his reign, the severe judge replied without the slightest hesitation, "Molière, Sire." "I should not have thought so," Louis XIV said. "But you know more about these things than I."

The following incident related by Cizeron-Rival casts light on Boileau's attitude toward Molière.

"Two months before Molière died, Boileau went to see him, and found him very uncomfortable, coughing badly and breathing only with great difficulty. It looked as though the end was near. Molière, who was rather cold by nature, was more friendly than usual to Boileau. This encouraged the latter to say, 'Poor M. Molière, I see you are in a sad way. Always worrying, straining your lungs on the stage—you should be more careful. Give up acting. Are you the only man in your company capable of playing the leading parts? Why not merely write plays, and leave acting to someone else in your company? The public will think the more highly of you for it—they will look upon your actors as men in your employ. Moreover, as it is, your actors are not too easy to get along with; when you are no longer one of them, they will have greater respect for you.' 'Ah, Monsieur,' Molière replied, 'how can you say such things! It is a matter of honor for me not to quit acting!' A fine point of honor, the satirist thought to himself—painting a black Sganarelle mustache on your face every day—and turning your backside to take a beating so that others may laugh! Is it possible that this man, supreme in our age for his mind and for the sentiments of a true philosopher, this inventive censor of every human folly, should be afflicted with a folly more extravagant than those he holds up to ridicule daily? What a poor thing man is!"

Boileau did not urge Molière to desert his comrades or to give up his activity as a stage director; being the head of a troupe of actors, Molière could have refused to do so on human grounds, as the saying goes, and for many other reasons. Boileau urged him only to give up acting on the stage, and it was the stubborn old actor in Molière that found this unthinkable.

Today we feel differently about the matter. Far from blaming these weaknesses and contradictions in our genius, we love him for them; they round off his portrait and make him more human in our eyes. We also feel him to be closer to us all in his amorous passions and domestic trials. Molière, the comedian, was by nature affectionate and prone to fall in love, just as Racine, so tender in his poetry, was by nature rather caustic and inclined to epigrams. Evidence of this sensibility is found in Molière's works, in his fondness for the genre of the noble romance, in many lines of his *Don Garcie* and *La Princesse d'Elide*, in the charming scenes of lovers' quarrels in the last-named play as well as in *Le Tartufe* and in *Le Bourgeois gentilhomme*, and in the moving scene in Act IV of *Don Juan* where Elvire appears veiled. Plautus and Rabelais, those great comic authors, similarly belie their reputations by passages disclosing a delicate sensibility which we are surprised and happy to discover in them, but this is particularly true of Molière; in this respect he is very much like Terence.

In 1662, about the time he was so amusingly portraying Arnolphe dictating the marriage commandments to Agnès, the forty-year-old Molière married Armande Béjart, Madeleine's younger sister, who was no more than seventeen. Despite his passion for her, and despite his genius, he did not escape the misfortune he had described with such gusto. Don Garcie was less jealous than Molière, and George Dandin and Sganarelle were less deceived. He began to be aware of his wife's unfaithfulness at the time he staged *La Princesse d'Elide*, and from that moment on his domestic life was one long torment. Told about the success ascribed to M. de Lauzun with his wife, he had it out with her. Her back to the wall, Mlle. Molière put him off the scent by denying his charges concerning M. de Lauzun but confessing an inclination for M. de Guiche, and ended the scene by bursting into tears and falling in a faint. Heartbroken and humiliated, our poet went back to his old love, Mlle. de Brie, or, more accurately, he made her the confidante of his sorrows—just as Alceste is driven back to Eliante by Célimène's rebuffs. At the time when he produced *Le Misanthrope*, Molière was estranged from his wife and saw her only at the theater. She played the part of Célimène and he that of Alceste, and it is probable that the play contained some allusions to their feelings and actual situation. Molière's troubles were further complicated by the presence of the older Béjart, who is said to have been imperious and unaccommodating. The great man thus had to cope with three women, and as Chapelle would tell him pleasantly, he was sometimes as badgered as Jupiter by the three goddesses during the siege of Troy.

Molière did not, in the manner of several great poets, compose sonnets on his personal feelings, his loves, his sorrows; but did he convey something of them in his comedies? And if he did, to what extent? According to M. Taschereau, his biographer, Molière's plays contain passages referring to his domestic troubles. "Molière," says La Grange, his friend and the first editor of his complete works, "made admirable use of his own family affairs in his comedies. He made game of everybody, of himself above all, in several passages . . . as has often been noticed by his closest friends." Thus, *Le Bourgeois gentilhomme* contains a lifelike portrait of his wife (Act III); *L'Impromptu de Versailles* refers facetiously to the date of his marriage (Scene 1); in *L'Avare* he laughs at himself for his fluxion and his cough (Act II, Scene 5) and makes La Flèche limp like the older Béjart; and in the *Précieuses* Jodelet is given the pale complexion of the actor Brécourt. Similarly, it is very probable that in portraying Arnolphe and Alceste, he had in mind his own age, his situation, and his jealousy, and that under the mask of Argan he gave vent to his personal antipathy for the Medical Faculty. But an important distinction must be made here, one that cannot be stressed too much, for it involves the very essence of dramatic genius.

The references to Molière's own life mentioned above come down to rather vague general similarities or minor details: in actual fact, none of Molière's characters is *himself*. In most cases, these references must be regarded merely as a superior actor's artifices and byplays, or else as momentary identifications between the actor and the character, such as are familiar to comedians of all times and are intended to provoke laughter. In short, Molière's characters are not copies, but creations.

In the family of minds which includes, over various epochs and at different levels of excellence, Cervantes, Rabelais, Le Sage, Fielding, Beaumarchais, and Walter Scott, Molière is, with Shakespeare, the most accomplished example of the dramatic gift, which is properly speaking creative. Shakespeare has this advantage over Molière that he is capable of pathos and flashes of terror, for instance in his characterizations of Macbeth, King Lear, or Ophelia; but Molière makes up to some extent for this lack by the inner coherence and depth of his principal characters. . . . Molière and Shakespeare are both "primitives," two brothers, with this difference, I imagine, that in ordinary life Shakespeare, poet of tears and terror, tended to display a more smiling, happier nature, whereas Molière, the amusing comedian, tended to melancholy and silence.

Mlle. Poisson, wife of the actor of that name, drew the following portrait of Molière (*Mercure de France,* May 1740), which is confirmed by Mignard's portraits in respect of physical features, and which pleases us by the image of a frank, open nature it suggests. "Molière was neither too fat nor too thin; he was tall rather than short; he had a noble carriage and a pretty leg. He walked slowly and had a very serious expression. His nose was big, his mouth large with thick lips, his complexion dark; his eyebrows were black and strongly marked, and his way of moving them made his face extremely comical. As for his character, he was gentle, kind, generous; he was fond of making speeches, and when he read his plays to the actors, he wanted them to bring their children, in order to observe and to be guided by the spontaneous reactions of these young persons." The virile beauty of Molière's face suggested by those few lines reminds me of a story told by Tieck about Shakespeare's "utterly human countenance." Shakespeare, young and still unknown, was waiting in an inn for the arrival of Lord Southampton, who was to become his patron and friend. He was listening silently to the poet Marlowe, as the latter indulged in boisterous talk without paying attention to the young stranger. When Lord Southampton arrived in the town, he sent his page to the inn. "Go to the common room," he said, "there you must carefully scrutinize all the faces; mind you, some will look to you like the faces of less noble animals, and others like the faces of nobler animals; but keep searching until you find a face that seems to resemble nothing but a human face. That is the man I want; greet him in my name and bring him to me." The young page hastened on his errand; he entered the common room and slowly examined the faces one by one. Finding the face of Marlowe the most beautiful of all, he decided he was the man and took him to his master. The fact is, Marlowe's features had a certain resemblance to those of a noble bull, and this impressed the page, child that he was. But Lord Southampton later pointed out his error to him and explained why the human and well-proportioned face of Shakespeare, though superficially less striking, was nonetheless the more beautiful. What Tieck says so ingeniously about faces, he means to apply, we feel, to the inner characteristics of genius.

For Molière, dramatic works were inseparable from

their representations; he was an excellent director and
actor as well as an admirable poet. He loved, as we have
said, the theater, the stage, the public; he valued his prerogatives as director, he liked to make speeches on certain
solemn occasions, to address the audience when the pit
was stormy, as sometimes happened. There is a story
about how he pacified a crowd of musketeers indignant
because they had been refused free admission. His contemporaries are unanimous in recognizing that as an actor
he achieved a high degree of excellence in comic plays,
but it was an excellence acquired through study and will
power. "Nature had denied him the outward gifts so indispensable on the stage, particularly for tragic roles,"
Mlle. Poisson says. "His voice lacked resonance, and because of his harsh inflections, his volubility, and too fast
delivery, he was, in this respect, inferior to the actors of
the Hôtel de Bourgogne. He was aware of his limitations,
and confined himself to a genre in which his defects were
more tolerable. Even there he had to surmount many difficulties, and he rid himself of his volubility, so unfavorable
to good articulation, only by continual efforts. As a result
he developed a hiccup which remained with him to the
day of his death, but which he knew how to turn to advantage on certain occasions. To vary his inflections, he
introduced certain unusual tones, for which he was at first
accused of affectation, but to which people eventually became accustomed. Not only was he liked in the roles of
Mascarille, Sganarelle, Hali, etc., he also excelled in high
comedy, as Arnolphe, Orgon, Harpagon. In these latter
roles, by truth of emotion, by his mastery of facial expression, and by all the subtleties of his art, he held the audience spellbound to the point where it no longer distinguished between the character represented and the actor
who represented him. For this reason he always reserved
for himself the longest and most difficult parts."

Molière, having reached the age of forty, was at the
peak of his art, and, it would seem, of his fame. He was
liked by the king, patronized and lionized by the high

nobility. Condé often sent for him; he went to M. de la Rochefoucauld's house to read *Les Femmes savantes* and to the old Cardinal de Retz's to read *Le Bourgeois gentilhomme*. Was Molière, apart from his domestic troubles, I don't say happy in his life, but satisfied with his social position? He certainly was not. That is clear, no matter how the facts are played down, attenuated, or disguised. He felt at times that he was denied serious, lofty consideration, treated as a comedian rather than a poet. Everyone was amused by his plays, but not all appreciated them sufficiently; he realized that too often people looked upon him merely as their best means of amusement.

He was sent for to cheer up "the good old cardinal," to ginger him up a bit: Mme. de Sévigné speaks of him in this tone. Chapelle called him *"grand homme";* but his influential friends, especially Boileau, deplored the buffoon in him. After his death, de Visé, in a letter to Grimarest, contested his title of *Monsieur*. At his funeral, a common woman, asked who was being buried, replied, "Eh, it's that Molière," whereupon another woman, who was standing by her window and overheard, cried out, "How dare you, you—! It's *Monsieur* de Molière!"

Molière, a clear-sighted and inexorable observer, certainly did not miss any of the thousand such trivial indignities, which, for all his contempt of them, reminded him of his social status. Certain honors were only mediocre compensation and often rather bitter. Such, I imagine, must have been the honor of making Louis XIV's bed, in his capacity as valet to the king. Or when Louis XIV, to stop slanderous rumors,[2] served (with the Duchesse d'Orléans) as godparent to Molière's first child, thus giving royal sanction to his marriage; or again, when he asked Molière to sit at his own table and said aloud, handing him a chicken wing, "Here I am giving supper to Molière, yet my officers do not find him good enough company." Was it possible for a man as proud as Molière to be as cheered by the royal reparation as he had been depressed

[2] Molière was, among other things, accused of marrying his own natural daughter.—*Eds.*

by the officers' affront? Vauvenargues, in a dialogue between Molière and a young man, makes the poet-actor
express his dissatisfaction with his status in a touching
and grave manner. It seems that the idea of this dialogue
was suggested to Vauvenargues by Grimarest's account of
an actual conversation in which the poet dissuaded a
young man from embarking on a theatrical career.

Ten months before his death, Molière, through the medi-
ation of mutual friends, made up with his wife whom he
still loved. He even became father of a child, which did
not survive him. The change caused by the resumption of
married life aggravated his respiratory trouble. Two
months before his death Boileau paid him the visit we
have referred to above. The day of the fourth performance
of *Le Malade imaginaire*, he felt worse than usual; but
I shall let Grimarest speak, who must have obtained the
details of the scene from Baron, and whose unadorned
naïveté seems to me preferable to the more concise correctness of those who have retold his story. That day,
then, "Molière, feeling much more tormented by his fluxion than usual, sent for his wife to whom he said, in the
presence of Baron: 'So long as life was a mixture of
equal parts of pain and pleasure, I have thought myself
happy; but today I am so overcome with suffering, that
I cannot expect a single moment of contentment and relief,
and I see clearly that I must quit the game; I can no
longer hold out against agonies which give me not a moment's respite. But,' he added after pondering a bit, 'how
much a man suffers before dying! And yet I am sure that
this is the end.' Molière's wife and Baron were deeply affected by M. de Molière's words, which they did not expect, however unwell he may have been. With tears in
their eyes they begged him not to act that day, but to rest
for his own good. 'How can I do that?' he said to them.
'There are fifty poor workmen who have nothing but their
wages to live on; what will they do if I don't act? I should
reproach myself if I failed to give them bread a single
day so long as I am really able to act.' Nevertheless he
sent for the actors and told them that, feeling worse than

usual, he would not act that day unless they were ready to begin at four o'clock sharp. 'Otherwise,' he said, 'I can't be there, and you must refund the money.' The actors had the chandeliers lighted and the curtain up precisely at four o'clock. Molière acted with the greatest difficulty, and half the audience noticed that at the moment he was saying *Juro*, in the ceremony of the *Malade imaginaire*, he was seized with convulsions. Having realized that his convulsions had been noticed, he made an effort and by a forced laugh concealed what had just happened to him.

"When the play was over, he took his dressing gown, went into Baron's loge, and asked him what people were saying about it. M. Baron replied that his plays always gained by being examined closely, and that the more often they were performed, the more they were liked. 'But,' he added, 'you seem to be sicker than you were before.' 'That is true,' Molière said. 'I have a cold that is killing me.' Baron, after touching his hands and finding them icy, covered them in his muff; he sent for his porters to carry Molière home promptly, and walked beside his chair himself, lest he meet with some accident between the Palais-Royal and the Rue de Richelieu where Molière lived. When he was in his room, Baron wanted to give him some broth of which Molière's wife always had a supply, for no one could have taken better care of him than she did. 'Eh, no.' Molière said, 'my wife's broths are like real spirits to me; you know all the ingredients she puts in them. I'd rather have a little piece of Parmesan cheese.' Laforest brought him some; he ate it with a bit of bread, and had himself put to bed. He had been there only a moment when he sent someone to ask his wife for a pillow filled with a drug she had promised to make him sleep. 'I am willing to try anything that does not enter the body,' he said, 'but remedies one has to swallow frighten me; it would not take much to make me lose what remains to me of life.' A moment later he was seized with a violent fit of coughing, and after spitting he asked for a light. 'Here is a change,' he said. Baron, seeing the blood he had spat out, cried out in terror. 'Don't be afraid,' Molière said to him. 'You've seen me spit up much more than that. However,' he added, 'go and tell my wife to come up.' He was left under the care of two nuns, members of the order who come to Paris to make collections during Lent, and to whom he used to give hospitality. In this last moment of his life they gave him all the edifying relief one could expect of their charity, and he showed the feelings of a good Christian and all the resignation he owed to the will of the Lord. Finally he gave up the ghost in the arms of these two good nuns; he was choked by the blood that poured from his mouth. When his wife and Baron came back, they found him dead."

It was Friday, February 17, 1673, at ten o'clock in the evening, an hour at the most after he had left the theater, that Molière thus breathed his last, at the age of fifty-one years, one month, and two or three days. The curé of Saint-Eustache, his parish, refused him ecclesiastical burial on the ground that he had not been reconciled with the Church. On February 20, Molière's widow addressed a petition to the archbishop of Paris, Harlay de Champvallon. Accompanied by the curé of Auteuil, she went to Versailles to throw herself at the king's feet; but the good curé seized the opportunity to justify himself against suspicion of Jansenism, and the king bade him be silent. And then—the whole story must be told—Molière being dead, he could no longer amuse Louis XIV; and the monarch's immense egoism, that hideous incurable egoism as revealed to us by Saint-Simon, took control. Louis XIV brusquely dismissed the widow and the priest, and wrote to the archbishop to find some compromise solution. It was decided that "a bit of ground" would be granted, but that the body would be buried directly, without being taken to the church. On the night of February 21, Molière's body, accompanied by two ecclesiastics, was carried to the Saint-Joseph cemetery in the Rue Montmartre. About two hundred persons followed, each bearing a torch; no funeral hymns were sung. On the day of the funeral a crowd of fanatics had gathered around Molière's house apparently with hostile intent; these people dispersed when someone threw them coins. It was to prove less easy to disperse the crowd at the funeral of Louis XIV.

Molière's genius will be forever one of the adornments, one of the very proofs of the genius of humanity. La Rochefoucauld said that absence extinguishes little passions but increases great ones, like a violent wind which blows out candles but fans fires: the passage of time similarly affects reputations, erasing the lesser and enhancing the greater. But even among the greatest men, whose fame survives, there are many who stand at a distance from us, so to speak—their names rather than their works remain in the memory of mankind. Molière belongs to the smaller number of those whose works are ever present, new to every new generation, every new stage of civilization. Famous men, geniuses, books may multiply; civilizations may transform themselves (provided they continue); but five or six great lifetime achievements are part of the inalienable treasure of human thought. Every man who learns to read makes one more reader of Molière.

To Love Molière

To love Molière—to love him sincerely, with all one's heart—do you know what that is? It is to have an inner safeguard against many defects, many failings and intellectual vices. Above all, it is to dislike whatever is incompatible with Molière, everything that was opposed to him in his own epoch, everything that he would find unbearable in our own.

To love Molière is to be cured forever not merely of base and infamous hypocrisy, but of fanaticism, intolerance, and callousness of the kind that makes for anathemas and condemnations. It is to moderate one's admiration even for Bossuet and for all those who, like him, gloat, if only in words, over their dead or dying enemies; who usurp some sort of sacred language and unconsciously put themselves in the place of the All Highest, thunderbolt in hand.

To love Molière is also to be safe and a thousand leagues away from that other fanaticism—political, cold, brusque, and cruel—which never laughs, which reeks of sectarianism, which, under the pretext of puritanism, manages to combine and blend all the venoms, and unite in one spiteful doctrine all the hatreds, resentments, and Jacobinisms of all times. It is to be just as far removed, on the other hand, from those flaccid and insipid minds who in the presence of evil cannot be aroused to indignation or to hate.

To love Molière is to rid oneself of complacency and excessive admiration for man; it is to realize that no matter what man does, human nature is frail. At the same time, it is to avoid contempt for this common humanity at which we laugh, to which we belong, and into which Molière's invigorating hilarity plunges us again and again.

To love and to cherish Molière is to dislike all mannerism in language and expression. It is to refuse to be amused by airs and graces, strained subtleties, laborious contrived effects, affectation of every kind, a style that is all false glitter.

To love Molière is to dislike overcleverness and pedantry; it is to see through our Trissotins and Vadiuses even in their most elegant disguises. It is to avoid being taken in by the eternal Philaminte, that *précieuse* who is found in every age in new shape and with new plumage. It is to love integrity and intellectual honesty in others as much as in oneself. I am only giving the key and the theme; it is up to the reader to carry on from here.

To love and openly to prefer Corneille, as do some persons I know, is no doubt a fine thing and in a sense perfectly legitimate. It is to aspire to the world of noble souls and to emulate them. And yet, does not preference for Corneille, with his grandeur and sublimity, expose us to the temptation of false pride? Does it not, also, perhaps entail the danger of condoning turgidity and bombast, of countenancing heroics indiscriminately? He who passionately loves Corneille may just possibly not be averse to a bit of boasting.

To love, on the other hand, and to prefer Racine, this is without a doubt to love elegance above all, and grace, and naturalness, and truth (at least relatively), and sensitivity —a love we find charming and can share. And yet, does not this unique type of perfection also open access to a certain conventional tame beauty, a certain exclusive, excessive softness and languor, refinements that are too dearly bought? In short, to prefer Racine is to risk overindulgence in what in France we call "good taste," which in the end leaves such a bad taste.

To love Boileau—but surely no one loves Boileau. Boileau is respected, he is appreciated; we admire his probity, his soundness, at moments his verve, and if we are tempted to love him, it is solely for his sovereign fairness, thanks to which he could so infallibly do justice to the great poets, his contemporaries, and particularly to Molière, whom he placed above them all.

To love La Fontaine is almost the same thing as to love Molière: it is to love nature, all nature, the candid portrayal of mankind, the great comedy "in a hundred different acts" unrolling before our eyes in a thousand graceful scenes which so faithfully reflect his character. But they also reflect his weaknesses and self-indulgences—as we never find them in the more virile straightforward genius of the supreme master. But why drive a wedge between them? La Fontaine and Molière are not to be separated, but to be loved as one.

> *Molière*, from *Portraits littéraires*. Originally a preface written in 1835 for an edition of Molière's works.
>
> *To Love Molière*, 18 July 1863 (*Nouveaux lundis*).
>
> Written almost thirty years apart, these two selections show that Sainte-Beuve consistently shared Boileau's opinion of Molière as the greatest star in the literary constellation of the *grand siècle*.

MADAME DE SÉVIGNÉ

THE CRITICS, particularly those outside France, who have lately judged our two literary centuries with the greatest severity, agree that the dominant characteristics of those periods, their brilliance and attraction, which are expressed in a thousand ways, are the fruits of the spirit of conversation and society—knowledge of the world and men, a keen discernment of what is proper and improper, subtle delicacy of feeling, and graceful piquancy and refinement of language. And indeed, until about 1789, those are, except in the cases of a very few writers, the characteristics that distinguish French literature from the other literatures of Europe. These brilliant qualities have sometimes been held up to us as a reproach; but such a mistake could be made only by persons incapable of appreciating their true meaning.

At the beginning of the seventeenth century, our civilization, and hence our language and literature were anything but mature or firmly established. Europe, after emerging from its religious upheavals and entering upon the Thirty Years' War, was laboriously giving birth to a new political order. France was eliminating the residues of her civil discords. At Court, a few salons, a few *ruelles* or coteries of wits, were already fashionable; but nothing great or original had yet begun to germinate; the monotonous spiritual nourishment was provided by Spanish novels and Italian sonnets and pastorals. Not until after Richelieu, after the Fronde, under the Queen Mother and Mazarin,

did there suddenly emerge, as though by miracle, amid the
fetes of Saint-Mandé and Vaux, from the salons of the
Hôtel de Rambouillet and the antechambers of the young
king, three first-class minds, three geniuses diversely endowed, but all of naïve and pure taste, perfect simplicity,
and felicitous abundance, nourished by their own native
graces and delicacies, and destined to open a glorious age
in which none was to surpass them. Molière, La Fontaine,
and Mme. de Sévigné belong to a literary generation which
preceded that led by Racine and Boileau, and they are
distinguished from the latter by various features, rooted
both in the nature of their genius and in the date of their
coming. We feel that by the turn of their minds as well as
by their position they are much closer to the France of
before Louis XIV, to the old language and the old French
spirit; that they were much more part of these by their
education and their readings, and that if they are less appreciated by non-Frenchmen than certain later writers,
they owe this precisely to elements in their accent and
manner which are the most intimate, the most indefinable,
and the most appealing for Frenchmen. We cannot too
highly venerate and uphold these immortal writers who
first gave French literature its original character, and who
have secured for it, down to this day, a physiognomy
unique among all literatures.

Molière extracted the strongest and highest poetry conceivable from the spectacle of life, from the living play of
human failings, vices, and follies. La Fontaine and Mme. de
Sévigné, on a more limited stage, had so fine and true a
sense of the things and life of their times, each in his own
manner—La Fontaine closer to nature, Mme. de Sévigné
to society—and they expressed this exquisite sense so freshly
in their writings, that we find it quite easy to consider them
as being not too far below Molière. Today we shall speak
only of Mme. de Sévigné; it seems that everything has
been said about her, and it is true that the details are nearly
exhausted; but until now she has been considered too much
in isolation, as was long the case with La Fontaine whom
she resembles so much. Today, as the society whose most

brilliant facet she represents is receding into the past and we can see it in clearer perspective, it is easier and at the same time more necessary to define Mme. de Sévigné's rank, importance, and milieu. It is doubtless for having failed to take into account the difference between her period and ours that many distinguished minds in our own day seem inclined to underestimate one of the most delightful geniuses who ever existed. I should be happy if this article helped to dispel some of these unfair preconceptions.

The excesses of the Regency have been stigmatized a great deal; but before the regency of Philippe d'Orléans, there had been another, not less dissolute, not less licentious, and even more horrible in the cruelty that characterized it—a kind of hideous transition between the excesses of Henri III and those of Louis XV. The immorality of the Ligue, which had smoldered under Henri IV and Richelieu, burst out anew. Debauchery was just as monstrous at that time as it had been at the time of the *mignons* or would be later at the time of the *roués;* but what brings this period closer to the sixteenth century and distinguishes it from the eighteenth, is above all assassination, poisoning, those Italian habits due to the Medicis, and the insane fury of duels, heritage of the civil wars. This is what the impartial reader will see in the regency of Anne of Austria; such is the dark and bloody background against which the Fronde loomed up one fine morning, the Fronde which is often called "a joke with a mailed fist." The conduct of the women of that time—ladies distinguished for birth, beauty, and wit—seems fabulous, and we should like to believe that historians have slandered them. But since excess always begets its opposite, the small number of women who escaped corruption plunged into sentimental metaphysics and became *précieuses;* hence the Hôtel de Rambouillet. This was an oasis of civilized manners in the midst of high society. Eventually it even led to good taste, as exemplified in Mme. de Sévigné who had frequented it.

Mlle. Marie de Rabutin-Chantal, born in 1626, was the daughter of the Baron de Chantal, a frenzied duelist who

one Easter Sunday left the holy table to serve as second to
the famous Comte de Bouteville. Brought up by her uncle,
the good Abbé de Coulanges, she received a solid education as a child, and learned Latin, Italian, and Spanish
under Chapelain and Ménage. At the age of eighteen, she
married the Marquis de Sévigné; he was unworthy of her,
treated her with little respect, and was killed in a duel in
1651. Mme. de Sévigné, a widow at twenty-five, with a
son and a daughter, never wished to remarry. She was
madly in love with her children, especially her daughter;
the other passions always remained unknown to her. She
was a smiling blonde, not at all sensual, very cheerful and
playful; wit flashed and sparkled in her lively eyes, her
paupières bigarrées, as she put it. She became a
précieuse. She went into society, she was loved, lionized, courted,[1] leaving in her path a number of unhappy
suitors to whom she paid little attention, and generously
keeping as friends even the men she had rejected as lovers.
Her cousin Bussy, her teacher Ménage, the Prince de Conti
(brother of the great Condé), the *surintendant* Fouquet
sighed for her in vain. But she remained inviolably faithful
to Fouquet after he was disgraced; and when she relates
his trial to M. de Pomponne, she speaks of *notre cher mal-
heureux* with great affection. Still young and unself-con-
sciously beautiful, she devoted herself to her daughter, and
her greatest pleasure was to watch her shine in society.
After 1663, Mlle. de Sévigné figured in the brilliant ballets at Versailles, and Benserade, the official poet who then
held the place at Court that Racine and Boileau took in
1672, composed more than one madrigal in honor of
that *bergère* and *nymphe,* whom a worshiping mother
called "the prettiest girl in France." In 1669, M. de Grignan

[1] Mme. de La Fayette wrote to her: "Your presence adds to
our festivities, and the festivities add to your beauty . . . in
short, joy is the true state of your mind, and sorrow is more
contrary to you than to anyone." Mme. de Sévigné had what
the English call a "sense of humor," one of the most cheerful
kind, colored and varied at every moment by the liveliest imagination. Her sparkling wit sometimes conceals her sensibility;
she could not help appearing graceful even in moments of grief.

obtained her in marriage; sixteen months later he took her to Provence where he served as *lieutenant géneral* in the absence of M. de Vendôme.

Thus, after 1671 Mme. de Sévigné was separated from her daughter, seeing her only at long and irregular intervals. She sought comfort in a daily correspondence, which continued until her death in 1696, and which covers twenty-five years, with gaps accounted for by the brief reunions of mother and daughter. Prior to this separation, we have only a small number of letters that Mme. de Sévigné wrote to her cousin Bussy and to M. de Pomponne concerning the trial of Fouquet. Thus it is only from that time on that we have complete data on her private life, her habits, the books she read, down to the most casual events in the society in which she lived and of which she was the soul.

From the first pages of this correspondence we find ourselves in a world very different from that of the Fronde and the Regency; we realize that what is called French society was at last constituted. No doubt (and even if we did not have numerous contemporary memoirs, the anecdotes related by Mme. de Sévigné would be evidence of it), no doubt the young nobility on which Louis XIV imposed dignity, courtesy, and elegance as the price of his favors still indulged in horrible disorders and crude orgies; no doubt, under the brilliant gilded surface, vice was sufficiently rampant to overflow into another Regency, particularly after it was set fermenting by the bigotry at the close of the reign of Louis XIV. But at least the proprieties were observed; opinion began to stigmatize what was unsavory and ignoble. Moreover, as disorder and brutality became less conspicuous, decency and wit were gaining in simplicity. *Préciosité* had gone out of fashion; the former *précieuses* now only smiled at the memory. Gone were the days when people discoursed interminably on the sonnet of Job or of Uranie, on the *carte du Tendre* or on the character of Romain; now they "conversed," they talked, exchanging Court news, evoking memories of the siege of Paris or the war in Guyenne. Cardinal de Retz related his

travels, M. de La Rochefoucauld made remarks on human
nature, Mme. de La Fayette analyzed feelings, and Mme.
de Sévigné interrupted them all to quote a smart saying
by her daughter or to recount a prank of her son's or an
amusing anecdote about the good d'Hacqueville or M. de
Brancas.

In 1829, our utilitarian concerns make it hard for us to
imagine what this life of leisure and conversation was really
like. The world moves so fast in our day, so many things
are by turns brought on the stage, that we scarcely have
the time to observe and grasp them all. Our days are spent
in studies, our evenings in serious discussions; as for friendly
conversations, *causeries,* there are few or none at all. The
noble society of our day, which has most largely preserved
the leisure habits of the two preceding centuries, seems to
be able to do so only by staying aloof from modern ideas
and ways. In the period under consideration, this leisurely
mode of life was not incompatible with interest in literary,
religious, and political events; it was enough to cast an occasional glance at them from the corner of an eye, without
leaving one's chair, and the rest of the time one could devote oneself to one's tastes and one's friends. Moreover, conversation had not yet become, as it was to become in the
eighteenth century, in the open salons presided over by
Fontenelle, an occupation, a business, a social requirement.
Wit was not necessarily the aim; geometrical, philosophical, or sentimental subtlety was not *de rigueur;* people
talked about themselves, about others, about trifles or nothing at all. As Mme. de Sévigné says, they were "endless"
conversations. "After dinner," she writes somewhere to her
daughter, "we went to talk in the pleasantest woods in the
world; we stayed there until six o'clock, engaged in several
kinds of conversation, so agreeable, so tender, so friendly,
so obliging for both you and me, that my heart is still
aglow."

In the midst of this social life, so easy, so simple, so
whimsical, and so gracefully animated, a visit, a letter received, insignificant in itself, was an event in which one
took pleasure, and which was reported eagerly. The way

this was done lent price to the least things; casually,
without being aware of it, these people turned living into
an art. (Recall, for instance, Mme. de Sévigné's report on
Mme. de Chaulnes' visit to Les Rochers.) It has often been
said that Mme. de Sévigné went to a great deal of trouble
with her letters, that writing them she had in mind, if not
posterity, at least the society of her day, whose approval
she sought. This is false: the days of Voiture and of
Guez de Balzac were a thing of the past. As a rule, she
set down whatever sprang to her mind, and as many things
as possible; and if she was in a hurry, she scarcely read
over what she had written. "The fact is," she says, "between friends we should let our pens trot along as they
please; I never pull hard at the reins of mine." But there
are days when she has more time and when she feels in
better form; then, quite naturally, she takes better care,
she arranges and she composes more or less as La Fontaine
composed his fables. This is, for example, what she does
in her letter to M. de Coulanges on Mademoiselle's marriage, and in the one to him about her lackey Picard, whom
she dismissed for having refused to help with the mowing.
Letters of this type, artistic and brilliant in form, which
did not contain too much malicious gossip or too many
little secrets, created a stir in society, and everyone wanted
to read them. "I mustn't forget what happened to me this
morning," Mme. de Coulanges wrote to her friend. "I was
told, 'Madame, a lackey from Mme. de Thianges is here.'
I ordered him to be admitted. This is what he had to tell
me: 'Madame, I have come from Mme. de Thianges who
asks you kindly to send her Mme. de Sévigné's letter about
the horse and the one about the meadow.' I told the lackey
that I'd bring them to his mistress, and I have passed them
on to her. As you can see, your letters make all the noise
they deserve; it is certain that they are delightful, and you
are like your letters." Thus, correspondence at that time
was important, just like conversation; neither was "composed," but people gave all their minds and hearts to them.
Mme. de Sévigné continually praises her daughter for her
letters: "Your ideas and your style are incomparable." And

she reports that "now and then" she reads passages to persons worthy of them: "occasionally I read a little excerpt to Mme. de Villars; she likes the tender passages, and her eyes fill with tears when she hears them."

Just as the candor of Mme. de Sévigné's letters has been doubted, so has the sincerity of her love for her daughter; on this score, too, no allowance has been made for the time she lived in, and for the fact that for persons whose existence is one of luxury and idleness passions may be very much like fancies, just as manias may often become passions. Mme. de Sévigné adored her daughter, and she became known for this; this is why Arnauld d'Andilly called her "a pretty pagan," a worshiper of idols. Separation served only to intensify her affection; she scarcely gave thought to anything else; the questions and compliments of people she saw invariably brought her back to her daughter. In the end, this almost exclusive attachment became the badge of her personality, and she could not do without it, carrying her maternal love about with her as one does a fan. For all that, Mme. de Sévigné was perfectly sincere, frank, an enemy of pretense; she was even one of the first to apply the adjective "real" (*vraie*) to a person, and she might have invented the expression for her daughter if M. de La Rochefoucauld had not forestalled her by applying it to Mme. de La Fayette; at all events she was fond of applying it to persons she loved. After we have analyzed that inexhaustible maternal love from every conceivable angle, we fall back on the explanation given by M. de Pomponne: "So it seems that Mme. de Sévigné loves Mme. de Grignan passionately? Do you know what is behind it? Shall I tell you? It is that she loves her passionately." It would indeed be most ungracious were we to find fault with Mme. de Sévigné for this innocent and legitimate passion, thanks to which we are able to follow step by step the wittiest of all women over twenty-six years of the most delightful period of the most attractive French society.[2]

────────────

[2] M. Walckenaer, in his memoirs on Mme. de Sévigné, observes very aptly that having been orphaned at an early age she had had no opportunity to develop filial feelings, so that all the

La Fontaine, painter of fields and animals, was anything
but unfamiliar with society, and often portrayed it with
subtlety and malice. Mme. de Sévigné, for her part, also
greatly loved the country; she went on long visits to Livry,
staying with the Abbé de Coulanges, or to her estate of
Les Rochers in Brittany, and it is interesting to note how
she saw and depicted nature. To begin with, we realize
that like our good fabulist she had read *Astrée* at an early
date, and that in her youth she had daydreamed under
the mythological trees of Vaux and Saint-Mandé. She was
fond of taking walks "by the rays of Endymion's beautiful
mistress," and of spending a couple of hours alone with the
"hamadryads"; her trees were decorated with inscriptions
and ingenious devices, such as are found in the landscapes
of *Pastor fido* and *Aminta*. "*Bella cosa far niente* says one
of my trees; another replies to it: *Amor odit inertes;* and I
don't know which I should listen to." Elsewhere she says:
"As for our inscriptions, they are not rubbed off; I go often
to look at them; there are even some new ones, and two
adjoining trees occasionally say opposite things: *La lonta-
nanza ogni gran piaga salda* and *Piaga d'amor non si sana
mai.* There are five or six pairs of this kind." These somewhat insipid reminiscences of pastorals and romances come
spontaneously from her quill, and her many entirely fresh,
original descriptions are all the more charming by contrast.
"I have come here [to Livry] for the last good weather in
the year, to say farewell to the leaves; they are still on the
trees, they have merely changed color; instead of being
green, they are now aurora, and so many shades of aurora
that they compose a magnificently rich gold brocade,
which we try to persuade ourselves is lovelier than green,
were it only for a change." And when she is at Les Rochers,
she writes: "I'd be very happy in these woods, if only I

---

passion of her heart was as though held in reserve in order to
be later concentrated on her daughter. Widowed early, in the
best years of her youth, she seems never to have loved a man.
What a treasure of love she had accumulated! Her daughter
inherited all of it, with compound interest.

had a leaf that sings—ah, how pretty, a leaf that sings!"
And how she depicts for us "the triumph of the month of
May," when "the nightingale, the cuckoo, the warbler usher
in the spring in our woods"! How she makes us feel, almost
touch "those fine crystalline days of autumn, which are no
longer hot, and not yet cold"! When her son, in order to
obtain funds for some extravagance, orders the ancient
woods of Buron cut, she is upset, distressed at the thought
of all the fugitive dryads and dispossessed sylvan deities:
Ronsard did not lament more eloquently the fall of the
Gastine forest, nor M. de Chateaubriand that of his paternal
woods.

Mme. de Sévigné's constant gaiety and playfulness must
not be interpreted as the mark of an essentially frivolous,
insensitive nature. She was serious, even sad, especially during her stays in the country, and she was given to solitary
musings. This is not to say that she indulged in melancholy
reveries, strolling along somber paths in the woods, like
Delphine or Oswald's sweetheart. That kind of revery had
not yet been invented; it was not until 1793 that Mme. de
Staël wrote her admirable book, *L'Influence des passions
sur le bonheur.* Until then daydreaming had been more
natural and more personal, and at the same time less self-
centered. To daydream was, for Mme. de Sévigné, to think
of her daughter in Provence, of her son in Crete or with
the king's army, of absent or dead friends; it was to say:
"As for my life, you know it; I spend it with five or six
friends whose company I like, and doing a thousand things
I am obliged to do, which is no small matter. But I am
vexed at the idea that while we do nothing the days go
by, and our poor life is made up of such days, and we
grow old and die. I think this is very bad."

In those days life was strictly regulated by religion, and
it was largely thanks to this that sensibility and imagination, which have since lost all restraint, were kept within
sensible bounds. Mme. de Sévigné took good care to "glide
over" certain ideas; she explicitly asserts her belief in
Christian ethics, and more than once poked fun at her

daughter's infatuation with Cartesianism.[3] As for herself, amid the insecurity of this world, she bows her head and takes refuge in a kind of providential fatalism, which bespeaks the influence of Port-Royal and such writers as Nicole and St. Augustine. The tendency to religious resignation increased in her with age, but did not alter the serenity of her disposition, though she expressed herself with greater restraint and her affection acquired a note of gravity. We feel this especially in her letter to M. de Coulanges on the death of the Minister Louvois, where she rises to the sublimity of Bossuet, just as in earlier letters she occasionally equaled the comic verve of Molière.

M. de Saint-Surin, in his meritorious works on Mme. de Sévigné, has lost no opportunity to contrast her advantageously with the famous Mme. de Staël. I, too, believe that the comparison between the two women is interesting and useful, but it must not be made to the detriment of either. Mme. de Staël represents an entirely new society, Mme. de Sévigné one that is a thing of the past; this accounts for the prodigious differences, which we are at first tempted to ascribe solely to the different turns of mind and temperament. However, without denying the profound innate dissimilarity between their two souls—one knew only maternal love, while the other experienced every passion, including the most generous and most virile—closer scrutiny shows that they shared many weaknesses and many qualities, which developed differently only because they lived in different centuries. What spontaneity full of grace and lightness, what pages of dazzling intellectual brilliance in Mme. de Staël, when sentiment does not mar them, when she

---

[3] Mme. de Grignan's merits have often been discussed, and her mother's adulation of her has done her harm in our eyes to some extent; to be loved so much is a thankless part to sustain before people who are indifferent. The son, who was rather free in his conduct and ideas, seems to us more lovable. I can easily imagine that each of Mme. de Sévigné's children inherited only one of the two qualities so harmoniously combined in her disposition: the son had her grace but lacked reasonableness and solidity; the daughter had her reasonableness, but was somewhat strait-laced and lacked charm and zest.

forgets her philosophy and politics! And does not Mme. de
Sévigné sometimes philosophize and discourse? Why else
should she make the *Essais de Morale, Socrate chrétien*,
and St. Augustine her daily fare? For this allegedly frivolous woman read everything and read well; a mind that
finds no pleasure in serious reading, she used to say,
acquires "a pale complexion." She read Rabelais and
Bossuet's *Variations des églises protestantes*, Montaigne and
Pascal, La Calprenède's novel *Cléopâtre*, and Quintilian,
St. John Chrysostom, and Tacitus and Virgil, not "traves-
tied," but "in all the majesty of their native Latin." When
the weather was rainy, she could read a folio volume "in
twelve days." During Lent, she enjoyed the sermons of
Bourdaloue. Her conduct toward Fouquet in his disgrace
suggests the devotion she would have been capable of
in a revolutionary period. If she shows herself vain and
boastful when the king dances with her one evening or
when, after the performance of *Esther* at Saint-Cyr, he
pays her a compliment—would anyone else of her sex have
been more philosophical in her place? We are told that
Mme. de Staël herself went to a great deal of trouble to
wrest a few words and a glance from the conqueror of
Egypt and Italy. Surely, a woman who, though associated
from early youth with men like Ménage, Godeau, Benserade, kept clear of their pedantries and insipidities by
the strength of her good sense, and seemingly without effort
evaded the more refined and seductive advances of men
like Saint-Evrémond and Bussy; who, though she was a
friend and admirer of Mlle. de Scudéry and of Mme. de
Maintenon, remained equally aloof from the sentimentalism
of the one and the somewhat overdone reserve of the other;
who, though connected with Port-Royal and steeped in
the works of *ces Messieurs*, had high regard for Montaigne
and quoted Rabelais, and desired no other inscription on
what she called her "convent" than "Sacred Freedom" or
"Do what you like," as at the Abbey of Thélème—surely,
such a woman may be frolicsome and playful, she may
"glide over" thoughts, and she may take things by their

familiar and amusing side, but for all that she gives evidence of intellectual strength and rare originality.

There is only one occasion when we cannot help regretting that Mme. de Sévigné indulged in her habit of lighthearted mockery, when we absolutely refuse to be amused by her, and, after looking for every possible excuse, still find it hard to forgive her. It is when she relates so cheerfully to her daughter the rebellion of the peasants of Lower Brittany and the atrocities which marked its repression. So long as she confines herself to poking fun at the *Etats*, at the rural squires and their noisy celebrations, at their enthusiasm for voting everything "between twelve and one o'clock," and all the other after-dinner follies of her "next-door neighbors" in Brittany, everything is fine, her jokes have point and substance, and occasionally she brings to mind the touch of Molière. But at a certain point she talks about "a little intestine warfare" in Brittany and "an attack of the stone" in Rennes—this is to report how M. de Chaulnes, the governor of Brittany, was driven back to his house by a hail of stones after he tried to disperse the people. Then she goes on to recount how M. de Forbin arrived with six thousand men, and how those poor devils of mutineers, catching sight of the royal troops from afar, took flight across the fields or fell on their knees, crying *Mea culpa* (the only "French" words they knew). She also relates that, in order to punish Rennes, its parlement was transferred to Vannes; that twenty-five or thirty men were seized "at random" to be hanged, and that the inhabitants of an entire long street, including women in childbed, old men, and children, were driven out and banished, and giving them shelter was forbidden under penalty of death. She speaks volubly of how people were broken on the wheel and quartered, and how the authorities, after they had had their fill of breaking and quartering, confined themselves to plain hanging. In the midst of such horrors perpetrated on innocent people or misguided poor devils, it is painful to see Mme. de Sévigné joke almost as usual. We should like her to display a burning, bitter, generous indignation; above all, we should like to erase from her letters lines such as these: "The rebels of Rennes fled along ago; and so the good will suffer in place of the wicked; but I find all this satisfactory, provided the four thousand soldiers who are at Rennes under M. de Forbin and M. de Vins do not prevent me from taking walks in my woods, which are of marvelous height and beauty." And in another letter: "Sixty burghers have been rounded up; tomorrow the hangings begin. The province will be a fine example to the others, and above all it will remind them that one must respect governors and governesses, that one must not insult them and hurl stones into their gardens"; and finally: "You speak very amusingly about our troubles; but we are no longer broken on the wheel so often; only one man a week, to keep justice functioning; hanging seems now like a treat." The Duc de Chaulnes, who ordered all these horrors to retaliate for the insults hurled at him (the gentlest and most familiar of them was "fat pig") and for the stones that had been thrown into his garden, did not as a result go down even a notch in Mme. de Sévigné's affection. To her and to Mme. de Grignan he remained "our good duke"; more than that, when he is appointed ambassador to Rome and leaves the province, all Brittany, according to her, "is sad" at his departure. All this certainly suggests many reflections on the customs and civilization of the *grand siècle;* our readers will easily supply these. All I shall say is that on this occasion Mme. de Sévigné's heart unfortunately failed to rise above the prejudices of her time. She might have done so, for her kindness equaled her beauty and her grace. Occasionally she intervened in favor of galley prisoners with M. de Vivonne or with M. de Grignan. Without doubt, the most interesting of her *protégés* was a gentleman of Provence whose name has not come down to us. "This poor boy," she says, "was devoted to M. Fouquet; he was convicted for taking a letter to Mme. Fouquet from her husband; and for this he was sentenced to the galleys for five years. This is a rather unusual case. You know he is one of the finest young men you could see; it is inconceivable that he should be sent to the galleys."

Mme. de Sévigné's style has been so often and so intelligently judged, analyzed, and admired, that it would be hard today to find any appropriate new praise; on the other hand, I do not in the least feel inclined to inject new blood into clichés by means of chicaneries and criticisms. I shall confine myself to one general observation, namely, that the great and beautiful style of the age of Louis XIV can be related to two different techniques, two opposite manners.

Malherbe and [Guez de] Balzac founded, in our literature, the austere, polished, worked, learned style; to achieve it, we proceed from thought to expression, slowly, by degrees, experimenting and erasing. This is the style that Boileau recommends for all purposes; according to him, the writer must go back to his work twenty times, constantly polishing and repolishing it; he boasts of having taught Racine to compose "easy verses with difficulty." Racine is indeed the perfect model of this style in poetry; Fléchier was less felicitous in his prose. But in addition to this kind of writing, always somewhat monotonous and academic, there is another, far freer, capricious and varied, without traditional method, and entirely in conformity with the diversity of talents and geniuses. Montaigne and Régnier had previously given admirable specimens of it, and Queen Marguerite a charming one in her familiar memoirs, the work of a few *"après-disnées."* This is the broad, loose, abundant style, which follows closely the current of ideas; the spontaneous or, as Montaigne himself put it, *prime-sautier* style, that of La Fontaine and Molière, that of Fénelon, of Bossuet, of the Duc de Saint-Simon, and of Mme. de Sévigné. Mme. de Sévigné excels in it: she lets her pen "trot," never "pulling hard on the reins," and as she goes she scatters a profusion of colors, comparisons, images, while wit and sentiment pour from her on all sides. In this way, without trying or suspecting it, she placed herself in the front rank of our writers.

And now, if a few overcritical minds find that I have gone too far in my admiration for Mme. de Sévigné, may I be allowed to ask them one question: Have you read

her? And by reading I mean, not perusing a random selection of her letters, not picking out two or three which enjoy
a classical reputation—the letters on the marriage of
Mademoiselle, on the deaths of Vatel, of M. de Turenne, of
M. de Longueville—but plunging into the ten volumes of
her correspondence and following her step by step, enjoying everything—in short doing for her as we do for *Clarissa
Harlowe* when we have two weeks of leisure and rain in
the country. After that trial, which is anything but terrible,
I am sure that you will have forgotten that you ever
criticized my admiration.

3 May 1829 (*Portraits de femmes*).

Sainte-Beuve's historical and moral sense is very
apparent here. His literary admiration for Mme.
de Sévigné does not blind him to, nor is it di-
minished by, her human insensitivity, which he
explains historically without excusing it.

VOLTAIRE AND THE PRÉSIDENT
DE BROSSES

AN ACADEMIC INTRIGUE IN THE EIGHTEENTH CENTURY

I AM ASSUMING, in order not to be unfair, that *Le Siècle de Louis XIV, L'Histoire de Charles XII*, the chivalrous feelings that inspire the tragedy *Tancrède*, the *Epître à Horace, Les Tu et les vous, Le Mondain, Les Systèmes,* the lovely stanzas *Si vous voulez que j'aime encore* are vividly present to your minds; I am assuming that you have recently reread many of the exquisite and natural, quick and definitive literary judgments scattered throughout Voltaire's letters and all his works: having thus made clear that I am not questioning the admiration we owe to the keenly intelligent and extraordinarily talented writer, I shall speak about the man and his weaknesses with greater freedom.

Voltaire had just come back from Berlin, having realized how foolish he had been to enter the lion's den. His adventure at Frankfurt had made him diffident; at the same time, his much-publicized quarrel with Frederick II made him appear more dangerous than ever before. He could not make up his mind where to settle: we find him successively in Strasbourg (August 1753), in Colmar, at the Abbey of Sénones, at Plombières in the Vosges, and then again in Colmar, trying to find out what was being said about him in Paris and looking for a safe retreat near the frontier. A year thus went by in worried waiting. He was sixty. In November 1754 he went to Lyon to confer with his friend, the Maréchal de Richelieu. The coldness with which he was received there by the archbishop, Cardinal de Tencin, though the latter was an uncle of his friend d'Argental, made him realize the extent of his disfavor at Court. This decided him forthwith to go to Switzerland with his niece. He stayed first at Lausanne, and then at Les Délices, near Geneva. His first years in Switzerland were happy and gay. Voltaire felt himself a free man again; he took part in the life of the country and made it accept his own life; he gave private performances of comedies and tragedies and easily found amateur actors, and not at all bad ones, for the principal roles in his plays. At the same time he resumed close contact with his friends in Paris, especially d'Alembert, with whom he began a lively exchange of letters that was never to stop. His correspondence with d'Alembert provides us with an essential key to his life; it should be read separately in its entirety, as it appeared in the early editions (in the later Beuchot edition it is merged with the rest of the correspondence). Voltaire's life is a comedy: his correspondence with d'Alembert shows us what was going on behind the scenes; the other letters are more or less for public consumption.

As soon as he settled in Switzerland, Voltaire sent d'Alembert articles for the *Encyclopédie*. The project had been carried on until then in a spirit of harmonious cooperation and without too many obstacles. Voltaire gave d'Alembert excellent literary advice, but soon began to add advice of a different, more general nature, such as: "Because of the fierce conflict between the Parlements and the Bishops, sensible people have every opportunity, and you'll be free to stuff the *Encyclopédie* with truths no one would have ventured to utter twenty years ago. When the pedants are at each other's throats, the philosophers are triumphant." Then trouble began. D'Alembert's article "Geneva" for the *Encyclopédie*, in which he questioned the sincerity of the Protestant ministers' faith in Christ, aroused indignation in Geneva, and Voltaire who lived there felt the effects of it. For all that, he wrote to d'Alembert: "You must never retract: do not give the impression of yielding to these wretches by resigning from the *Encyclopédie*." In fact, d'Alembert was sick of the whole project, which was beginning to meet with serious opposition in Paris. At this juncture, Voltaire, while leading in Switzerland the life of an aristocrat and seemingly wholly given to intellectual pleasures, in his letters to d'Alembert displays passionate interest in the common cause. On every occasion he acts as the fervent zealot, the grandmaster or the general who harangues his lieutenants—d'Alembert was the chief of them in Paris. "I cannot understand why those who work [for the *Encyclopédie*] do not join forces and declare that they will renounce the whole thing unless they are supported. . . . Form a body, gentlemen: a body is always respectable. . . . Run as a pack, and you will be masters."

I have said elsewhere that when Montesquieu died, the army of men of letters had not yet been put on a war footing; it was to mobilize them that Voltaire worked with such ardor.

In his youth Voltaire had been alone, without adherents, without support; when he looked back at this period of his life, which had been marked by so many upsets, he felt how important it was to have a party and an army of his own. He wanted to organize them from a safe distance, without overexposing his own person to the fire, and hence he urged d'Alembert and his friends to bestir themselves. The *Encyclopédie*, which rallied the men of letters, seemed an excellent opportunity. Whenever the existence of this big machine was threatened, he insisted that all of them must join forces and rush to its defense. In the meantime, he led a carefree pleasant life in his country houses on the lake; he gave dinners to the very ministers of Geneva whose feelings and conscience had been offended by d'Alembert: "It isn't enough to make game of them," he wrote, "one must also be polite. Make game of everything, and be gay."

D'Alembert, for his part, less petulant but steadier, more coolheaded and cautious, at once restrained Voltaire and kept him in line. Often exhorted by him, he exhorted and cheered him in turn when he saw him flagging; he played on Voltaire's pet aversions and deliberately nursed his resentments, designating his victims by name. All this correspondence has an ugly side: it smells of clannishness, intrigue, underhanded scheming; from whatever angle you look at it, it scarcely redounds to the credit of these men who raised lying to the rank of a principle and who felt deep contempt for their fellow men whom they had set out to enlighten: "Enlighten and despise mankind!" was their motto, and "Brothers, march ever sneering on the road of the truth!" was their perpetual refrain.

However, Voltaire who had often got himself into trouble, thought of his safety. His house, Les Délices, was very near Geneva, and he knew that his reputation would not be enhanced if, after falling into the clutches of a king in Berlin, he were to fall into those of a little republic and its sovereign burghers. "I have a house nearby and I have spent more than 100,000 francs on it," he wrote in January 1757. "It has not yet been demolished." Apparently, the idea had occurred to him that he might be ill-treated by the citizens of Geneva. It was then that he thought of providing additional refuges or fortresses for himself. He purchased the estate of Ferney (October 1758), and at the same time wrote to the Président de Brosses offering to buy, in one form or another, the latter's property of Tourney, situated in the Franche-Comté near the Swiss border, which would provide him with a foothold in France. He made this proposal in the tone of a whimsical neighbor: "I cannot see you devoting much time to the care of your Tourney property; your tenant farmer there, Chouet, does not wish to continue and is about to cancel his lease. Would you consider leasing it to me for life? I am old and sick; I am aware that I am making a bad bargain; but this bargain will be useful to you and please me. The following are the conditions that my imagination which has always been my guide would submit for your wise consideration." And he proposes a little contract, quite attractive and quite ideal. De Brosses replied to these proposals point by point, with accuracy and precision, in a businesslike manner, with a touch of wit; he adroitly referred to Voltaire's real motive —his desire not to be entirely at the mercy of Geneva: "One must live in one's own country. . . . One must not live abroad. . . . The more I think of that republic, the more I am fond of monarchies." On receiving the Président's precise reply, Voltaire seems to forget his own earlier proposals: he hesitates, he retreats, he makes new ones, as though through forgetfulness. He adds, however: "I still persist in my intention of owning land in France, in Switzerland, in Geneva, and even in Savoy. It is said, I don't know where, that a man cannot serve two masters; I want to have four in order to have none at all and to enjoy to the full that most noble prerogative of human nature, which is called freedom."

After some haggling over terms, the deal was concluded. Voltaire purchased a lease for life on the château and the lands of Tourney with all the manorial rights and privileges attached to the property. In several letters written following this purchase he mentioned that his independence would now be complete and secure. When Thieriot congratulated him on adding Ferney to Les Délices and on having two footholds, Voltaire replied joyously: "You're mistaken, my feet are planted in four places, not two: one in Lausanne, in a very fine house, for the winter; one at Les Délices, near Geneva, where respectable people come to see me—so much for my front feet. My rear feet are at Ferney and at Tourney, which I acquired on the basis of a long-term lease from the Président de Brosses." He was elated at the thought of being so cleverly and politically astride so many frontiers; he had successfully carried out his scheme and now gave vent to his satisfaction. "If you go to the country of the Pope," he wrote to d'Alembert, "pass this way. You will see that the preachers of Geneva respect the towers of Ferney, the moats of Tourney, and even the gardens of Les Délices." —"Use the regular mail service, and address boldly: *A Voltaire, gentilhomme du Roi, au château de Ferney, par Genève;* for I shall stay a few weeks at Ferney. We have Tourney for our theater, and Les Délices is the third string of our bow. Philosophers should always have two or three underground holes, to protect themselves against the dogs that are after them."

In making his deal with the Président de Brosses, Voltaire had stipulated explicitly that he would be entitled to all the manorial rights attached to Tourney; in this period he signed some of his letters, "Voltaire, Comte de Tourney." He had two parish priests who were his "subjects," and he enjoyed this hugely: "I have two curates, and I am very satisfied with them. I am ruining one and giving alms to the other." And: "My curates take my orders, and the Geneva preachers dare not look me in the face." A furious storm broke out in Paris against the Encyclopedists. D'Alembert withdrew from the undertaking; Palissot was preparing to produce his satirical play, *Les Philosophes;* but Voltaire who, the moment he took over the property, had a little theater built at Tourney, and who staged comedies there under the noses of Geneva and Rousseau, exclaimed in triumph: "When anyone worries about what I am doing in my cottages, when I am asked, 'What are you doing there, you rogue?' I reply, 'I reign,' and I add that I pity the slaves." Here the philosopher's zeal is thrown overboard, and his attitude is indistinguishable from the rich man's pride. Voltaire's happiness was of the insolent kind.

This is a crucial moment in Voltaire's life: it marks his true accession to universal literary rule; he "reigns" and will reign during the twenty years that remain to him. In this essay however, we shall confine ourselves to an account of his business relations with the Président de Brosses.

The correspondence between them, published by M. Foisset in 1836, provides us with all the necessary exhibits. As I said, Voltaire leased for life the lands and the château of Tourney. He had great plans for demolishing, rebuilding, and embellishing, and he set about them at once with his natural vivacity, beginning, as was only fair, with the theater. It had been stipulated that Voltaire, in his capacity as life tenant, would treat the property like a good father, would not fell trees, and would exercise moderation in his plans for remodeling and relandscaping. I shall spare the reader the original documents that anyone can consult, and confine myself to the spirit of the affair. It must be granted that the transfer of property, which took the out-

ward form of a lease for life, lent itself easily to chicanery
of every kind; it was a very complicated document. As
soon as he took over the estate, Voltaire began to harass
the Président under every conceivable pretext. It is interesting to observe how, in Voltaire's letters to him, the cause
of humanitarianism is always invoked side by side with the
pettiest private concerns. The priest of Moëns, the parish
adjoining Ferney, had started a lawsuit against the poor of
his parish who thought themselves entitled to some tithe
or other (although, under ancient law, a community of inhabitants could not be entitled to a tithe). Voltaire grew
passionate about this and appealed to the Président: "Pity
the unfortunates; you are not a priest. In the name of
humanity, see what can be done for the idiots of Ferney.
Enlighten me, I beg of you." "The idiots of Ferney," i.e.,
the parishioners: note this perpetual cruel method of de-
spising those he claims to be serving, and of substituting
the insolent satisfaction of pride for human charity. At the
same time, Voltaire did not forget the Président's promise
to send him four thousand vinestocks from Burgundy; in
fact, he hoped to get five thousand instead of the four he
was entitled to: "By God! four thousand vinestocks, or
rather five thousand! You'll profit a hundredfold. All I am
interested in, is the good of the property. You and your
son will drink the wine."

These sweet words, mingled with requests and insinua-
tions that the Président had outsmarted him, never
stopped. The Président reassured him as best he could:
"We have negotiated as gentlemen and as men of the
world, not as pettifogging lawyers. I know that you would
be incapable of acting otherwise than as a man of honor
and that you will treat the property as if it were your own
patrimonial estate, as a careful owner and good father.
And so, trust me, just as I trust you; let this be taken for
granted between us once and for all."

But this was not at all the way things were going. Voltaire would not let himself be appeased, nor would he
leave others in peace. "I've been reading and rereading
your contract, and the more I reread it, the more I see

that you have imposed your terms on me, like a conqueror; but I don't mind it at all. I like to improve the places I live in, and I am acting both for your good and for my pleasure. I have already given orders that half of the château be torn down and the other half remodeled." He wanted, at the château, deep and regular moats and drawbridges; pitilessly he cut down old trees. "Your old trees will be put to better use in my remodelings than as firewood for the citizens of Geneva." However, the agents who were on the spot and M. Girod (great-uncle of M. Girod of the Ain), the notary, alerted the Président. The latter was in no hurry; it was agreed that an inventory and a survey of the grounds would be made. But when the agents were about to begin this survey, Voltaire stopped it. He proposed to de Brosses to purchase the land for good, and while this new project, which was nothing but a red herring, was under consideration, the survey was not started. In this way Voltaire gained time to proceed with his plans before the condition of the grounds at the time he took over was recorded. This tactical ruse is very apparent when we read all the documents.

When we read only one or two of these letters more or less attentively, we might think that Voltaire's changes of mind are only natural in so imaginative a man, that he cannot control himself, and that all we can blame him for is his nerves. But on closer inspection we see very clearly that the restlessness that seizes him is both nervous and calculated. He knows perfectly well why he asks for changes and revisions in the contract; he seems to be quoting, as if they were explicitly stated, clauses which he knows do not exist or which he alters deliberately. To begin with, he pleads, he cavils, he protests in order to avoid paying his share of the transfer duties.

He wrote about it to the Président and summoned him to act as if the latter had agreed to exempt him from paying these duties, which had nothing in common with the real-estate and some other taxes from which the Tourney estate was exempted. Voltaire, who did not want to pay, pretended that he did not know the difference between these two kinds of tax and refused to give in: "We must bestir ourselves, act, talk, and have our way. [This was indeed his motto.] I have embellished Tourney, I have improved the grounds; but I'll burn everything if I am robbed of the slightest of my rights. I am Swiss, and I don't listen to reason when I am provoked. I have enough to live on without Tourney, and I'd rather let it go to brambles than be persecuted." Thus he became Swiss when he wanted to avoid paying at Tourney, while at Geneva he remained the lord and count of Tourney, and was treated as such.

These titles mattered a great deal to him. The day he entered the château of Tourney as its lord, he wore a gala coat and was accompanied by his two nieces (Mme. de Fontaine and Mme. Denis) "covered with diamonds." The priest greeted him with a speech, the tenant farmer treated him to a splendid dinner, his "subjects" fired salvos from their muskets and heavier pieces as well: artillery and a gunner had been borrowed from Geneva for the occasion. Girls brought oranges in baskets decorated with ribbons. In short, it was a great occasion for rejoicing. But a few months later, when the lord of the manor and judge was asked to pay the costs of a criminal affair in which one of his "subjects" (a native of the village of La Perrière, in the territory of Geneva) was involved, Voltaire refused on the ground that La Perrière was not part of the Tourney estate, and that offenses committed there by one of his "subjects" (and this one was a very bad lot) did not concern him in the least. He would lose a privilege rather than incur an expense which was a consequence of it. It is instructive to see how, at that moment, he philosophically renounced all the prerogatives attached to his title: "The more I know this property, the more I think that I shall be concerned with rural rather than manorial matters. My business is to improve everything, and I don't intend to have anybody hanged. An honor that yields no income is a very poor honor at the foot of the Jura. . . . I have no ambition to be the lord of a provincial hole!" Never has a man undergone a more rapid and more opportunistic change of heart.

All this time, Voltaire, though posing as a generous and unselfish man, the victim of a disadvantageous transaction, did everything he pleased with Tourney. He readily found excuses for his avarice as well as for his wanton depredations. "I take pleasure in rendering fertile a land which was far from fertile before, and on my deathbed I shall have no occasion for self-reproach concerning the way I used my fortune. . . . Unquestionably, I am steadily improving the land by enlarging the meadows at the expense of a few trees. . . . I have every reason to believe that you will not object to the services I am rendering you and your family." At the moment the contestation was at its sharpest, he went so far in his buffoonery as to say: "I am doing good for the love of good itself, and Heaven will reward me for it: I shall live a long time because I love justice."

It is impossible to go into all the details here; let us now come to the biggest and most unsavory incident, which led to the break between the two men. Before Voltaire took possession of Tourney (December 1758), the Président had sold some timber to a local peasant, a dealer in wood, by name of Charlot Baudy. One day, Voltaire in a conversation with the Président complained that he had not enough firewood; the Président said that Baudy might supply it to him, and that he would speak to him about it himself. As a result, Baudy delivered to Voltaire fourteen *moules* (the local unit of measurement) of firewood. After the wood was delivered and burned, Voltaire took it into his head not to pay the dealer and to pretend that de Brosses owed him the wood or had given it to him as a present. This miserable business, coming as it did on top of the others, took on extreme proportions because of Voltaire's stubbornness and insincerity. After the Président had addressed him a polite and firm letter on the subject, Voltaire, in keeping with his usual procedure, launched into another question, one that seemed of interest to mankind. "What this letter is about," he wrote from Ferney on January 30, 1761, "is no longer Charles Baudy and the four moules of firewood [note how he changes, without seeming to do so, fourteen into four]. I am writing about something that concerns the public good. I am demanding retribution for blood that has been spilt, for the ruin of a man under your protection, for the crime of a priest who is the scourge of the province, for sacrilege added to murder." Alas! the word "priest" gives it all away. Hatred of priests was merely another of Voltaire's passions, which made him temporarily forget his avarice. The priest in question was the parish priest of Moëns whom we mentioned before. He seems to have committed a grave offense: one night he had posted peasants to intercept and cane the son of a local notable, as he was leaving the house of a loose woman. But Voltaire wanted more than reparations or justice: he wanted publicity. In a letter to d'Alembert dating from that period he lets the cat out of the bag when he writes these horrible words: "I am trying to send a priest to the galleys." After his unsuccessful efforts to obtain the Président's help in this matter, Voltaire went back to his secret vice, avarice, and to the fourteen *moules* of firewood. Furthermore, he had been stung by the Président's very wise reply to his letter concerning the priest of Moëns. After pointing out that extrajudicial declamations make a deplorable impression in such cases, de Brosses added a remark concerning those unfortunate logs: "I don't think," he wrote, "that fourteen *moules* of firewood has ever been given as a present to anyone, unless it be to a Capuchin monastery." To compare Voltaire to a Capuchin monastery, at the very time he was threatening a priest with the galleys! This was enough to unleash his rage.

Now Voltaire was seized with one of those fits which he unfortunately never tried to control. He wrote to all his friends of the Parlement de Bourgogne, asking them to arbitrate his quarrel with the Président. In the account of it he addressed to them, he deliberately confused everything, distorted and falsified the facts, and lied boldly—he had acquired a despicable facility for lying. To hear him, one might think that he had been utterly reluctant to start such a quarrel and that he had been drawn into it against his will. For shame! That a writer like Voltaire should lower himself to these petty things! And since he was at the time working on his commentary on Corneille, he exclaimed: "Corneille reproaches me for deserting him in favor of firewood." He passed all bounds in his invectives against the Président: "Let him tremble! What I want is no longer to ridicule him, but to dishonor him." Thus he was ready to turn all the resources of an infuriated and dishonest genius against his enemy.

A letter he wrote to the Président in this connection brought a reply which will remain memorable, and which should be put beside the noble letter the great Haller had once addressed to Voltaire urging him to stop the maneuvers and intrigues in which he was trying to implicate him.

"Remember the counsels of prudence I have lately given you in conversation," de Brosses wrote, "when you related to me the reverses of your life and you added that you had a 'naturally insolent' character. I have given you my friendship; one proof that I have not withdrawn it is this warning I am giving you now, never to write at moments when you are not yourself, so that you won't have to blush when you have come back to your senses for what you did during your delirium."

And after giving a correct account of their previous dealings, he went on to say:

"Only a prophet can foresee whether a lease for life will turn out to be profitable or not: this depends on things that are beyond human control. I can say, truthfully, that I wish with all my heart that you should enjoy your property for a long time, and I hope that you will continue being an ornament of this century for another thirty years; for despite your weaknesses, you will never be anything but a very great man . . . in your writings. But I wish that you would instill into your heart some small fraction of the morality and philosophy these writings contain."

As for Voltaire's demand for arbitration, the Président says that the matter is not one for arbitration: Voltaire owes the money for the fourteen *moules* of firewood to the dealer who had delivered it to him, and if he fails to pay, this dealer will summon him to court without further ado.

"There has been no transaction between you and me, and since there has been no transaction, there can be no arbitration. M. le Premier Président, M. de Ruffoy, and our other mutual friends whom you mention cannot help shrugging their shoulders seeing so wealthy and famous a man going to such lengths in order to avoid paying 280 francs to a peasant for wood he delivered. Are you trying to write a sequel to your story with M. de Gauffecourt, to whom you refused payment for a post chaise you bought from him? Verily, I pity mankind when I see such a great genius with so small a heart, continually torn by petty jealousy and avarice. It is you yourself who poison a life otherwise so perfectly made for happiness. Read and re-read the letter from M. Haller, it contains true wisdom."

Voltaire had insinuated that the Président was relying on his position of authority to make him—or his niece and heir—lose his case in court; to this the Président replied as a man conscious of the dignity of his office:

"It is very improper for you to insist on the authority you say I have as a judge. I don't know what 'authority' means in such cases, and even less what it is to make use of it. It is inadmissible to speak in such fashion; have the good sense in the future not to say anything like that to a magistrate."

M. de Brosses wrote all this on the margin of Voltaire's insolent letter, which he sent back to him, with these words in the place of the usual complimentary ending:

"Once and for all, you are never again to write to me concerning this matter, particularly in this tone. —My wish to you, Monsieur, is, in the words of Persius: *Mens sana in corpore sano.*"[1]

To conclude this matter, I shall add that the Président may have been severe at some points, and that he showed himself more just than generous. It seems to me that in his letters to Voltaire, when he speaks of the more or less favorable possibilities of a lease for life, he insists a little too often on the possibility—always unpleasant—of death. But

[1] The quotation is actually from Juvenal (Satire X).

there can be no doubt that he acted justly and correctly;
and when he wrote his final letter on this matter he had
been exasperated by the continual importunities and hypocrisy of his adversary. After both died, Mme. Denis,
then Mme. Duvivier, Voltaire's heir, had to pay to the
Président's son approximately forty thousand francs after
experts had estimated the depredations and deteriorations
of the property—proof that Voltaire had abused his position
as life tenant.

Eventually the storm blew over, but Voltaire did not
forget it. He remained owner for life and usufructary of
Tourney, but soon tired of it, preferring to be the patriarch
of Ferney. Years went by. In 1770 a number of members
of the French Academy died in quick succession, including
Moncrif, the Président Hénault, the Abbé Alary; Mairan
was ill, and about to follow them. There were many vacancies, and the Président de Brosses had the natural idea
of presenting himself as a candidate to succeed Hénault;
but at this point he once again ran into Voltaire. He had
been warned during the quarrel: "Look out! He is dangerous!" To this he had replied: "Is this a reason for letting
him be malicious with impunity? On the contrary, it is
people of this kind who should be chastised. I am not
afraid of him: I am not a Pompignan. He is admired for
his excellent verse. Certainly it is excellent; but it is his
verse that should be admired. I too admire it, but I shall
despise him as a man if he acts in a despicable way."
However, de Brosses had forgotten what an honest man
forgets so easily, namely, that an opponent might resort to
lies and slander. Voltaire did not shrink from such methods. During those nine years d'Alembert and he had come
into ever closer league. Voltaire's wish had come true: "I
should like the philosophers to form a body of initiates,
and I'd die happy. —Brothers, unite! —Let the true philosophers support one another, let them be loyal to the confraternity, and then I am ready to be burned at the stake
for them. —No, I'll send to the stake or at least expel anyone I please." The moment Voltaire got wind of the Pré-

sident's candidacy, he wrote to d'Alembert (December 10, 1770):

"I hear that the Président de Brosses is in the running. I know that in addition to *Fétiches* and *Terres Australes*, he wrote a book on languages, in which his borrowings from others are fairly good, while his own contribution is detestable.

"I sent him a Consultation of nine lawyers, all of whom concluded that I could charge him with fraud before his own Parlement. [A lie.] He acted very sordidly toward me, and I still have the letter in which he tells me in veiled terms that should I take him into court, he would denounce me as author of seditious works, which I certainly never wrote. [A lie.] I can submit these fine things to the Academy. I don't think such a man is suitable for you."

D'Alembert, like any other party man, accepted at their face value the prejudices of his chief and colleague. In the eyes of any confraternity or party, the greatest crime is not to belong to it. To remain independent, "to go it alone"[2]—especially when you are in sympathy with it—almost amounts to having denounced and betrayed it. The Président de Brosses, who on many points came close to the Philosophical School, had never allied himself with it, and had even refused to join it. When he published his work on fetishism, Voltaire, hastily seeing in it more than the Président had claimed to show, had written to him: "I think that the anti-fetishists should stand together as the initiates used to; but they are at one another's throats." These words were thrown out as though casually, in connection with a very minor affair; Voltaire seemed only to be joking, while actually sounding out his correspondent. The Président had not taken the bait, and had turned a deaf ear to Voltaire's overtures. This was enough for the leaders of the Order, even those who had no personal grudge against him, to think themselves dispensed from the

[2] Voltaire says so explicitly in a letter to d'Alembert about Rousseau: "It is your Jean-Jacques who infuriates me most. This archmadman who might have been somebody if he had let himself be guided by you, chooses to go it alone."

need of treating him with justice or correctness. D'Alembert hastened to warn Voltaire that the Président had many friends in the Academy, and hence that it was necessary to alienate them from him at all costs. In their letters of this period they never stop discussing the Président; they refer to him as *plat, nasillonneur, petit persécuteur nasillonneur, le fripon de Président.* They looked for a candidate who might win against him; they considered a certain M. Marin, the chief censor, whom Beaumarchais later stigmatized in his memoirs; they considered the Abbé Delille, then very young, who had recently translated the *Georgics.* "If you don't take him," Voltaire wrote, "couldn't you have some *grand seigneur?*" What they wanted was not only to defeat de Brosses, but "to discourage him once and for all." Voltaire set all his machines in motion. Attempts were made, in his name, to delay and to intimidate the learned Foncemagne, who supported the Président's candidacy. Voltaire wrote letter upon letter to the Maréchal de Richelieu, who also favored the Président: "You don't know him at all, but I know him for having deceived me, for having caused me trouble, and for having wanted to denounce me." On finding that his wishes were resisted, Voltaire authorized d'Alembert to be his spokesman and to say anything he pleased. He gave him a free hand, and empowered him, if need be, to cast all anathemas in his name. "I am crossing the Rubicon to drive out the *nasillonneur délateur et persécuteur;* and I declare that I shall be obliged to resign my seat if he is given one. I have so little time left to live that I have no reason to be afraid of war."

I won't quote all these ignominies. The excommunication was fully effective; the four vacancies were filled by M. de Roquelaure, bishop of Senlis, the historian Gaillard, the Prince de Beauvau, and the Abbé Arnaud. Because the Président had refused to give Voltaire the fourteen *moules* of firewood as a present, he could never become a member of the French Academy, and, what is more serious, his memory would still be stained by an odious imputation of fraud, so shamelessly circulated by Voltaire, if the Correspondence, now brought up to date, did not show clearly which of the two was honest and which the liar and slanderer.

Note that these calumnies which Voltaire whispered to so many persons did not prevent him five years later from resuming his relations with M. de Brosses, who had become the Premier-Président of the Parlement de Bourgogne, and from recommending certain matters to his attention (November 1776): "As for me, at my age, I have no other desire than that of enjoying your favorable opinion when I die . . ."

On one occasion de Brosses had to pass judgment on Voltaire as a writer, and he did it with fairness, without a trace of resentment. In his *Life of Sallust,* speaking of the Latin writers who imitated the style of Sallust, exaggerating his mannerisms, he reviews the modern writers who try to imitate the two most brilliant men of their epoch (Fontenelle and Voltaire), borrowing from the latter his "philosophical tone, his brilliant, rapid, superficial manner, his sharp, trenchant, epigrammatic style, his way of pairing antithetical ideas, which are so often surprised to find themselves together. But Voltaire," he hastens to add, "the greatest colorist who ever lived, the most pleasant and most seductive, has a manner entirely his own, of which he alone possesses the magic secret, although he makes use of the same manner in treating subjects which require another. He is a unique, original writer who begot a great number of mediocre copyists." Whereas de Brosses grants too much to Voltaire when he calls him the greatest colorist in the world, he makes a very good point when observing that he uses the same manner indiscriminately in his treatment of all subjects. Indeed, Voltaire has only one prose: whether he writes history, a novel, or a letter, his tone remains the same.

What is the moral of this distressing tale? In my opinion, it is this, that of all defects, the worst is that of insincerity, untruthfulness, and habitual lying. "Lying is a vice only when it hurts others," Voltaire wrote to Thiériot. "It is a very great virtue when it does them good." In writing this,

his sole purpose was to disclaim authorship of his *Enfant prodigue.* "If you have disclosed the secret to Sauveau," he added, "make him lie too. Lie, my friends, keep lying; I shall do the same for you if the occasion requires." When we play with lies so early and so gaily, we easily use them as an instrument of all our passions. Slander is but one more lie; it is a tempting weapon; every liar has it in his quiver, and cannot resist using it, particularly when his enemy will never know. We flatter ourselves that we are far better in this respect than the Encyclopedists; I am, however, very much afraid that when it comes to schools, sects, or parties, men remain unchanged.

As for Voltaire, when we know him well and when we have seen him in his various fits of rage, it is impossible not to look upon him as a demon of grace, wit, and very often also (this must be granted) of good sense and reason, as a blind and brilliant elemental force, which is often luminous, a meteor that cannot be controlled, rather than a human and moral being.

8 November 1852 (*Causeries du lundi*).

Nothing pertaining to literature is alien to Sainte-Beuve. He loves every aspect of it. A true aficionado, he is interested not only in the final product, in what everyone sees on the public stage, but also in what goes on behind the scenes. Now and again, with more enjoyment than malice, he takes his readers on an excursion into the sculleries of some past literary world, acting as an experienced guide. Discretion kept him from raising the curtain on similar intrigues and deals in the literary society of his own day.

This essay, and those on Mme. Geoffrin and Grimm, illustrates a particularly rich vein of Sainte-Beuve's work—the evocation of the atmosphere of an earlier time.

MADAME GEOFFRIN

MADAME GEOFFRIN was one of the most famous and most influential women of the eighteenth century. Only four or five letters she wrote were published; a number of her apt and pithy sayings are often quoted; but what she is really remembered for is her salon—the most complete, best organized, and, if I may say so, most efficiently run in her day. Since the founding of the first salon, the Hôtel de Rambouillet, none other surpassed Mme. Geoffrin's in importance. It was one of the institutions of eighteenth-century France.

Some may think that to form a salon all that is required is to be wealthy, to have a good chef, a comfortable house situated in a fashionable quarter, a great desire to see people, and affability in receiving them. But in this way one succeeds only in gathering people indiscriminately: you fill your salon, you don't create one. If you are very wealthy, very active, very ambitious, and resolved at all costs to have all the reigning stars of the season in your home, you may at best achieve what a number of Americans achieve in Paris every winter: they give brilliant parties, people drop in or even rush in, and the next winter these brilliant parties are forgotten. How different are such invasion tactics from the art of creating a true salon! This art was never better known and more efficiently practiced than in the eighteenth century, within the placid and self-contained society of Paris, and no one carried it further, conceived it more grandly, and applied it with greater skill

and refinement than Mme. Geoffrin. A Roman cardinal
could not have displayed more political sagacity, more
cleverness and subtlety than she displayed for thirty
years. When we study her closely, we become convinced
that a great social influence is always justified: behind the
famous successes that are later summed up in an oft-re-
peated name, there will always be found to be a great
deal of work, study, and talent; and in the case of Mme.
Geoffrin, we must add, there is a great deal of good sense.

The first mentions of Mme. Geoffrin occur when she is
already old; her youth escapes us in a remote past that we
shall not try to penetrate. Of unadulterated bourgeois
origins, born in Paris in 1699, Marie-Thérèse Rodet, on
July 19, 1713 was married to Pierre-François Geoffrin,
a substantial citizen, one of the lieutenant colonels of the
national guard of his day, and one of the founders of the
Manufacture des glaces. A letter written by Montesquieu
in March 1748 shows that Mme. Geoffrin at that time
gathered a choice company in her house; already she was
the center of the circle which was to continue and to grow
for twenty-five years. What was the background of this
distinguished and clever woman, who scarcely seemed destined for such a role by her birth or her position in society?
What was her early education? One day the Empress
Catherine of Russia addressed this very question to Mme.
Geoffrin, who replied to her by a letter that should be
appended to Montaigne's celebrated passages on education.
She wrote:

"I lost my father and mother as an infant. I was brought
up by an old grandmother who was full of intelligence
and common sense. She had very little schooling, but her
mind was so enlightened, so clever, so active, that it
never failed her; it always served her in place of learning.
She spoke so pleasantly about things she did not know,
that no one wished she knew more about them; and when
her ignorance was too obvious, she extricated herself so
humorously that the pedants intent upon humiliating her
were confused. She was so happy with her lot, that she
looked upon erudition as something very useless for a

woman. She would say, 'I have done so well without it, that I never felt the need for it. If my granddaughter is a fool, erudition will make her overconfident and unbearable; if she is intelligent and sensitive, she will do as I did, she will replace what she does not know with cleverness and feeling; and when she reaches the age of reason, she will learn what she is most suited for, and she will learn it very fast.' Thus, all she taught me as a child was how to read; but she made me read a great deal; she taught me how to think properly by making me explain things; she taught me to know people by making me say what I thought and by telling me her opinions about them. She asked me to account for all my actions and all my opinions, and she corrected me with so much gentleness and grace that I never concealed anything from her: she saw what went on inside me as clearly as what was outside. My education was continuous . . ."

As I said above, Mme. Geoffrin was born in Paris; she never left it except once, in 1766, at the age of sixty-seven, when she made her famous trip to Warsaw. Otherwise she never went farther than the suburbs; even when she visited a friend in the country, she usually returned at night and slept at home. In her opinion, "there was no better air than that of Paris," and no matter where she was, she preferred the gutters of the Rue Saint-Honoré, just as Mme. de Staël was homesick for those of the Rue du Bac. Mme. Geoffrin adds one more name to the list of the brilliant Parisians highly endowed with the virtue of social affability, who contributed so readily to the spread of civilization.

Her husband seems to have counted for little in her life, unless it was to provide her with the fortune which was the starting point and primary instrument of the consideration she came to acquire. We have descriptions of M. Geoffrin as an old man, silently attending the dinners given in his home to men of letters and scholars. We are told that attempts were made to make him read books of history or travel. He was usually given only the first volume of some such work; he never asked for the following volumes, and his reaction was usually confined to a terse remark: "The work is interesting, but the author is somewhat repetitious." On one occasion, perusing a volume of the *Encyclopédie* or of Bayle which was printed in double columns, he read straight across the two columns line by line, and declared that "the work seemed good to him, though somewhat abstract." This is the kind of story inevitably circulated about every husband who is outshone by a famous wife. One day a foreigner asked Mme. Geoffrin what had become of the old gentleman who had used to attend her dinners regularly and was seen there no longer. "That was my husband, he died," she said.

Mme. Geoffrin had a daughter who became the Marquise de la Ferté-Imbault. She was an excellent woman, we are told, but lacking her mother's moderation and poise. The latter used to say: "When I look at her, I feel like a hen who laid a duck's egg."

Mme. Geoffrin thus inherited her grandmother's qualities, and she seems to have been unlike any other of her ancestors. Her talent, like all talents, was entirely personal. Mme. Suard depicts her as a person who gently imposed respect "by her tall stature, by her silvery hair covered with a coif knotted under her chin, by her noble and discreet way of dressing, and by her expression combining reasonableness and kindness." Diderot played a game of piquet with her after dinner at Grandval, in the house of the Baron d'Holbach in October 1760. He wrote to a friend: "Mme. Geoffrin was splendid. I am always impressed by this woman's noble and simple taste in dress; that day she wore an austerely colored gown of a simple material, with broad sleeves; her linen was of the plainest and finest, and all the rest exquisitely neat." She was then sixty-one. This way of dressing like an old lady, so exquisite in its modesty and simplicity, was one of her distinguishing characteristics, which brings to mind the very similar art of Mme. de Maintenon. But Mme. Geoffrin did not have to make the most of her beauty, which was still remarkable when the light was not too bright; she was frankly old at an early age, and, so to speak, she had no autumn. Whereas the majority of women are intent upon retreating in good

order and prolonging their age of yesterday, she forestalled
the future of her own accord and accepted without a mur-
mur her age of tomorrow. It was said that all women
dressed as for yesterday, and that only Mme. Geoffrin always dressed as for tomorrow.

Mme. Geoffrin is said to have learned her worldly ways
from Mme. de Tencin, and to have been formed in
the latter's school. Noticing her assiduity in visiting her
during her last days, Mme. de Tencin is reported to have
said to her habitués: "Do you know why *la Geoffrin* comes
here? She comes to see what part of my inventory she can
salvage for herself." This inventory was well worth the
trouble, since it included Fontenelle, Montesquieu, and
Mairan. Mme. de Tencin deserves less to be remembered
for her sentimental and romantic stories, which her nephews may have helped her write, than for her spirit of
intrigue, for her cleverness in manipulating people, and for
the boldness and range of her judgment. A not very esti-
mable woman, some of whose actions even come close to
crime, she captivated those who frequented her by her air
of sweetness, almost goodness. When her own interests
were not involved, she gave sure and practical advice,
which could be put to good use in life. She knew the ins
and outs of everything. More than one great statesman
would have been helped, even in our own day, if he had
kept in mind this maxim which she often repeated: "Intelligent men make mistakes because they never realize that
people are as foolish as they are." The nine published letters she wrote to the Duc de Richelieu during the campaign of 1743 show her in the thick of her ambitious maneuvers, determined to seize power for herself and her
brother, the cardinal, during the brief moment when the
king, emancipated by the death of the Cardinal de Fleury,
had not yet taken an official mistress. Louis XV was never
judged more thoroughly and with more farsighted and
better motivated contempt than in those nine letters. As
early as 1743 this *intrigante* had flashes of insight into the
future. "Unless God visibly intervenes," she wrote, "it is
physically impossible that the monarchy should not be

overthrown." It was this clever teacher whom Mme. Geoffrin consulted and from whom she received good advice, especially that of never refusing any acquaintance, any friendly advance; for even if nine out of ten turn out to be unprofitable, a single one can make up for them all. Moreover, as this resourceful woman would say, "Everything can be made to serve, if you know how to use your tools."

Thus Mme. Geoffrin inherited part of Mme. de Tencin's salon and tactics; but while confining her arts to the private sphere, she expanded them singularly and in a very honorable manner. Mme. de Tencin moved heaven and earth to make her brother a prime minister; Mme. Geoffrin ignored politics, never took sides in matters pertaining to religion, and thanks to her infinite art and steadiness of purpose, she became herself a kind of skillful administrator, almost a prime minister of society, one of those ministers who are the more influential for being less acknowledged and more permanent.

To begin with, she conceived of this complex mechanism which is called a salon in all the fullness of its potentialities, and she succeeded in organizing it completely; its cogs moved gently and imperceptibly for all their intricacy, and she kept everything in good order by dint of constant care. She took pains to gather not only men of letters in the strict sense, but also artists, sculptors, and painters, establishing contact between those two groups and between them and people of society; in short, her salon was a kind of *Encyclopédie* in action and in conversation. Every week she gave two regular dinners. Mondays were reserved for artists; these included Vanloo, Vernet, Boucher, La Tour, Vien, Lagrenée, Soufflot, Lemoine, several distinguished art lovers and patrons, and a few men of letters, such as Marmontel, to keep up conversation and act as liaison between the various others. The Wednesday dinners were for men of letters; they were attended by d'Alembert, Mairan, Marivaux, Marmontel, the Chevalier de Chastellux, Morellet, Saint-Lambert, Helvétius, Raynal, Thomas, Grimm, d'Holbach, and Burigny of the Académie des Inscriptions. Only one woman was admitted in addition to the mistress of the house—Mlle. de Lespinasse. Mme. Geoffrin had noticed that the presence of several women at a dinner distracted the guests and broke up conversation; she loved unity, and to be herself the center of things. Her doors remained open well into the night, and the evening ended with a little supper, very simple and very refined, attended by five or six close friends at the most, and at this hour also a few women, the flower of society. There was no foreigner of distinction, either resident in Paris or a visitor, who did not desire to be admitted to Mme. Geoffrin's. Princes came to her house as private individuals; ambassadors never failed to return once they had been invited. Europe was represented there by Caracciolo, Creutz, Galiani, Gatti, Hume, and Gibbon.

As can be seen, of all the eighteenth-century salons, Mme. Geoffrin's was the most complete. It was more so than that of Mme. Deffand, who, after the defection of d'Alembert and others following the departure of Mlle. de Lespinasse, lost almost all her men of letters. The salon of Mlle. de Lespinasse, apart from five or six faithful friends, was formed of people who had little in common with one another, chosen here and there with infinite art. By contrast, Mme. Geoffrin's salon appears to us as the great center and meeting place of the eighteenth century. In its respectability and seemly animation, it served as a counterweight to the licentious little dinners and suppers given by Mlle. Quinault, Mlle. Guimard, and financiers like Pelletier and La Popelinière. During Mme. Geoffrin's last years, there were formed, in emulation of her salon and to some extent in competition with it, the salons of the Baron d'Holbach and of Mme. Helvétius, composed in part of Mme. Geoffrin's guests and in part of a few men whom Mme. Geoffrin thought too unpredictable to be admitted to her dinners. In the end, the century refused her restrictions and her apron strings: it insisted on discussing everything openly and freely.

The spirit Mme. Geoffrin brought into the administration and economy of this little empire that she had conceived so broadly, was a spirit of naturalness, justness, and refinement, which went into the smallest details, a spirit of cleverness, activity, and gentleness. Just as she ordered the sculptured decorations of her apartment to be removed, she pursued an analogous aim in the moral sphere: "Nothing in relief" seemed to be her motto. "My mind is like my legs," she used to say, "I like to walk on even ground. I do not want to climb a mountain merely to have the pleasure of saying, when I reach the top, 'I have climbed this mountain.'" She liked simplicity, and if need be, she would have affected it a little. Her activity was of the discreet kind, quiet and efficient. As the mistress of the house, she kept an eye on everything; she presided, and she scolded, but she scolded in a way that was hers alone; she wanted people to end their remarks at the right moment, she policed her salon. With the words, *"Voilà qui est bien,"* she would interrupt a conversation that was straying toward risky subjects or would restrain minds that were becoming overheated; the culprits feared her and went elsewhere to celebrate "their Sabbath." As a matter of principle, she herself spoke only when necessary, intervening only at certain moments, and always without monopolizing the conversation for too long a time. These were the moments she chose for her wise maxims, piquant stories, and moral anecdotes, usually seasoned by some familiar expression or image. This sort of thing was becoming only to her, and she knew it: that is why she said that she did not want "anyone else to preach her sermons, tell her stories, or touch her fire tongs."

Having at an early date established herself as an old lady and "mother" of the people she received, she had a means of ruling them, a little artifice that eventually became a tic and a mania: this was to scold them. But with her, scolding was a favor, the greatest mark of her interest. Not everyone could be scolded by her; those whom she liked best were scolded the most. Horace Walpole, before going over with flying colors to the camp of Mme. du Deffand, wrote from Paris to his friend Thomas Gray (January 25, 1766):

"Madame Geoffrin, of whom you have heard much, is

an extraordinary woman, with more common sense than I almost ever met with. Great quickness in discovering characters, penetration in going to the bottom of them, and a pencil that never fails in a likeness—seldom a favorable one. She exacts and preserves, spite of her birth and their nonsensical prejudices about nobility, great court and attention. This she acquires by a thousand little arts and offices of friendship; and by a freedom and severity, which seem to be her sole end of drawing a concourse to her; for she insists on scolding those she inveigles to her. She has little taste and less knowledge, but protects artisans and authors, and courts a few people to have the credit of serving her dependents. She was bred under the famous Madame Tencin, who advised her never to refuse any man; for, said her mistress, though nine in ten should not care a farthing for you, the tenth may live to be an useful friend. She did not adopt or reject the whole plan, but fully retained the purport of the maxim. In short, she is an epitome of empire, subsisting by rewards and punishments."

The duties of major-domo in her salon were usually entrusted to Burigny, one of her oldest friends, and the one who was most scolded of all. When rules were infringed or imprudent words uttered, she commonly blamed him for not having intervened in time.

Her guests laughed at these things and joked with her about them, but they submitted to her rule; it was fairly severe, but tempered with kindness and generosity. She had ways of justifying her right to correct others: occasionally she would endow one of them with a nice little pension, and she never forgot the annual gift of a pair of velvet breeches.

Her charity was great and ingenious: in her case it was a true gift of nature: she had "a giving disposition," as she put it. Her motto was, "Give and forgive." Her generosity was perpetual. She could not stop herself from making presents to everyone, from the poorest man of letters to the empress of Germany, and she made them with that art and accomplished delicacy that turns refusal into

an act of rudeness. Her active generosity and her exquisite
social tact were the culminations of her sensibility. Like her
other qualities, her kindness had something singular and
original about it, something that was entirely her own. A
thousand charming and unexpected remarks by her have
been quoted, which might have been used by Sterne; I
shall recall only one. One day she was told that everything
in her house was perfect, everything that is, except the
cream she served, which was far from good. "What can
I do?" she replied. "I can't change my milkwoman." —"Why
can't you change her?" —"Because I gave her two cows."
Some time earlier, when this milkwoman had lost her cow,
Mme. Geoffrin had given her two cows to comfort her,
and from that day on she felt she could not refuse her
services. A rare example of delicacy: many persons would
have been capable of giving a cow or even two cows; but
who else would have continued to patronize an ungrateful
or negligent milkwoman who supplied poor cream? Mme.
Geoffrin did this for her own sake, so as not to spoil the
memory of a charming action. Just as she scolded her
guests not in order to correct them but for her own pleasure,
so she was generous not in order to make the recipients of
her gifts happy or grateful, but rather to please herself.
Her kindness had a certain brusqueness and impatience
about it. She abhorred thanks; someone said that "thanks
put her in a state of amiable and almost serious anger."
She had a paradoxical theory of gratitude, even going so
far as to praise ingratitude. Clearly, even when she obliged
others, her purpose was to please herself. It seems to me
that in this she displays a strain of selfishness and aridity
characteristic of the eighteenth century. She was the pupil
of Mme. de Tencin and the friend of Fontenelle even when
she followed the bent of her own heart; even then she did
not forget herself, and calculated everything. She reminds
one of Montesquieu, who on one occasion, after treating
a man with the utmost generosity, dismissed him harshly.
On such occasions contempt of humanity manifests itself
even in kindness. I know that even when generosity is
practiced for selfish reasons, all sorts of arguments can be

advanced in favor of this charming and respectable virtue.
When Mme. Geoffrin was challenged on the subject, she
had a thousand good answers, as shrewd as herself. "Those
whose kindnesses are rare need no special maxims; but
those who do good often, must do it in a manner most
pleasant to themselves, for we should do comfortably what
we do every day." Let us respect and honor Mme. Geoffrin's natural and rational liberality; but let us recognize
that all this goodness and this kindness lack a certain
heavenly fire, just as all eighteenth-century spirit and
sociability lack imagination and poetry, a background of
heavenly light. One never glimpses the blue on the horizon
nor the brightness of the stars.

Mme. Geoffrin's dominant quality was discrimination and
common sense. Horace Walpole, whom I like to quote, a
good judge and beyond suspicion, had often seen Mme.
Geoffrin before going over to Mme. du Deffand; he greatly
enjoyed her company and speaks of her always as one of
the most intelligent persons he had ever met, one who had
the greatest knowledge of the world. In a letter to Lady
Hervey written shortly after an attack of gout (October
13, 1765), he says:

"Madame Geoffrin came and sat for two hours last night
by my bedside: I could have sworn it had been my Lady
Hervey, she was so good to me. It was with so much sense,
information, instruction, and correction! The manner of the
latter charms me. I never saw anybody in my days that
catches one's faults and vanities and impositions so quick,
that explains them to one so clearly, and convinces one
so easily. I never liked to be set right before! You cannot
imagine how I taste it! I make her both my confessor and
my director, and begin to think I shall be a reasonable
creature at last, which I never intended to be. The next
time I see her, I believe I shall say, 'Oh! Common Sense,
sit down: I have been thinking so and so, is it not absurd?'
—for t'other sense and wisdom, I never liked them, I shall
now hate them for her sake. If it was worth her while, I
assure your Ladyship she might govern me like a child."

On every occasion he speaks of her as the very embodiment of Reason.

Mme. de Tencin called her brilliant habitués her "stable": Mme. Geoffrin regarded them a little in the same way. She judged her friends and her guests with impartiality, and occasionally she let slip terrible words, seriously meant, which are remembered to this day. It was she who said of the Abbé Trublet when someone called him a wit: "He, a man of wit! It's a case of a little wit rubbing off on a fool." On one occasion Rulhière was reading aloud his manuscript of Russian anecdotes; she suggested that he throw it into the fire, and offered to compensate him by a sum of money. Rulhière indignantly invoked all the great sentiments—honor, disinterestedness, love of truth. She replied by saying merely, "You mean you want me to raise my offer?" We see that Mme. Geoffrin was sweet only when she chose to be, and that behind her benign disposition and kindness was a bitter experience of the world.

Some of her maxims remind us of Benjamin Franklin—they disclose the same calculating common sense and practicality. On the chips used at her gaming tables she had engraved the words: "Thrift is the source of independence and freedom." And she said: "Don't let grass grow on the path of friendship."

She was one of those intuitive minds Pascal speaks of, which are accustomed to judging at first sight and hardly ever take time to correct themselves. Such minds tend to fear weariness and boredom and are not always sound and penetrating. In this respect, Mme. Geoffrin differed entirely from Mme. du Châtelet, who liked to follow an argument to its last consequences. Such sensitive and quick minds are particularly suited for understanding society and people; their eyes like to wander about rather than alight at one place. In order not to weary, Mme. Geoffrin needed a great variety of persons and things. When a visit threatened to be overlong, she would turn pale and wish she were dead. Anything protracted, even a pleasure, was unbearable to her. On one occasion, she saw that the good Abbé de Saint-Pierre was preparing to pass a long winter evening with her. She had a moment of panic and, finding inspiration in her despair, she actually succeeded, with enormous effort, in making the abbé amusing. He was himself greatly surprised, and when she complimented him on his entertaining conversation as he left, he replied, "Madam, I am just an instrument that you played marvelously well." She was indeed a great virtuoso.

The great event in Mme. Geoffrin's life was her trip to Poland (1766), undertaken to visit the king, Stanislas Poniatowski. She had met him as a young man in Paris and lavished her bounties on him, as she did on so many others. No sooner had he ascended to the throne of Poland than he wrote to her, "*Maman, votre fils est roi*," and urged her to pay him a visit. She did not resist the invitation, despite her advanced age; she passed through Vienna, where she was treated with great consideration by the sovereigns. It has been thought that she was charged with a diplomatic mission on that occasion. We have the letters she wrote from Warsaw. They are charming; they were passed from hand to hand in Paris, and anyone who did not see them cut a poor figure in society. Voltaire chose that moment to write to her as to one of the powers that be: he asked her to recommend the Sirven family to the good graces of the king of Poland. Mme. Geoffrin's head was firmly set on her shoulders, and she did not lose it during the voyage. Marmontel, when writing to her, seemed to suggest that the consideration with which she, a mere private person, was treated by monarchs might revolutionize her ideas; she put him straight:

"No, neighbor," she replied ("neighbor," because Marmontel was living in her house), "no such thing. What you think will not happen. Everything will remain as when I left, and you will find my heart, too, just as you have always known it, very responsive to friendship."

Writing to d'Alembert, also from Warsaw, she said, soberly congratulating herself on her fate:

"By the end of this trip, I shall have seen enough people and things to be convinced that they are everywhere more or less the same. My store of reflections and comparisons is well stocked for the rest of my life." And she adds these touching and noble words about her royal ex-protégé: "It

is a terrible lot, to be king of Poland. I dare not tell him
how unhappy I think he is; alas, he feels it only too often.
Everything I have seen since I left home will make me
thank God to have been born French and a private
individual."

Back from this trip, laden with honors and attentions,
she was more cleverly modest than ever before. Perhaps
in her this modesty was but a gentler and more refined
method of asserting her self-respect and pride; but in any
case discretion was something she excelled in. Like Mme.
de Maintenon, she belonged to the race of the *glorieuses
modestes.* When she was complimented on her trip or
questioned about it, whether she answered or not, she remained unaffected in her words or silence. No one was
more skillful than this Parisian *bourgeoise* in the art of
making use of the great, of getting out of them what she
needed without being overhumble or overproud, and of
behaving in everything and with everyone with as much
naturalness as decorum permitted.

Like all powers that be she had the honor of being attacked. Palissot tried twice to depict her in his plays as
a patroness of the Encyclopedists. But of all the attacks,
the one that most distressed her must have been the
publication of Montesquieu's letters to his family, undertaken by the Abbé de Guasco in 1767 in order to be disagreeable to her. A few words Montesquieu wrote against
Mme. Geoffrin sufficiently indicate what might have been
suspected, namely, that there is always some intrigue
and maneuvering wherever people are to be manipulated,
even if it be a woman who undertakes the task. Mme.
Geoffrin, however, was influential enough to stop the edition, and the passages referring to her were replaced with
blanks.

Her last illness was marked by some curious incidents.
While liberally subsidizing the *Encyclopédie,* she had always preserved a background or a corner of religion. La
Harpe relates that one of her devotees was a Capuchin
confessor, a very broad-minded one, whom she kept for the
convenience of her friends who might have need of him;
for just as she did not like to see her friends have them-

selves sent to the Bastille, she did not like them to die
without confession. As for herself, though she lived with
the philosophers, she went to Mass as one goes to a rendezvous, and she had her pew in the church of the Capuchins,
just as others had their *petites maisons*. This serious or
decorous disposition grew more pronounced with age. Following too exact observance of a jubilee in the summer of
1776, she suffered a paralytic stroke, and her daughter,
profiting from her condition, closed the door to the philosophers, fearing their influence on her mother. D'Alembert,
Marmontel, and Morellet were rudely kept out; it is easy
to imagine the stir this created. Turgot wrote to Condorcet:
"I pity poor Mme. Geoffrin for being so tyrannized over,
and for having her last moments poisoned by her horrible
daughter." Mme. Geoffrin was no longer her own mistress;
even in her lucid moments she felt that she had to choose
between her daughter and her friends, and blood proved
the stronger: "My daughter is like Godefroy de Bouillon,"
she said, smiling, "she wants to defend my tomb against
the Infidel." She secretly sent the same infidel friends her
greetings and regrets, and even gifts. Her reason had weak-
ened, but her character remained unchanged, and she kept
waking to say things that showed that she was still herself.
On one occasion there was talk at her bedside about the
means which governments could use to make their peoples
happy, and everyone present invented fantastic schemes.
"Don't forget that they have to be kept amused," she said.
"That's something that's often overlooked."

She died in the parish of Saint-Roch, on October 6, 1777.

22 July 1850 (*Causeries du lundi*).

Ever since the Hôtel de Rambouillet, rendezvous
of the *précieuses*, salons presided over by ladies
of wit, taste, or fashion have played an important
role in French literary life. Sainte-Beuve has
chronicled a number of them. Certain French
critics believe that the autocratic Mme. Geoffrin
suggested to Proust certain aspects of his Mme.
Verdurin.

GRIMM

I

GRIMM's *Correspondance littéraire* is one of the books which I consult most often for my short studies dealing with the eighteenth century. The more I read it, the more I discover that Grimm—in the literary, not the philosophical sense—had a sound, perceptive, firm mind, not given to infatuations; he was an excellent critic in a number of respects, one who never waited to know his colleagues' opinions before expressing his own.

That last-mentioned characteristic is to be particularly noted. Once the reputation of an author has been established, it is easy to speak of him: all one needs to do is to be guided by the general opinion; but to judge a beginning author correctly and tactfully, without exaggerating his importance, to foresee his development when he himself is still incompletely aware of his powers, still experimenting, still growing, and to sense his limitations, as well as to formulate intelligent criticisms of an author who is at the height of his popularity—all this is the hallmark of the born critic. Grimm had this gift of perspicacity, a gift so useful to a critic's contemporaries, and so little apparent to later generations. He was too close to the Encyclopedists to be able to judge them impartially (though he was aware of their weaknesses), but otherwise he is remarkable in appreciating his contemporaries at their true value.

Grimm has been treated unfairly; his name is never mentioned without some disobliging qualification. My own opinion was formerly unfavorable in certain respects until

I discovered that in these it was inspired solely by Rousseau's testimony in the *Confessions*. But Rousseau never hesitated to lie when his morbid vanity was at stake, and I have become convinced that he lied about Grimm. His lies are the more dangerous because, in his madness, he advanced them in good faith, distorting the facts and ascribing a number of petty indignities to his former friends. Grimm, who saw all these things in print and who survived Rousseau by many years, had enough self-respect never to answer the accusations. What I wish to do here is to express my gratitude to Grimm as one of our most distinguished critics. I shall attempt to show his true features, without enthusiasm (he scarcely arouses any), without favoring him, but also without denigrating him.

Grimm was German by birth and by education; but we do not notice this in the least in his writings: his thought and his mode of expression are completely clear and completely French. Born at Ratisbon in December 1723, the son of a prominent Lutheran pastor, he studied at the University of Leipzig. One of his teachers was the famous critic Ernesti, whose detailed lectures on Cicero and classical literature Grimm turned to good account. He never flaunted his erudition, but his knowledge of ancient authors was greater than that of most French writers; his was a solid classical background, in the thorough German manner. He expresses his surprise at Voltaire's deprecating remarks on Homer: Homer, Voltaire says in the *Essai sur les moeurs,* was far inferior to modern epic authors. "If this verdict had been given by M. de Fontenelle," Grimm writes, "it would scarcely be worth mentioning; but that it should be M. de Voltaire who utters such a judgment is really inconceivable." And he goes on to give his own arguments in favor of the ancient poet. The fact is that Grimm could speak of Homer in this way because he had read him in Greek, whereas Voltaire was acquainted with him only through a French translation.

Grimm's earliest writings were in German; he composed a tragedy which became part of the German repertory of the time. Many years later, at Potsdam, Frederick the Great

paid him the compliment of reciting its beginning to him
from memory. Born twenty-five years before Goethe,
Grimm belonged to the generation preceding the great
awakening of German literature, a generation which
sought to model itself on the ancients and the modern
French and English classics. Soon after settling in France,
Grimm published several letters on his country's literature
in the *Mercure*, mentioning and praising the young Klopstock for the first songs of his *Messias*, and predicting the
advent of a new literary springtime in his native land.
Thirty years later, on receiving from Frederick an essay on
German literature in which this monarch, a little behind
the times on this point, foretold an imminent flowering of
the national literature, Grimm, in his reply dated March
1781, respectfully called his attention to the fact that this
had already taken place and was no longer a matter for
predictions: "The Germans say that the gifts which Frederick promises to send them have for the most part already
arrived." Though he had become French and long since
declared himself incompetent in Germanic matters, Grimm
had apparently watched the progress of the great literary
revolution that had begun in his country in 1770. This
naturalized Parisian deserves to be recognized as one of the
forerunners of Lessing and Herder.

Grimm arrived in Paris as a young man in modest circumstances without a post. For some time he was attached
to the young hereditary prince of Saxe-Gotha; then he
served as tutor to the sons of Count Schomberg and as
secretary to the young Count Friesen, nephew of the
Maréchal de Saxe. In this subordinate and difficult position
he succeeded in winning respect thanks to his tact, his
good bearing, and the natural reserve which he dropped
only among intimates. Grimm had a genuine understanding of music. He passionately championed Italian against
French opera, and in doing so he showed himself, with an
enthusiasm characteristic of his country and his youth, to
be a man of taste. He thought that French music as it was
at the time departed from the recitative or plain chant only
to "shout," not to sing. He recognized as real singers only

Jelyotte and Mlle. Fel, particularly the latter, and he clashed with those who saw in her no more than a *"joli gosier."* "A great and fine voice, a unique voice," he exclaimed, "always dependable, always fresh, brilliant and light! Thanks to her talent this singer has taught her country that it is possible to sing in French, and with the same boldness she has given an original expression to Italian music." He never left her performances "without exaltation, without being in the mood thanks to which one feels capable of saying or doing beautiful and great things." Hence his passion for her, which is no more surprising than that of certain dilettanti of our own day for singers like Sontag or the Malibran sisters. This passion does credit to Grimm, though certain writers have taken pleasure in ridiculing him for it.

While Grimm was attacking the boredom and false method of French opera, the Italian actors came to Paris in 1752 and gave performances at the Opera itself. This occurred at a moment when the quarrels between the parlement and the Court were at their fiercest; thirty years later dissensions of the same kind led to the French revolution. A wit said that thanks to the arrival of Manelli, the Italian singer, in 1752 France avoided civil war, because the idle minds that would otherwise have further inflamed the political scene spent their fury instead on the musical quarrel. Grimm caught the public's fancy with a witty pamphlet entitled *Le Petit Prophète de Boehmischbroda.* Under the form of a prophecy he told the French many a hard truth about their music and many a pleasant one about their literature.

By this time he was thirty. He had proved himself master of the language and was welcomed in the best circles. Equipped with a good mind and the most diversified points of comparison, he was soon more capable of judging France than the French themselves. This is often true of an intelligent foreigner who remains in France a sufficiently long time. In the eighteenth century, Horace Walpole, Benjamin Franklin, and Galiani were able to judge us perfectly and surely after passing beyond their first impressions. But Grimm judges us more knowledgeably than anyone else; he is more at home with us than Horace Walpole, and, unlike Galiani, he does not insist on being witty at all costs. He adds calm and reflection to discernment. I find infatuation in Grimm only in relation to Diderot. Even taking his friendship into account, the praise he lavishes upon him remains somehow Germanic. In becoming the most French of Germans, Grimm, by virtue of a kind of natural affinity, grew fond of Diderot, the most German of Frenchmen. Otherwise, Grimm was entirely cured of his national failings, and he did not acquire any of ours.

His literary correspondence with the northern courts and various German sovereigns began in 1753, when the Abbé Raynal, who had been engaged in this task, ceased his labors and asked him to carry on. It opened with a review of a work by the same Raynal, of whom Grimm speaks objectively, tempering his praise with some words of truth. This Correspondence, which was kept up uninterruptedly until 1790—i.e., for thirty-seven years, and ended only, so to speak, under the impact of the French Revolution, with the end of the old French society—is a monument all the more valuable because it is unpretentious and follows no preconceived idea. It has been said very justly that in Paris it is virtually impossible to speak one's mind freely about writers who have achieved a certain position. This was true then and is still true today. Grimm, who moved in society, escaped this difficulty by keeping his Correspondence secret; but whereas publicity is an almost insurmountable obstacle to frank criticism of one's contemporaries, secrecy is a trap that encourages temerity and scandalmongering. Grimm had a mind elevated and fair enough not to fall into such pettiness and not to surrender his judgment to passion or malicious gossip. In short his letters were confidential, but not clandestine.

He began by simply informing his princely correspondents about current literary developments and new books. Gradually he increased his influence and gained in authority. This authority was entirely established and consecrated when the Empress Catherine of Russia took him as her favorite and confidential correspondent. The German courts at the time had their eyes turned toward France; the sovereigns visited Paris incognito and on returning home wanted to continue to be in touch with a world that had charmed them. Grimm, before holding an official diplomatic post, was a kind of chargé d'affaires whose task was to keep foreign sovereigns informed concerning French opinion, and a confidential observer of French intellectual life. He worthily fulfilled this double mission.

While Grimm was still at this early moment in his career, Rousseau, who was beginning to be famous, introduced him to Mme. d'Epinay, an attractive and intelligent woman. She was young, rich, and unhappily married; she was devoid of guidance, and in search of a sympathetic soul. "M. Grimm came to see me with Rousseau," she wrote. "I asked him to dinner for the next day. I was very pleased with him; he is gentle, polite; I think he is timid, for he seems to be too intelligent to be so easily embarrassed for any other reason. He passionately loves music; we made music with him, Rousseau, and Francueil all afternoon. I showed him a few pieces I had composed, which he seemed to enjoy. If there is anything I dislike in him, it is the exaggerated praise he lavished on my talents, which I am quite aware I do not deserve."

A short time later, Mme. d'Epinay was involved in certain family troubles: her relations loudly questioned her honesty. Her sister-in-law had commissioned her before dying to destroy a packet of compromising letters, and she was accused of having burned an important business document. This document was later found, but in the meantime she was the talk of the town, and people took sides for or against her without knowing what it was all about. At a dinner in the house of Count Friesen, Mme. d'Epinay was sharply attacked and Grimm spoke up in her defense. One of the guests persisted, the discussion grew heated, and Grimm, at the end of his patience, remarked, "One must have very little honor oneself to need to dishonor others so rashly." This led to a duel; both antagonists were wounded. This duel changed Grimm's relationship with Mme. d'Epinay. Her gratitude overflowed in tenderness, and before long they were on an intimate footing.

Grimm was by this time completely certain in his mind concerning Rousseau's character. He was the first among his group to see clearly the beginning of Rousseau's madness and to call it by its true name. When he saw that Mme. d'Epinay, naturally generous and impulsive, was becoming oversolicitous for the welfare of this unfortunate genius, he warned her rather severely of her imprudence. One day Rousseau went to see Mme. d'Epinay. He told her that he had received letters urging him to return to Geneva, where he was offered the post of librarian with a salary, the possibility of living honestly and peacefully. "What am I to do?" he asked her. "I neither wish to nor can I remain in Paris; I am too unhappy here. I am willing to spend a few months in my republic; but I am asked to settle there, and if I accept the offer, I shall have to stay for good. I have acquaintances there, but no close friends. These people hardly know me, yet they write to me as to their brother; I know this is the advantage of the republican spirit, but I mistrust such warm friends; there is some purpose behind all this. On the other hand, my heart melts when I think that my country wants me. But how can I leave Grimm, Diderot, and you? Ah, my kind friend, I am so tormented!"

At once Mme. d'Epinay bestirred herself. After looking around a bit, she found for Rousseau what he wanted above all else—a country cottage. She or her husband owned a little house called The Hermitage in the forest of Montmorency. She conceived the idea of suggesting to Rousseau that he live in it; she would furnish it comfortably, taking care not to seem to be doing it especially for him. She made the offer. Rousseau at first took fright and balked, but finally accepted. In her happiness she spoke to Grimm about it. "I was very much surprised to find," she later wrote, "that M. Grimm disapproved of what I was doing for Rousseau. He disapproved in a way I thought at first very unfeeling. I tried to argue against him; I showed him the letters we had exchanged. He said, 'In all this I can see only hidden pride; you are doing him no good letting him stay at The Hermitage, and you are hurting yourself even more than him. Solitude will make him more embittered than ever; he will find all his friends unfair, ungrateful, and you above all the rest, if you refuse even once to do his bidding . . . In the style of his letters you have shown me I can already see the germ of his accusations. They will not be true, of course, but they will not be entirely devoid of truth, and this will be enough to put you in a bad light.' "

Never was a forecast more accurate. Grimm had a complete insight into the sick soul that was joined to so marvelous a talent; he untiringly corrected the mistaken, overindulgent opinions of his gracious and overhasty friend. "I am persuaded," Mme. d'Epinay said of Rousseau, "that there is only one way of treating this man to make him happy: it is to pretend that one doesn't notice him and to devote oneself to him incessantly." At this Grimm laughed. "How little you know your Rousseau!" he said."If you want to please him, you must do the very opposite: do nothing for him and pretend that you are doing everything; keep talking about him to others, even in his presence, and don't be deceived if he pretends to be annoyed." He added and never stopped repeating that Rousseau was afflicted with a secret madness, and that the absolute solitude of The Hermitage would bring about his complete mental derangement. Toward the end of Rousseau's stay at The Hermitage, when he had begun openly to voice his extravagant suspicions, Grimm wrote: "I cannot say it often enough, my dear friend, by far the lesser evil would have been to let him return to his native land two years ago instead of sequestering him at The Hermitage. I am convinced that his stay there will sooner or later cause you grief." In fact, this stay was responsible for a mortal calumny contained in certain poisonous pages of the *Confessions*, which one may read there in close proximity to some of the book's most inspired passages.

This is not the place to go into this affair. When we read Mme. d'Epinay's *Mémoires* on the one hand, and the *Con-*

fessions on the other, it is clear that the letters quoted in these works, which might help clarify the question, are differently reproduced in the two books; they were altered by one of the parties: someone lied. I do not think that it was Mme. d'Epinay. As for Grimm, his character emerges in a favorable light because of his very indifference. As Mme. d'Epinay depicts him in her *Mémoires,* he was never a meddler, and though capable of speaking out bluntly on occasion, he generally kept somewhat aloof, even in intimacy—not because he was overcareful or diffident, but simply because he "disliked arguments and needless complications." Rousseau had more than one motive for resenting him. First of all, Grimm and Diderot paid Thérèse [the mother of Rousseau's children] and her mother a pension of four hundred francs a year. Grimm never spoke of it, and Mme. d'Epinay discovered it only by accident. Now, Rousseau did not like gifts, and even less those who made them. Surely, he reasoned, anyone who would pay a pension to persons close to him must be a great schemer. In the second place, Grimm's exact mind had often seen through Rousseau's pretensions, and this at the most sensitive points. For instance, one day Rousseau brought M. d'Epinay copies of twelve pieces of music he had made for him. He was asked whether he could do as many more in two weeks. Rousseau, combining the vanity of the copyist and the casualness of the amateur, replied:

"Perhaps I can and perhaps I can't; it depends on my mood, my health."

"In that case," said M. d'Epinay, "I'll give you only six to do, for I must be sure to have them."

"Very well," Rousseau said, "you'll find that these six will spoil you for the other six that someone else will do. I challenge anyone to match the accuracy and perfection of mine."

"You begin to sound like a professional copyist," Grimm said, smiling. "Everyone knows that your writings are perfect to the last comma, but when it comes to copying music, I'll wager that you make some mistakes."

Rousseau blushed, and his confusion deepened when, on examination, it was found that Grimm was right.

That scene took place at Mme. d'Epinay's, at La Chevrette. Rousseau said scarcely a word all evening; next morning he returned silently to The Hermitage, and never forgave Grimm for having discovered errors in his copies. Such grievances (not to go further) nursed in solitude and magnified by a morbid imagination, could only produce monstrous results.

"Being a recluse," Rousseau confesses to us, "I am more sensitive than others. If I give offense to a friend who leads a normally social life, he thinks about it for a moment, and a thousand distractions make him forget it the rest of the day; but nothing distracts me from his offenses; I lie awake all night thinking about them; on my solitary walks I worry about them from sunrise to sunset; my heart has not a moment of respite, and an unkindness from a friend causes me years of grief in a single day." There you have the sickness and the wound plainly disclosed. Grimm's sole offense lay, perhaps, in treating this wound, from a certain day on, as if it were physically incurable, and in paying too little attention, because of his perspicacity and firmness, to this other moving remark made by his former friend: "There has never been a fire in my heart that a single tear could not extinguish." It is more than doubtful that Grimm would have succeeded in extinguishing the fire in Rousseau, even with tears, but the fact is he never tried.

The love affairs that were carried on so easily and publicly in eighteenth-century society were not easily reconciled with morality. Although Mme. d'Epinay was married to an unworthy man, she was nonetheless not free; the consideration of duty was not entirely absent; she had children, and she took pride in being a good mother and bringing them up properly. Concerning their education she consulted Rousseau, Grimm, and all her other friends; but it is questionable whether her children were given the example of virtue and the good life that was preached to them. Grimm, we may say to his credit, was not as insensitive as might be supposed to this incompatibility between life as it was lived and the moral precepts that were constantly uttered, and he suffered from it. "One of the things, my sweet friend," he wrote, "which make you most precious in my eyes is the restraint and circumspection that you display in the presence of your children . . . Children are very keen. They seem to be playing, but they hear and see. How often my fears on this score have spoiled the sweetness of moments spent beside you!" This impulsive confession, by one who was so proud of being above conventional morality, is in itself a homage to duty.

In his relations with Mme. d'Epinay, Grimm quickly revealed himself as a critical guide and judicious adviser; he possessed these qualities to a remarkable degree, even in his friendships. She would often write after a talk with him, "How sound he is, how objective!" He guided her in a line of conduct designed to counteract her tendency to frivolity and impulsiveness. He judged those around her with great sureness and gave her the best possible advice as to how to treat them; he reminded her of her shortcomings: "Don't rush into anything, I beg of you! it is one of your old mistakes always to go too fast. My dear friend, nature acts slowly and imperceptibly; this same nature has endowed you with beautiful eyes; use them, and do as nature does." He did everything he could to impart some wisdom to "this lovely, intelligent creature with such beautiful eyes." Mme. d'Epinay, whose mind was above all notable for honesty and discernment, fully appreciated Grimm's sureness of insight: "Once M. Grimm has given his judgment, all my doubts are put to rest," she wrote. All master critics tend naturally to speak as oracles, and Grimm could not help displaying this tendency in his words and methods, for all his courteous and worldly air. In every gathering he liked to be the one who set the tone. He had the qualities of rigorousness and common sense that are seldom unaccompanied by a certain dryness. His friends facetiously nicknamed him "the Tyrant." Was not Malherbe, too, called "the tyrant of words and syllables"?

Grimm's letters dealing with the break between Rousseau and Mme. d'Epinay, which occurred when Rousseau left The Hermitage, are masterpieces of tact, precision, and insight into this sick soul. He attempted to communicate to his friend some of his own perspicacity and firmness. In order to free himself from all obligation to Mme. d'Epinay, Rousseau pretended to suspect her of a cruel and base action, namely, of being the author of an anonymous letter about him that had been sent to Saint-Lambert. He used this as a pretext for addressing her an insulting letter, which is a veritable maze of tortuous accusations.

"The harm is done," Grimm wrote. "You asked for it, my poor friend, even though I always warned you that he would cause you grief . . . I am sure all this will end in some hellish adventure; it is bad enough that you should be exposed to insulting letters. We can forgive our friends everything except insults, because insults can come only from contempt . . . You are not sensitive enough to insults, I have often told you that. Insults should be felt, though never avenged. I consider this a principle."

Mme. d'Epinay, whose lungs were not strong, went to Geneva to consult Dr. Tronchin. Grimm, forced to remain behind because of urgent work with Diderot, could not join her at once; while waiting for him she visited Voltaire, then at Les Délices. "So you dined with Voltaire?" Grimm wrote her. "I am glad of it. I don't see why people resist his invitations; one should try to get along with him and profit from him as the most seductive, most agreeable, and most famous man in Europe; provided you do not try to make him your close friend, all will be well."

Rousseau and Voltaire were the most famous writers of his time, and we see how shrewdly he judged them; he knew the others just as well.

It was about this time (1759) that Grimm's literary occupations assumed a greater place in his life. The months he spent in Geneva with Mme. d'Epinay during her illness were a period of daily intimacy, which seeemed to him a moment of supreme happiness, one never again to be experienced with such intensity. As a man of foresight, he resolved, while cultivating friendships, to store up occupations for the years of seriousness and austerity ahead; he wanted to prove to himself that he was no longer an idler useless to society. One of the northern courts, which he does not identify, made him the offer of being its correspondent. "I like this occupation," he said, "and it suits me perfectly because it gives me the opportunity to show how these things can be done." The Correspondence, as we have said, goes back to 1753, though at first Grimm may have carried it on in the name of the Abbé Raynal rather than in his own. In any case, he was to become, to an ever increasing extent, the confidential critic-in-ordinary and the literary chronicler of the century. The voluminous collection of his letters, in spite of errors, lack of organization, and the inclusion of pieces by different hands, forms a coherent whole that deserves to bear the name of Grimm. It was his spirit that dictated the principal parts, and it is not difficult to discover in it an original strain of thought, which is completely unlike that of La Harpe or Marmontel; it is of an entirely different order, and in his best moments Grimm need fear no comparison with Voltaire.

II

Grimm's Correspondence is generally held to be severe, a little arid in its soundness, and even slightly satirical; but at the beginning of his career Grimm possessed the enthusiasm and the love for the beautiful that are the true inspiration of criticism. In a letter disparaging the opera *Omphale* (1752) he said: "I confess that I look upon the admiration and respect I have for true talent, in whatever field, as my greatest possession next to my love of virtue." He wrote this sentence only a short time after he came from Germany to Paris. In the opening pages of his Correspondence he still has the same attitude. His tone and intention are anything but frivolous. In the promise given him that his letters would remain confidential, he sees only an additional incentive for speaking his mind in full freedom. "Love of truth," he says, "requires this severe justice as an indispensable duty, and even our friends will not have the right to complain about it, because criticism that aims only at truth and justice and is not inspired by the fatal desire to find bad what is good may be erroneous and subject to correction, but can never offend anyone."

At that time articles about books were still called *Extraits,* and these *Extraits,* authorized and consecrated by the example of the *Journal des Savants,* were most often confined to an accurate and dry analysis of a given work: "under the pretext of giving its substance, the writers usually presented its mere skeleton." Grimm was not at all in favor of this ponderous, routine criticism which was like a legal summary. According to him, important books should not be known by excerpts, but must be read: "Bad works need only to be forgotten. Hence it is to take unnecessary trouble to give excerpts of them; and as a matter of policy, journalists should be forbidden to discuss a work, good or bad, when they have nothing to say about it." "To examine" and "to correct"—such is his purpose in these pages; "and this should be the purpose of all journalists." In this Grimm is to some extent an innovator, and he correctly defines the function of journalistic criticism.

It is interesting to note the excesses and extremes of this type of writing. The method first adopted by the *Journal des Savants,* the oldest of the literary journals, was one extreme—the giving of a simple account, a kind of description of a given book, often differing very little from a table of contents. This method, however, had a useful purpose: in an epoch when communications were less easy than today, it served to keep scholars of different countries informed about new writings and to offer them at least reliable and faithful excerpts until they were able to obtain the work itself. An opposite extreme, of which many are guilty today (and I am speaking here of serious criticism, that exemplified in certain English and French magazines) is to give almost no idea of the book which is the occasion of the article, but to look upon it only as a pretext for developing new considerations, more or less relevant, and for new essays. The author of the book disappears; it is the critic who becomes the principal and true author. What we have is books inspired by the appearance of other books. Grimm's method lies between the two and is a golden mean.

"What is a literary correspondent?" the Abbé Morellet asked one day. He had been rather humorously criticized by Grimm, and in his old age had the disagreeable experience of seeing this banter in print. Morellet answered his own question: "It is a man who, for a sum of money, undertakes to amuse a foreign prince every week at the expense of current literary productions and their authors." Morellet obviously had his reason for speaking thus; but Grimm, in spite of inevitable lapses, does not fall into this inferior type of writing to which the economist relegates him. As a rule he seeks to inform his princely correspondents rather than to amuse them; a man whose letters were read by Frederick the Great and Catherine of Russia had a public that could scarcely be bettered and that asked for substance as well as entertainment. It was a truly honorable occupation to please such minds as these.

Grimm can unhesitatingly be classified as belonging to the school of the masters of criticism, the school of Horace, Pope, Boileau; he has their sharp, passionate, irritable sensitivity in matters of taste. His severity is in direct ratio to his capacity for admiration. According to him, there are three deadly things—a tragedy whose lines ring false, a painting whose colors are false, and an operatic aria falsely sung.

"Anyone who can tolerate such things," he says, "should know how limited he is in matters of taste: he will never be strongly affected by what is truly beautiful and sublime. A man able to feel beauty and to grasp its character will not be satisfied with mediocrity; what is bad will make him suffer and torment him to the degree that he is enchanted by the beautiful. Therefore it is false to say that our taste must not be exclusive, if this means that we should tolerate mediocrity in works of art and even find some enjoyment in what is bad. People so charitably disposed can never

have had the good fortune of experiencing the enthusiasm
inspired by great masterpieces; it is not for them that
Homer, Sophocles [I omit Richardson, whom Grimm
places in too high company], Raphael, and Pergolese did
their work. If this indulgence toward poets, painters, mu-
sicians becomes general among the public, it is a sign that
taste has been absolutely lost."

A man endowed by nature with such keenness and sensibility as that, when those qualities are not accompanied
by creative imagination, is a born critic, a lover and judge
of other people's creations.

As we open the volumes of Grimm's letters today, let
us not forget that these pages were originally written for
non-Frenchmen. Reading him, Byron and Goethe acquired
a correct and complete idea of the literature and mode of
life of that period; and Byron gave him the highest praise
when he casually wrote in his diary or *Memorandum* at
Ravenna words that are a veritable consecration, declaring
him to be a great man in his domain. We Frenchmen, who
know in advance and by tradition many things found in
Grimm, need not read him page by page, but only choose
the significant passages. A well-made index would be sufficient for this purpose. For example, what does Grimm
think of—I won't say Homer, Sophocles, or Molière (he
speaks about them only incidentally)—but Shakespeare,
Montaigne, and all the eighteenth-century writers, Fontenelle, Montesquieu, Buffon, Voltaire, Rousseau, Duclos,
etc.? When we question him about them, we soon learn to
know the quality of his mind and the excellence of his
judgment.

On Shakespeare, Grimm is the most advanced and the
clearest of the French writers of his day. His opinion of
Shakespeare has all the more weight because he has a
deep understanding of the genius of the great French
dramatists, and because he holds them to be more in tune
with the genius of French society itself. He never urges the
French to give up their form of tragedy in favor of imitations of foreign models: "On the contrary: Frenchmen,
cherish your tragedies, and remember that although they

may lack the sublime beauties admired in Shakespeare, they also lack the gross defects that mar his work." In judging the French tragedy of his own day, he is aware of its weakness and dullness. In four or five pages (January 1, 1765) Grimm formulates the true relations and the fundamental differences between ancient and French tragedy. Shakespeare, for all his defects, often seems to him closer to the ancients than do the French. Grimm puts him among the greatest for his luminous construction, for the energy of his action, and for his powerful theatrical effects, for "the way he can break off an interesting thread of development and confidently pick it up again just as forcefully." According to him, Shakespeare has no equal in the art of outlining character and endowing his protagonists with life:

"What genius has ever penetrated more deeply into human types and passions? It is quite obvious from his works that his knowledge of antiquity was imperfect; if he had been thoroughly acquainted with its great models, the organization of his plays would no doubt have been improved; but if he had studied the ancients as carefully as did our greatest masters, if he had lived intimately with the heroes he loved to portray, could he have rendered their characters with greater truth? His Julius Caesar owes as much to Plutarch as Racine's Britannicus to Tacitus; and for all that he was not the most learned of historians, it must be said that he had historical intuition, at least where his characters are concerned, to a greater degree than any historian."

It is not surprising that English critics, particularly the judicious Jeffrey in the *Edinburgh Review,* made great use of Grimm as a valuable auxiliary in the war they were preparing to renew at that time (1813) against the dramatic authors of the Continent. But, once again, Grimm, though aware of the defects of French tragedy, does not sacrifice it to that of our neighbors. He recognizes that every type of drama is adapted to the nation and the class that it moves and interests: "The one [English drama] seems intent only on strengthening the character and way of life of the nation, the other [French drama] on refining them." Grimm goes further: he thinks that certain scenes that one of the two nations could watch without any risk, however terrible and frightening their truth may be, might very well involve dangers if shown to the other, which would immediately misinterpret them. "Could this not even result," he asks, "in effects very contrary to the moral aim of the theater?"

When it comes to Montaigne, Grimm is in the heart of France—*la vieille France*—and he is quite at home there. Despite all that has been written on the author of the *Essais,* he says things about him that no one else has said so effectively. He observes that although the *Essais* contain countless facts, anecdotes, and quotations, Montaigne was not a scholar in the proper sense of the word: "He had read scarcely more than a few Latin poets, a few travel books, and Seneca and Plutarch." Plutarch especially "is the true encyclopedia of the ancients; Montaigne has transmitted to us the choicest part of him and enriched it with subtle reflections, the fruits of his profound study of himself."

The eight pages that Grimm devotes to Montaigne's *Essais* are perhaps the most accurate, best thought out and best formulated in French criticism. I could quote some of his striking phrases, but it is the very meaning and movement of this delightful piece that make it valuable. Montaigne's mind, he says, "has the assurance and attractive frankness found only in wellborn children whose easy and natural impulses were not checked by social constraint and education . . . The truths [in his book] are wrapped in so many fantasies, if I may say so, so many childish traits, that we are never tempted to ascribe to him a serious intention . . . His philosophy is a charming labyrinth where everyone enjoys losing his way, but of which only one thinker possesses the guiding thread. By preserving the candor and artlessness of childhood, Montaigne has preserved its privileges and its freedom. He is not one of those redoubtable masters we call philosophers or sages, he is a child who is allowed to say anything, and whom we applaud rather than reprove even when he speaks out of turn." When Charron, Montaigne's friend and disciple, attempted to order and systematize his master's thoughts and reflections, he met with difficulties despite his caution: what was tolerated in the master because of his charming vivacity, was censored in the grave disciple.

Grimm's philosophy is cheerless and arid; he is a skeptic, and on days when he philosophizes on his own, he is unsmiling; we will come back to this. But when he speaks of Montaigne, he relents. Human knowledge being so limited, and we so powerless to extend it, what is a philosophical author to do if he wants to be interesting? According to Grimm, he has only two alternatives: either he will try to conceive as clearly as possible the small number of truths we can know (this is what Locke did); or else he can vividly describe his own individual impressions of the same truths; this serves at least to multiply the points of view, and this is what Montaigne did. The majority of so-called authors confine themselves to developing other people's ideas, which they adjust to the taste of the moment; nothing is rarer than vivid and bold expression of one's own thoughts and feelings, which makes for originality. Montaigne is original even in his erudition, even in his borrowings, "because he makes use of them only when he discovers in them an idea of his own, or when they strike him in a new and individual manner."

To excuse Montaigne's egotism, Grimm finds an argument that testifies to his keen powers of observation. Noting that egotism is less offensive when it manifests itself openly and good-naturedly, he adds: "Far from excluding altruistic feelings, it is often the surest sign of their presence. We are interested in our fellow men only to the extent that we are—and expect others to be—interested in ourselves." And he quotes a remark by Rousseau who one day, after pouring out his heart to a friend (perhaps Grimm himself) and noticing that the other listened to him without pouring out his own heart in turn, exclaimed, "Do you dislike me? You have never told me anything good about yourself!"

Concerning Montesquieu, Grimm expresses himself
with admiration and respect, though briefly; on the occasion of his death he eulogized him as a genius full of
virtue. All of Montesquieu's major works had appeared
before Grimm began his Correspondence. There is little
doubt that he would have raised some objections to Montesquieu's historical method, for, referring to some book
of political considerations, he says: "I am not too enthusiastic about these outlines of political theory a priori, even
though the authority of Montesquieu, who had a special
fondness for them, is in their favor. It always seems to me
that if the author who applies this method had not known
the historical events a posteriori, the principles from which
he claims to have deduced them would not have made him
foresee a single one of them; this proves clearly that these
principles are made *ad hoc* and *post facto*, that they are
more ingenious than solid, and that they are not the true
motive springs of the developments ascribed to them . . .
In politics, nothing occurs twice the same way."

Grimm's politics is dull, skeptical, or readily negative,
like his philosophy. He has little faith in progress; social
advances, or interruptions in the process of decline, seem
to him due chiefly to exceptional individuals, great geniuses, legislators, or princes, thanks to whom mankind takes
unexpected steps forward or is spared relapses that are
inevitable sooner or later. His ideas on the origins of society seem scarcely different from those of Hobbes, Lucretius, Horace, and the ancient Epicureans. Beyond the
stage of the primitive social group, progress leading to
true civilization seems to him possible only thanks to the
marvelous passions of a few individuals and the heroic
power of genius. "The earliest legislators of even the most
imperfect societies must necessarily have been supernatural
men or demigods." Thus, in politics Grimm is much closer
to Machiavelli than to Montesquieu, who grants more to
the genius of mankind itself.

Voltaire, the man and the writer, is nowhere more accurately defined than by the anecdotes and judgments
recorded in Grimm's letters. He shows convincingly how

and why Voltaire fails to achieve comical effects in his comedies; for instance, in the *Ecossaise*, he did not succeed in making his character Frélon, who tells himself all sorts of truths, a comic figure: "This comedy, and generally speaking all of Voltaire's lighter works, show that he never understood the difference between the ridiculous traits we discover in ourselves and those that others discover in us." And it is the latter that are the true object of comedy. Grimm also sees what qualities Voltaire lacks to be a true historian: "In general, history requires a profound and grave genius. Lightness, facility, the graces, everything that makes Voltaire such a seductive philosopher and the foremost wit of the century, all this is little suited to the dignity of history. Even rapidity of style, which may be valuable in the description of a battle or the outline of a scene, cannot be long sustained without displeasing." In philosophy, he treats Voltaire with the scorn of a man who was never afraid to go all the way, and whose skepticism, at least, was not inconsistent. Voltaire, on the contrary, stops halfway, and while continuing to misbehave is occasionally frightened by his own boldness. "He reasons about these things," says Grimm, "like a child, but like the charming child that he is." Beginning with *Tancrède*, Voltaire's plays seem to him marked by the signs of old age. On the occasion of his death, however, Grimm reviewed his career as a whole, and spoke of him with the admiration he deserves. Writing to Frederick (January 1784), he says that Voltaire held back the decline of literature, which will now rapidly ensue: "Since Voltaire died, a vast silence has prevailed in this land, and it continually reminds us how impoverished his loss leaves us."

Grimm's attitude is classical according to him, a nation can have only one great age in respect of the imagination and the arts. He does not try to understand why this is so, but he feels that it is borne out sufficiently by all past experience. "After this age ends," he says, "there are no more geniuses; but since the taste for the arts persists in the nation, people try to do by intelligence what their masters did by genius, and as intelligence becomes more widespread, soon everyone claims to possess it; hence true intelligence becomes rare, and the epigram, false wit, and pretentiousness take its place." For this reason he thinks that in France the age of Louis XIV cannot be surpassed; and in the eighteenth century he finds only one class of superior men, of a particular kind, the only one that the *grand siècle* did not have: "I shall call these men philosophers of genius; such are Montesquieu, Buffon, etc." Voltaire is the only one among the pure writers and poets who upholds true taste by his grace, his imagination, and his natural fertility; but according to Grimm, what he upheld was already tottering.

Rousseau is not maltreated by Grimm, as one might expect; Grimm consistently praises him for his talents, and at the same time refutes his systems. He pays special attention to the *Discours sur l'Inégalité*, where Rousseau's system is already present in its entirety, and from which all the rest will follow. In a very judicious and very honorable discussion, he tries to find the point where this eloquent and extravagant writer went astray, where his doctrine becomes excessive; he applies himself to refuting and correcting the idea behind it. Rousseau always tries to take man back to some primitive golden age and regrets that our species did not stop there: "Let us assume with Rousseau that the human species has now reached old age, an age that corresponds to the age of sixty or seventy in an individual; is it not self-evident that we must not consider it a crime for a man to be sixty? and is it not just as natural for a man to be sixty as it is to be fifteen? Now, what is not a reproach in the case of an individual, cannot be a reproach in the case of the species either." I recommend as a very fine moral chapter, to be opposed to Rousseau's assertions, the chapter that begins the year 1756 with the words: "I have often been surprised by man's vain pride . . ." Grimm sometimes begins the year with general reflections that are beautiful in their severity. In the kind of biography he sketches of Rousseau on the occasion of the appearance of *Emile* (June 15, 1762), Grimm breaks off at a point where his recollections would involve indiscreet revelations and a violation of the former friendship. After retracing the main epochs of Rousseau's life and his first more or less bizarre efforts, he says: "His private and domestic life would be no less curious; but this is written down in the memories of two or three of his former friends who have had enough self-respect not to record it." If Grimm had been perfidious, the traitor that Rousseau believed him to be, what a fine opportunity he had here, in these confidential letters, to relate what Rousseau had done with his children—what a contrast with the precepts in *Emile!* Similarly, he might have recalled many other details that became known only later, from the *Confessions.* Instead, he observed a dignified restraint; he confined himself to giving the main traits of Rousseau's character and closely analyzing his writings.

Now for a glimpse of the reverse of the medal. In judging the most detestable, most pernicious writings of his century, Grimm most often contents himself with showing them to be defective merely from the point of view of taste or originality. Helvétius and Holbach seem to him to present no danger to morality: "I find their only danger is boredom: all this begins to be so stale that it exasperates you. In the meantime, the world goes on as usual, and the influence of the boldest opinions amounts to zero." Grimm is mistaken; in attributing all public morality to a nation's institutions and laws, he forgets that during peaceful intervals books have a great influence. On this point he even contradicts himself, for, as he justly observes in another context, one of the greatest differences that separate the moderns from the ancients is this, that in order to know the latter, "A knowledge of their laws, their customs, and their religion is of very great service" whereas "We would judge the moderns much more correctly on the basis of the spirit of our theater, the taste shown in our novels, the tone of our societies, our little stories and our bon mots." On such nations, on the French in particular, books—good books and especially bad ones—have a great influence.

Between Grimm and Diderot, despite their close friendship and mutual admiration, there is the essential differ-

ence that Diderot is a professor and Grimm is not. A very
curious conversation between them makes us clearly perceive the point that separated them. One evening (January 5, 1757) when they were together, Diderot was in
one of his frequent moments of exaltation and philosophical prognostication: he saw the world through rose-
colored spectacles, with the future governed by Reason
and what he called "the lights"; he exalted his century as
the greatest mankind had so far known. Grimm was dubious and tried to bring the man of enthusiasm back to
earth. "We never stop praising our century," he said, "and
in this we are doing nothing new. At every moment in history man has preferred his own period to the immense
span of time that preceded it. By virtue of some sort of
illusion, perpetuated by successive generations, we look
upon the period of our life as an epoch favorable to mankind and distinguished in the annals of the world . . . It
seems to me that the eighteenth century has surpassed all
others in the praises it lavishes upon itself . . . Even the
best minds are close to believing that the gentle and peaceful rule of philosophy will follow the long storms of un-
reason and establish the tranquillity and happiness of mankind for all time to come . . . Unfortunately, the true
philosopher has ideas that are less reassuring and more
correct . . . I am far from imagining that we are about
to enter the age of reason, and I am more than half inclined to think that Europe is threatened by some sinister
revolution . . ."

I abridge, but such is the tone of the conversation as it
was recorded by Grimm that January of 1757. Diderot resisted his friend's objections; he became inflamed and in-
creasingly exalted: the century of philosophy was decidedly about to regenerate the world. The door opened,
a valet entered, looking frightened: "The king has been
murdered," he said. (This was the almost successful attempt of Damiens on the life of Louis XV.) Grimm and
Diderot looked at each other in silence, and this time
Diderot made no reply.

At about the age of fifty Grimm became a courtier; he

was appreciated by distinguished or eminent German ruling princes and by the empress of Russia, and he did not
feel constrained to decline their favors and their gifts. In
this respect he re-became somewhat Germanic. The duke
of Saxe-Gotha appointed him his minister at the Court of
France; the Court of Vienna made him a baron of the Holy
Empire, and that of St. Petersburg made him colonel, then
state councillor, and decorated him with the order of St.
Vladimir. We have a part of his correspondence with Frederick the Great; that which he carried on with the Empress
Catherine, particularly the letters he received from her,
would be of great interest. Catherine had the highest
opinion of him and his intelligence. "Following the hereditary prince of Darmstadt," she wrote to Voltaire (September 1773), "I had the pleasure of receiving M. Grimm.
His conversation is a delight to me; but we still have so
many things to tell each other that up until now our talks
have had more warmth than order and coherence." In the
midst of these engrossing chats she would suddenly rise
and say gaily that she had to go and earn her living such
was her way of referring to her imperial profession. If
these letters are published some day, they will reveal a new
and interesting angle of Grimm's character. Such close
relations with sovereigns often enabled him to be useful to
persons of merit, and while we occasionally find him severe
or somewhat satirical in his judgments, those who knew
him best say that he could be discreetly benevolent. He
often called the attention of his august correspondents to
talented writers and artists who deserved to be honored or
patronized.

Among the grants bestowed by Catherine at his recom-
mendation, there is one that seems to me touching. Toward
the end of her life, Mme. d'Epinay saw her fortunes crum-
bling; Necker's financial reforms had considerably reduced
her income. Informed of this by Grimm, Catherine chose
to help the intellectual lady, and in doing so she displayed
a combination of feminine delicacy and royal grandeur. On
this occasion Grimm expressed his gratitude by saying,
"Who has ever carried further than Catherine the great art

of kings, that of taking and giving!" In the way of exquisite flattery, Voltaire could not have done better.

A biographer relates that as a young student at the University of Leipzig Grimm had been deeply impressed by
Cicero's treatise on duties. Between then and the day he
addressed those thanks and words of praise to Catherine,
Grimm had gone a long way; we might say that he had
come full circle in the domain of moral experience.

The French Revolution deeply affected Grimm, but did
not surprise him. We have seen what his political ideas
were. From the very first day his attitude was critical; to
the illusory high hopes inspired by the almost universal
revolutionary movement, he formulated coldly rational objections, but he failed to understand the movement's
deeper causes. His own ideal of a constitution was entirely
formulated in these lines by Pope:

> The forms of government let fools contest;
> Whate'er is best administered is best.

The events that followed served only to confirm him in his
favorite idea that "the cause of mankind was desperate,"
and that the only hope lay in some great and good prince
such as occasionally appears on this earth—"one of those
privileged souls," who repairs the world's evils for a time.
Several years earlier, writing to Mlle. Volland, Diderot's
companion, and speaking to her about Truth and Virtue as
two great statues that Diderot dreamed of seeing rise on
the earth's surface, unchanging in the midst of ravages and
ruins, he exclaimed: "I, too, can see them . . . but the
eternity and immutability of these statues matter little if
no one is left to contemplate them or if the fate of those
who see them does not differ from the fate of a blind man
walking in darkness!" His doctrine was essentially aristocratic; he believed that truth and freedom, as he understood them, were in this world the privilege of a minority,
an elite, and at that only "under the express condition of
enjoying them without boasting of them." These gloomy
ideas, which had always been his, and in which the majority of mankind was held of little account, must have

gained ascendancy in the sad years of his old age, after he had lost all his friends, and when the world, seemingly shaken to its foundations, was being renewed around him in such a strange fashion. Grimm, almost blind, vegetating, having survived his friends and himself, died at Gotha on December 19, 1807, at the age of eighty-four. His already slumbering mind was not awakened by the roar of the guns of Jena. We have few details concerning his last years, and possibly there were none interesting enough to be recorded. As he himself had been wont to say, "I seem somehow to have missed the occasion of my own funeral."

Grimm: Sa Correspondance Littéraire, 10 and 17 January 1853 (*Causeries du lundi*).

Here, in addition to being given another interesting glimpse behind the scenes of literary history, we find some of Sainte-Beuve's ideas of the proper role of the literary critic—a statement of the standards that he always endeavored to observe in his own career. Independence, cool-headedness, impartiality, many-sidedness: such were Sainte-Beuve's ideals. If he did not always succeed in living up to them, he was always ready to admit what he came to consider past errors.

JEAN-JACQUES ROUSSEAU'S *CONFESSIONS*

THE WRITER who brought about the greatest single change in the French language since Pascal, and who ushered in, linguistically speaking, the nineteenth century, is Rousseau. Before him, from Fénelon on, there had been a number of writers who attempted to go beyond the pure seventeenth-century manner. Fontenelle had a manner all his own, if any writer ever had, and Montesquieu had also—a stronger, firmer, more striking manner, but a manner nonetheless. Voltaire alone was free of mannerism, and his lively, incisive, swift language ripples as though but a stone's throw from the spring. "You say that I express myself quite clearly," he writes somewhere. "I am like a little brook that is transparent because it is not too deep." He says this jokingly, expressing a half-truth as we all do on such occasions. But the eighteenth century was not content with this; it wanted to be stirred, enthused, rejuvenated by ideas and feelings as yet not clearly formulated, for the expression of which it was still groping. Buffon's prose, in the first volumes of the *Histoire naturelle*, provided something of what the century was searching for, but it was a prose more majestic than spontaneous, a little beyond the ordinary grasp, and too closely associated with scientific subjects. Then came Rousseau: the day he bared himself wholly to himself, the century recognized in him the writer most capable of giving expression to the unformed ideas which had been agitating it, the writer best able to state them with originality, vigor, and impassioned logic. In his efforts to master the language and make it docile to his purposes, he forced it a bit and left his indelible mark upon it. However, he more than made up for whatever it lost as a result of his influence, and in many respects he regenerated it and gave it new vigor. The mold of language he created and gave currency to has stamped all the greatest writers who came after him, whatever their innovations and attempts to outdo him. In them, the pure seventeenth-century form of French, as we like to recall it, became little more than a lovely relic, to the great regret of many cultivated persons.

Although the *Confessions* did not appear until after Rousseau's death, at a time when his influence was already enormous, this is the work that enables us most conveniently to examine the manifold merits, brilliancies, and defects of his talent. In what follows we will confine ourselves to consideration of the writer, but will feel free to make observations on the man and his ideas. The present moment is not too well-disposed toward Rousseau. He is condemned as the author or originator of the many evils from which we currently suffer. "There is no writer," it has been rightly said, "more apt to infuse the poor with arrogance." But for all that may be said on this score, in this study we shall try not to be too influenced by quasi-personal feelings, such as induce otherwise well-intentioned persons to hold a grudge against him in our present painful circumstances.* Men who have influenced posterity as powerfully as Rousseau are not to be judged solely by emotional reactions which are, after all, ephemeral.

It seems so natural to us that Rousseau should have written his "confessions," so consonant with his disposition and his talent, that it comes as a surprise to learn that the idea was not his own. The fact is, however, that it was first suggested to him by his publisher, Rey of Amsterdam, and then also by Duclos. Having completed *La Nouvelle Héloïse* and the *Emile*, Rousseau began to compose the *Confessions* in 1764, at the age of fifty-four. This was after

---

* This essay was written during the tense, bleak period preceding the *coup d'état* of December 1851 which led to the proclamation of the Second Empire. (*Eds.*)

he had left Montmorency and was staying at Motiers in Switzerland. The latest issue of the *Revue suisse* (October 1850) contains an early version of the opening pages of the *Confessions,* from a manuscript in the library of Neuchâtel. It was Rousseau's first draft. The original version is far less rhetorical and less elaborate than the final one. Here we do not hear "the trumpet of the day of judgment," nor is there any apostrophe to "the Eternal Being." In the older text, Rousseau develops at greater length, in a more philosophical spirit, his plan to set down a description of himself and to make public confession, whatever the consequences. He shows very clearly that he understands the originality, the singularity of his intentions:

"The story of a man's life can be written only by himself. His inner being, his true life, is known to no one else. However, when he tries to describe his life, he is false to it; what he calls his life becomes an apology for it; he shows himself as he wants to be seen, not as he is. The most sincere [autobiographers] are at best truthful in what they say; where they lie is in what they leave out, and their reticences alter the value of their frank statements to such a degree that when they give us only part of the truth, they give us nothing. I put Montaigne at the head of these 'pseudo-sincere' persons who, while speaking the truth, aim to deceive. He shows himself to us with his failings, but only with likable ones; now, no man but has some hateful ones. Montaigne draws a good likeness of himself, but only in profile. Who can tell whether a saber cut on the other cheek—perhaps with the loss of an eye— did not make him look very different, seen in full face?"

It is clear that Rousseau is embarked on something no one before him had ever undertaken, ever dared to attempt. As for the style, he tells us that he must invent a style as new as the task he has set himself, one adapted to the diversity and disproportionateness of the many things he proposes to describe:

"Were I trying to produce a work as carefully composed as my other works, I should not be depicting myself but playing a part. What I have in mind is a portrait, not a book. I shall work in camera oscura, so to speak; the only art I shall need is the ability to trace exactly the features as outlined. Therefore I have no choice with respect to style, any more than with respect to subject. I shall not try to make it uniform; I shall use whatever style seems best to fit the given episode, and I will change it according to my mood, without a qualm. I shall say what I have to say in the way I feel about it, as I see it, without effort or embarrassment, not worrying about being consistent. As I recollect my original impressions and set down my present feelings about them, I shall depict my state of mind at the moment the given event occurred as well as at the moment I describe it. The style, uneven but natural, now rapid and now diffuse, now sensible and now extravagant, now grave and now gay, will itself be part of my story. Apart from the manner of its writing, this book will by its subject prove valuable to philosophers; I repeat, it is a work destined for the comparative study of the human heart, the only existing work of its kind."

Rousseau's mistake lay not in his belief that public confession, in a spirit very different from that of Christian humility, was something unique, indeed, of very great interest as a study of the human heart. His mistake was to think that it would be useful. He did not realize that he was like the doctor who might set out to describe to ignorant laymen, in an intelligible, attractive way, some specific mental infirmity or illness; such a doctor would be partly to blame for the maniacs and madmen his book would produce by imitation or contagion.

The opening pages of the *Confessions* (as finally published) are too rhetorical and rather labored. They contain a number of awkward expressions and clichés. And yet, alongside touches of crudity, there is something else—a new, familiar, and penetrating simplicity:

"I felt before I thought; it is the common fate of humanity. I have proved it more than anyone. I am ignorant of what passed until I was five or six years old. I know not how I learned to read; I remember my first studies only, and their effect on me. . . . My mother left some romances; my father and I read them after supper. At that time the point was merely to use these entertaining books to give me practice in reading; but very soon the interest in them became so strong, that we read them by turns without ceasing, and passed whole nights at this employment. We could never leave off but at the end of the volume. Sometimes my father, on hearing the swallows in the morning, would say, quite ashamed: 'Come, let us go to bed; I am more a child than you.'"

Take good note of those swallows; they are the harbingers of a new springtime in our language; they did not appear before Rousseau. The feeling for nature in eighteenth-century France begins with him.

The same is true of his feeling for domestic life, the everyday life of the family in all its homeliness, its poverty, and its intimacy, its virtues and its satisfactions. There are a number of details in bad taste, as when he speaks of "volerie" and "mangeaille"—"swiping vittles," but they are more than made up for by that old childhood song of which he remembers only the tune and a few random words, but of which he has always been trying to remember the rest—and even now that he is old he still cannot remember it without being moved to tears.

"It is a caprice I don't understand," he says, "but I cannot sing it to the end without being choked by tears. I have a hundred times intended to write to Paris, to get the remaining words, in the hope that someone may still know them. But I am almost sure the pleasure I take in recalling them would be spoiled if I had proof that any other than my poor Aunt Suzon sang them."

This is what is new in the author of the *Confessions,* what enchants us and opens up to us unexpectedly the whole range of intimate, domestic sensibility. The other day I spoke to you of Mme. de Caylus' *Souvenirs.* What do her recollections of childhood amount to? What did she care about? What were her regrets at leaving the home where she had been born and brought up? It never even occurred to her to tell us. These refined, aristocratic breeds, endowed with such exquisite tact and so keen a sense of

raillerie, either did not care for such simple things or did
not dare to show that they did. We recognize and enjoy
their wit, but where is their heart? One has to be of the
people and to have been born in the provinces—in short to
be a "new man" like Rousseau—to be able to display one's
own natural feelings.

When we note with a certain regret how Rousseau
wrestled with the language, plowing it and harrowing it,
so to speak, we are nonetheless obliged to recognize how at
the same time he reclaimed it, fertilized it, and made it
give forth new growths.

M. de Chateaubriand, descendant of a proud, aristocratic family, but who sat at Rousseau's feet as a writer
and had nearly as little fear of making a fool of himself as
his master, employed the same more or less direct manner
of personal confession in *René* and his *Mémoires,* and he
achieved surprising, magical effects with it. But there are
differences between them. Rousseau lacks innate nobility;
he was not quite—far from it!—what is called a "wellborn"
child; he had a penchant for vice—and for the baser vices
besides. He had shameful secret desires which are remote
from our notions of gentlemanliness. After long periods of
timidity he suddenly bursts out violently with all the im-
pudence of a *polisson* and a *vaurien,* as he puts it. In
short, he lacked that inner check, a sense of honor, which
Chateaubriand possessed from childhood, and which
served as a rein on his failings. However, for all his shortcomings—shortcomings we no longer fear to call by their
right names, because he taught us to do so—Rousseau is
superior to Chateaubriand in that he is more human and
manly, with deeper feelings. He lacks Chateaubriand's in-
credible hardness of heart (a truly medieval trait), as
evidenced in the emotional unawareness with which the
latter speaks of his father and mother, for instance. When
Rousseau discusses his father's shortcomings—describing
him as a decent man who was given to pleasure, a bit
frivolous, and who abandoned him when he married again
—with what delicacy Rousseau treats this sore point, with
what sensitivity he puts himself in the other's position!

There is nothing chivalric about this delicacy—but it is genuine, a true inner delicacy, specifically moral and human.

It is inconceivable that this inner moral sense with which he was endowed, and which made him so alive to other people's feelings, should not have warned Rousseau to what extent he derogated from it in his behavior and in many of the locutions he affected. His style, like his life, never quite rose above what had been vicious in his early life and surroundings. After a normal childhood spent in the bosom of his family, he went to work as an apprentice and was subjected to hardships which spoiled his taste and depraved his delicacy. He never thinks twice about using such words as *polisson, vaurien, gueux, fripon;* indeed, there seems to be a certain complaisance in the way they come again and again to his pen. His language always kept something of the commonness of his early years. I distinguish two kinds of impurity in his language. One is traceable merely to his provincial background, to the fact that he speaks French like someone born outside France. He articulates strongly and harshly; at moments it is as though he speaks with a goiter. But this defect is readily forgiven, so completely did he overcome it in his most felicitous passages. By dint of hard work and deep feeling he made his organ more supple and succeeded in giving his intricate, difficult style the semblance of ease and spontaneity. The other kind of impurity or corruption that can be noted in him is more serious, in that it is of a moral nature: he never seems to have suspected that there are certain things which should never be given expression: certain ignoble, disgusting, cynical phrases that decent men dispense with or are ignorant of. Rousseau had actually been employed as a lackey at one time, and this is sometimes reflected in his style. He detests neither the term nor the thing the term denotes. "If Fénelon were still alive, you would be a Catholic," Bernardin de Saint-Pierre said to him one day when he saw him deeply moved by some religious ceremony. "Oh, if Fénelon were still alive," Rousseau exclaimed in tears, "I would try to be his lackey in

the hope of one day being worthy of becoming his valet."
We see that he lacked taste even in matters of feeling.
Rousseau is not only a craftsman of language, who had to
be an apprentice before he could become a master, and
whose works occasionally show traces of the labor involved; more than that, he is, morally speaking, a man
who in youth had an extremely rude experience of life,
and he is not disgusted himself when he writes of certain
ugly and sordid things. I shall say no more about this essential vice, this blemish which it is so painful to have to
come upon and to denounce in so great a writer, so great a
painter, such a man.

Slow to think, prompt to feel, burning with suppressed
desires, continually suffering at being held back, Rousseau
portrays himself as follows on reaching the age of sixteen:

"Thus I reached sixteen, uneasy, discontented with
everything including myself, without love for my trade,
deprived of the pleasures of youth, tormented by desires
whose object I was ignorant of, weeping without reason,
sighing without knowing for what; in short, cherishing my
illusions for want of seeing anything around me that could
match them. On Sunday, my companions came to fetch
me after sermon to join them in their games. I would have
gladly refused them if I could; but once I began to play,
I was more eager and went further than the others; it was
as difficult to stop me as it had been to get me started."

Always extreme! We recognize here in their original
form the thoughts of René—and in very nearly the same
words:

"My disposition was impetuous, my character uneven.
By turns noisy and joyous, silent and sad, I gathered my
young companions around me and then, suddenly deserting them, I would go off by myself and lie staring at some
stray cloud or listen to the raindrops pattering among the
leaves. . . ."

And:

"When I was young, I cultivated the Muses; there is
nothing more poetic, in the freshness of its passions, than a

heart of sixteen. The morning of life is like the morning of time, all purity, the sights and sounds alike."

Indeed, René is simply that other young man of sixteen transposed, set in another natural environment and another social condition; no longer an apprentice engraver, son of a humble burgher of Geneva, but a noble knight embarking on distant journeys, in love with the Muses. From the very first everything in Chateaubriand takes on greater lushness, more poetic color; the unexpected landscape and background enhance the character and define a new manner, but the prototype of the sensitive young man is where we found him first. It was Rousseau who discovered him, looking into himself.

René makes a more flattering model for us, because in him all the more sordid aspects of humanity are veiled; there is a tinge of Greece, of chivalry, of Christendom about him which makes for a different play of light over his features. In this masterpiece of art words have taken on new magic, they are luminous and harmonious. The horizon now stretches out in every direction, touched with gleams from Olympus. At first glimpse, there is nothing of this in Rousseau, but at bottom his is the truer work, more real, more alive. This tradesman's child who runs off to find his playmates "after sermon" or goes off by himself when he can to wander and dream his dreams—this slim, graceful youth with the bright eyes and fine features who always bears down a bit more heavily on life than we should prefer him to do, is a real person; he is in touch with the world around him. Besides feelings, he has physical presence. Both René and Rousseau have their morbid side; in them excessive passion co-exists with passivity and a disposition to idleness; their imaginations and sensibilities turn inward and feed on themselves. But of the two, Rousseau is the more genuinely sensitive, the more original and sincere in his chimerical impulses and vain regrets, in his idealizations of a bliss he might have known but turned his back upon. At the close of Book One of the *Confessions*, when he is about to leave his native land, he evokes a simple and touching picture of the modest happiness he might have known had he stayed. He tells us: "I should have passed, in the bosom of my religion, of my native country, of my family and my friends, a calm and peaceable life, such as my character wanted, in the uniformity of a labor suited to my taste and in a society according to my heart; I should have been a good Christian, a good citizen, a good father, a kind friend, a good artist, a good man. I should have liked my condition, perhaps been an honor to it, and after having passed an obscure and simple life, but even and calm, I should have died peaceably on the breast of my own family. Soon forgot, doubtless, I had been regretted at least whenever I was remembered." When he tells us this, we believe that he is sincere: that he did desire such a life and that he is sorry things turned out otherwise. His words exhale a profound feeling for the gentle, untroubled joys of a modest life lived far from the madding crowd.

We of this century, all more or less sick from the sickness of introspection, often tend to behave like newly created nobles who are ashamed of their ancestors; we forget that before we became the unworthy sons of the noble René, we were much more unmistakably the grandsons of the obscure citizen Rousseau.

Book One of the *Confessions* is not the most remarkable, but Rousseau is already fully present, in all his conceit, his budding vices, his bizarre and grotesque moods, his meannesses and salaciousness; but we have him also in his pride and independence, the firmness of purpose that will raise him above himself. Already in the account of his happy, healthy childhood and his tormented adolescence, we anticipate the apostrophes to society and the vengeful reprisals which he will later be inspired to make. His wistful evocation of the joys of life in the bosom of his family (which he did not long enjoy), like his intimations of sensitivity to nature and the seasons, will both come to flower in the literature of the following century. Today we risk being insufficiently sensitive to these first picturesque pages of Rousseau; we have been so spoiled by more colorful treatments of these motifs that we forget how fresh and new they seemed at the time, how extraordinary an irruption they represented in the midst of a very witty and highly refined, but extremely arid society, which was as devoid of imagination as of true sensibility—a society that lacked utterly that inner sap which by its circulation brings forth new flowers in every season. It was Rousseau who first brought back this potent vegetal sap and infused it into the fragile, dessicated tree. The French public, accustomed to the factitious climate of the salons—"urbane" readers, as he called them—were enchanted by the fresh mountain air he brought with him from the Alps, breathing new life into a literature which had been sterile for all its distinction.

It was high time, and this is why Rousseau was no corrupter of the language, but, all in all, a regenerator.

Before him, in France only La Fontaine had known and felt the life of nature, the pleasures of idle revery in the open countryside, to any such degree. His example, however, had scarcely been followed. The gentle old man with his fables was allowed to come and go, but the public stayed in the salons. Rousseau was the first to get fashionable people out of them, to persuade them to leave their stately formal gardens and take a real walk in the country.

The beginning of Book Two of the *Confessions* is delightfully fresh: Mme. de Warens appears for the first time. In portraying her, Rousseau's style softens and becomes more graceful; at the same time we are made acquainted with one more of his basic traits of character, namely, his sensuality. "Rousseau had a voluptuous mind," one good critic has noted. Women played a great role in his life; absent or present, their persons occupied him, inspired him, and moved him, and in everything he writes we find something feminine. "How, in approaching for the first time an amiable, polite, and dazzling woman," he says of Mme. de Warens, "a lady in a superior situation to mine, and such as I never had access to before . . . how did I at once find myself as free, as easy, as if perfectly sure of pleasing her?" Though he usually was far from feeling so easy in the presence of women, his style always exhibits ease and freedom when he writes of them. The most adorable pages of the *Confessions* are those devoted to his first meeting with Mme. de Warens, as well as those in which he describes how he was received by Mme. Basile, the pretty tradeswoman in Turin: "She was brilliant and dressy, and despite her charming manner all this luster intimidated me. But she received me with such kindness, she spoke to me so gently, compassionately, and even caressingly, that I was soon brought to myself. I saw I was succeeding, and that made me succeed the more." What a touch of Italian sunshine that passage conveys! And he goes on to relate the lively wordless scene that no reader ever forgets, a scene all gestures, just stopped in time, full of blushes and youthful desire. One might add to this the walk with Mlle. Galley and Mlle. de Graffenried just outside Annecy, every detail of which is ravishing. In the history of French literature, pages like these mark the discovery of a whole new world, a world of sunshine and fresh air that had never been taken proper notice of before, though it had always been just at hand. This mixture of sensibility and naturalness, in which sensuality is kept within conventional bounds, was necessary to liberate us at last from a false metaphysics of the heart and conventional "spirituality." The sensualness of the artist's brush, when carried no farther than this, cannot displease; there is sobriety, and there is no more than meets the eye. Rousseau is thus a good deal more innocent than many painters who have come after him.

As a painter, Rousseau has in all things a sense of *reality*. He has it whenever he speaks of beauty. Even when it is an imaginary beauty, as in *Julie ou la Nouvelle Héloïse*, it takes on very visible body and form; it is never an impalpable Iris suspended in midair. His sense of reality is such that every scene he recalls or invents, every character he introduces, is given a specific habitation in which to develop, the smallest details of which remain engraved in our memories. One of the criticisms leveled against the great novelist Richardson was that he never linked his characters with a recognizable locale. Rousseau, on the other hand, gave his Julie and his Saint-Preux their perfect setting in the Vaud country, on the shores of the lake to which he remained forever attached. His clear, firm mind serves always as a burin to his imagination, so that nothing essential is ever left out. And lastly, his sense of reality manifests itself in the care with which, in the midst of whatever circumstances or adventures he depicts—even the most romantic ones—he never forgets to mention that people had something to eat; he gives the details of their healthy, frugal fare, designed to rejoice the heart as well as the mind.

This feature is basic, rooted in Rousseau's nature as a burgher and man of the people, as I noted above. He had known hunger: in the *Confessions* he mentions, with an expression of gratitude to rescuing Providence, the last time he was literally too poor to buy food. This was why he never forgot, even in the idealized picture of his happiness that he later painted, to introduce elements of our common humanity, the simplest facts of life. Such details, combined with his eloquence, catch our sympathy and engage it.

Nature sincerely felt and loved for herself is the source of Rousseau's inspiration, whenever his inspiration is healthy, not morbid. When he comes back from Turin and seeks out Mme. de Warens again, he stays for some time in her house, and from his room he looks out over the garden and has a view of the countryside. "It was, since Bossey [a village where he had been put out to board as a child], the first time I had seen verdure from my window." Until then, it had been a matter of indifference to French readers whether or not there was greenery before their eyes; Rousseau made them notice it. He was, so to speak, the first to introduce greenery into our literature. Living in the house of a woman he loved, but to whom the nineteen-year-old Rousseau did not dare declare his passion, he was filled with a sadness "which had, however, nothing gloomy about it, and which was allayed by flattering hope." One day, a religious holiday, while everybody was at vespers, he went for a walk outside the town.

"The sound of the bells," he says, "which always singularly affected me, the singing of the birds, the clearness of the weather, the sweetness of the landscape, the houses scattered and rural, in which I placed in fancy our common abode; all this struck me with an impression so lively, so tender, so melancholy, and so touching, that I saw myself, as in a trance, transported to those happy times, and in those happy abodes, where my heart, possessing every felicity that could delight it, tasted them in raptures inexpressible, without ever thinking of sensual voluptuousness."

That is what the boy from Geneva felt at Annecy in the year 1731, when Paris was reading Montesquieu's *Le Temple de Gnide.* That very day he made the discovery of *rêverie,* the sort of inward reflection which had hitherto been recognized merely as a peculiarity of La Fontaine. Rousseau was to introduce it successfully into a literature whose only subjectivity was in the realm of eroticism. *Rêverie:* this was Rousseau's innovation, his personal discovery, his New World. The dream he dreamed that day came true a few years later, while he was staying at Les Charmettes. On St. Louis' Day he took another walk, and he describes it as no one had ever done before:

"Everything seemed to contribute to the happiness of the day. It had lately rained, there was no dust, and the brooks ran full. A gentle wind stirred the leaves, the air was pure, the horizon without a cloud; serenity reigned in the heavens as in our minds. Our dinner was served at a peasant's, and shared with his family, who heartily blessed us. What good people these poor Savoyards are!"

That moment at Les Charmettes, when a freshness of feeling as yet untried blossoms for the first time, is the most divine in all the *Confessions.* There is nothing like it again —not even when Rousseau has gone into seclusion at The Hermitage. His description of the Hermitage years and of the passion that comes to him there is doubtless deeply moving—and all the more so for all that has gone immediately before. Yet Rousseau was quite right to exclaim that, after all, "It was not the same as Les Charmettes!" The misanthropic suspiciousness he was already filled with plagued him even in his solitude. He kept thinking back to the people he had left behind in Paris, especially the Holbach clique; he enjoyed his retreat despite them, but thoughts of them poisoned his purest enjoyments. These were the years when he grew embittered and contracted the illness that proved incurable. To be sure, he still knew moments of delight right up to his death. On the Ile de Saint-Pierre, in the middle of the Lake of Bienne, he had a peaceful interval that inspired some of his finest pages. Indeed, the Fifth Promenade in the *Rêveries du promeneur solitaire,* together with the third letter to M. de Malesherbes, must be grouped with the most divine passages of the *Confessions.* And yet nothing equals in lightness, freshness and cheerfulness the description of his life at Les Charmettes. Rousseau's true happiness, the happiness that no one—not even himself—could take away, lay in his ability to evoke and recapture in brilliant detail such images of his youth as these—an ability he still possessed in his most troubled, most harassed later years.

Rousseau's evocations of nature are firm, clear, and restrained, even at his most luxuriating; his colors are always laid on over a well-defined drawing; in this respect, the native of Geneva falls within the purest French tradition. Although at times he lacks the warmer, more brilliant light of Italy or Greece, and—as happens sometimes along the shores of the lovely Lake of Geneva—a wind from the north brings a sudden chill to the air, or a cloud suddenly casts a gray shadow over the mountains, there are hours and whole days of perfect serenity. Subsequent writers have attempted to improve on this style, have even believed they could surpass it, and certainly have been successful with some effects of color and sound. Nevertheless, so far as modern innovations are concerned, Rousseau's style remains the firmest and surest, his language is the most balanced. His successors have gone further; they have not only transferred the seat of the empire to Byzantium, they have often carried it as far as Antioch, into the heart of Asia. In them, imagination degenerates into pretentiousness.

The portraits in the *Confessions* are sharply drawn,

lively, and witty. His friend Bâcle, the musician Venture, the judge-magician Simon are shrewdly observed. Less boldly drawn than the portraits in *Gil Blas*, they seem more like engravings. In this connection, Rousseau went back to the trade he practiced first.

I have confined myself to brief mentions of Rousseau's major traits. A master of the French language, he created *rêverie*, taught us to feel the presence and moods of nature, and sired the literature of home and family life realistically portrayed. It is unfortunate, of course, that such achievements are tinged with overweening pride and misanthropy, and that a note of cynicism spoils many a passage of charm and beauty. But Rousseau's follies and vices do not outweigh his solid merits and originality, nor do they overshadow his continuing superiority to those who have come after him.

4 November 1850 (*Causeries du lundi*).

Sainte-Beuve was always more interested in Rousseau as a human being and writer than as the political thinker whose ideas influenced the American and French revolutions. This essay is an early recognition of Rousseau as a harbinger of Romanticism in the realms of language and sensibility.

STENDHAL

I

THIS TIME we shall deal with a chapter in Restoration literary history. For some time there has been much talk about the witty writer, M. Beyle, who disguised himself under the somewhat Teutonic pseudonym of Stendhal.[1] When he died in Paris on March 23, 1842, there was a silence around him; mourned by a few, he seemed to be quickly forgotten by the majority. Now, only ten years later, a whole new generation has begun to be infatuated with his works, to single him out and study him very nearly as exhaustively as we study classic older authors. That there should be something like a Stendhal Renaissance would have very much surprised him. Those who knew M. Beyle personally and who most enjoyed his wit are happy to find themselves obliged to discuss this distinguished writer, though they sometimes do so less enthusiastically than such a critic as M. de Balzac, who knew him only at the end and who used his imagination freely. However, this is no reason to do him less than justice, to deny either his notable originality and influence or his type of literary usefulness.

There are two distinct persons in M. Beyle, the critic and the novelist; the critic began as early as 1814, but the novelist came only later. Today I shall deal with the critic, and he well deserves to be considered as such for his singu-

[1] Steindal is a town of Prussian Saxony, the birthplace of Winckelmann. Beyle probably had it in mind when he assumed the name under which he became a *guide de l'art* in Italy.

larly fresh, pungent, paradoxical, and often sensible habits of mind. It is for these that he is attracting so much attention, not with the public at large, but among the professional writers and the more alert readers of the day.

Henri Beyle was one of the very few who, like Paul-Louis Courier, at the fall of the Empire in 1814, was prepared for the new regime then taking its first faltering steps. Moreover, he had the advantage over men such as Courier in that he was not a malcontent or a grumbler. He had served the Empire zealously as a functionary and was about to become an administrator when his post was taken away from him, as it was from so many others. He landed on his feet immediately, a clever and intelligent writer, full of ideas and opinions on letters and the arts, including the theater, and he was willing and able to impart them to others. Beyle was one Frenchman (and one of the first) who had gone outside France, literarily speaking, and made comparisons. Traveling in the wake of the Grande Armée across Europe as a member of M. Daru's civilian staff (he was related to M. Daru), he looked with interest at everything that came his way: operas by Cimarosa and Mozart, paintings and sculptures, whatever was new and fine in the production of the various peoples of Europe. He underwent a quiet reaction against the art and literature of his own country, though he was a true son of France when he passed judgment on French taste, his own conversation serving to revive and regenerate it. This is why I can say that he was fully equipped for a change of regime as early as 1814, at a moment when very few men were. Within a short time he had brought a fresh approach to music, painting, and literature; he was above all an intellectual stimulator.

His activity along these lines, at which he distinguished himself for about twelve years, suggests a metaphor. Once the great European wars of conquest and invasion had come to an end, there opened a period of wars fought with words and pens. Now, in this new order of things, imagine some Hussar or Uhlan, a Light Horse in the vanguard who often gallops up to the enemy's positions to insult him face to face, but who also, no sooner has he got back to his own lines, needles the other troops to speed up their advance. Such was Beyle's role and method of maneuvering. He was a romantic Hussar, wrapped in some Scandinavian cloak under his pseudonym of Stendhal, shouting defiance of stuffiness and sentimentality. He was brilliant, adventurous, and loved to taunt; he was fairly strong in riposte, and an excellent skirmisher.

He was born in Grenoble, January 23, 1783, son of a lawyer, grandson of a physician who belonged to the upper bourgeoisie of the region. From his family he inherited something of the pride characteristic of the citizens of this fine, generous province. In his grandfather's house he received a good education, though his schooling was very irregular. He lost his mother when he was seven, and his father lived rather apart from the children. He learned Latin from his teachers, and picked up the rest at random, as can well be imagined in those years of France's upheaval. Italian poets were read in his family, and he liked to believe that his grandfather's ancestors had come from Italy. At the age of ten he secretly wrote a prose comedy, or at least a first act. His grandfather's house had a terrace with a magnificent view of the hills at Sassenage. It was the family gathering place on summer evenings and —he tells us—the scene of his principal pleasures during the ten years from 1789 to 1799. His character began to take shape when he attended classes at the Ecole Centrale, an institution founded in 1795 under a law passed during the convention, and largely according to the plans of M. Destutt de Tracy. I mentioned the latter because he was one of Beyle's intellectual godfathers; Beyle was always grateful to him and admired him to the end. Our writer was quite conscious of belonging to the philosophical school of Cabanis and Tracy and indeed flaunted his allegiance at the most unexpected moments. Advanced romantic that he was, Beyle was nonetheless opposed to— really hostile to—Chateaubriand's literary revival of Christianity and Mme. de Staël's effort to promote a spiritual renascence. Beyle was a direct descendant of the eighteenth

century. One of his bad habits was to carry this to the
point of affectation. Just when he was speaking most in-
terestingly about painting or music, when mention of
Haydn led him on to speak of Milton, or when he had just
movingly recited some beautiful lines from Dante or Petrarch, he would suddenly think better of it and pin a little
cockade of impiety on his hat. He would carry this idio-
syncrasy to astonishingly petty lengths, for his mind and
his heart were really above it.

M. Colomb, a friend and relative, has written an excellent biography of Beyle. On leaving the Ecole Centrale,
where toward the last he had become a passionate student
of mathematics, he went to Paris for the first time. He was
just seventeen when he arrived on November 10, 1799, the
day after the Eighteenth Brumaire—a memorable date, well
calculated to leave its stamp on a young man! In 1800,
having accompanied M. Daru to Italy, where he traveled
with the headquarters staff of the Napoleonic armies, he
witnessed the Battle of Marengo. After such exciting experience, life in an office began to seem pretty dull. Beyle
entered a regiment of Dragoons with the rank of sergeant;
he was a second lieutenant when he resigned two years
later, after the Peace of Amiens. During his stay in such
Lombardian cities as Milan, Brescia, and Bergamo, a young
man still under twenty, caught up in the strong feelings of
wartime and discovering the incidental delights of climate,
pleasure, and beauty, he completed his true education and
took on the character which henceforward he would merely
modify and cultivate. He had acquired his own ideals of
art and nature, and had found the country where he felt
most at home. The reason his novel *The Charterhouse of
Parma* seems his best, and the reason it grips the reader
from the outset, is that from the very first pages it renders
vividly and convincingly his memories of that brilliant era.
It was Montaigne, I think, who said, "Men make themselves worse than they are capable of being." Beyle, the
skeptic, the dreaded *frondeur*, was actually a very sensitive
man. "My sensibility has grown too keen," he wrote two
years before his death. "What only grazes others cuts me to

the quick. I was like that in 1799 and I am still like that in 1840, but I have learned to hide it under an irony imperceptible to the vulgar." His irony was not as imperceptible as he thought, being almost obvious, a bad habit which detracted from many good qualities and even compromised his talent. There we have the key to Beyle. Speaking of his impressions when he looked at the Forum from the top of the ruins of the Colosseum, and indulging his enthusiasm for Rome, he suddenly fears he may have gone too far in the eyes of his Parisian readers, and adds: "I am not speaking of the vulgar who are born to admire the pathos of *Corinne;* unfortunately, in the nineteenth century when a sensitive person is confronted with an exaggeration he reacts with irony." Thus, from a declamatory tone not far removed from elegance, Beyle suddenly shifts to the very opposite. He goes so far as to despise Bossuet and what he calls the latter's "phrases." Because there are sheepish minds who in their admiration for Racine do not discriminate between weak passages and magnificent ones, he comes close to detesting *Athalie.* Because some believers are hypocrites, he is sure he cannot ever be too much the unbeliever; and because there are social hypocrites, he sometimes risks falling into indecency and cynicism. In all things, fear of being taken in keeps him in check and dominates him: this, he says, is his defect. His pride would be outraged if he thought his real feelings showed. But when this defect is not too much in evidence, when he is relaxed and lets himself be the Milanese or the Parisian of "the good old days," or when he is among people who understand him and of whose kindliness he is sure (for this aggressive scoffer—you must note this—had a secret need for kindness), then Beyle's mind sparkles with lively sallies and daring views, felicitously and gaily expressed. And when he discusses the arts, their charm for the imagination, and the sublime happiness derived from them by sensitive persons, he may exhibit a certain gentleness and sweetness in his feelings, or at least the flash of a fleeting melancholy. "A drawing room containing eight or ten amiable persons," he said, "where the conversation is gay and the stories are good, and where a light punch is served at half past midnight[2]—that is the place I had rather be than any other. There . . . I am infinitely more pleased to listen than to speak myself; I gladly fall into 'a happy silence,' and if I speak it is only to 'pay my ticket of admission.' "

In that year of Marengo, two weeks before the battle, he attended a performance of Cimarosa's *Matrimonio segreto* at Ivrea: this was one of his great pleasures, a never-to-be-forgotten date in his life. Forty years later, he wrote: "I would walk many leagues on foot and agree to spend many days in prison to be able to hear *Don Giovanni* or the *Matrimonio segreto!* And I don't know what other works would be worth such an effort."

I shall not follow him in his travels across Europe under the Empire. His correspondence, soon to be published, will show that he participated in many memorable events; for instance, he was in Moscow in 1812. In 1814 he resigned from his official post and embarked on his career as wit and cosmopolite—or rather as a gentleman living south of the Alps who sometimes came to Paris. At the beginning of his *Life of Rossini,* Beyle writes: "After the fall of Napoleon, the writer of the following pages felt he would be cheated if he spent his youth amid political hatreds, and so he began to travel." Although he occasionally tried to conceal the fact, his fourteen years under the Consulate and the Empire left an indelible imprint on Beyle; indeed, it is this that distinguishes him from the rest of the innovators of his generation, among whom he was the most outstanding. Although he had to pay lip service to the dominant liberalism of the day, he succeeded in resisting the kind of moral pressure that liberalism, in so far as it represented a party, was then exerting on his most eminent contemporaries, and he preserved his independence of thought and action. "The French gave up in 1814," he often said,

[2] He says "half past midnight," because according to him the bores and the "regulars" always leave the drawing room at midnight; only a small group of pleasant people who are really enjoying themselves stay on.

with the regret and discouragement of a man who has known a more glorious era. But is it not an essential characteristic of the Frenchman never altogether to "give up," but always to begin again?

Beyle's first published work came out in 1814: *Lettres écrites de Vienne en Autriche sur le célèbre compositeur Joseph Haydn, suivies d'une Vie de Mozart, etc., par Louis Alexandre-César Bombet.* He had not yet thought of donning the mask of "Stendhal." One of Beyle's peculiarities or weaknesses as a writer, originating in the source mentioned above (fear of being laughed at), was nearly always to appear in public in disguise. He took pride in being a mere amateur. The life of Mozart in this volume is alleged to be no more than a translation of a German life by M. Schlichtegroll—but that is true only up to a certain point. The letters of Haydn, on the other hand, are in part translated and imitated from the Italian of Carpani, but this the author does not tell us, though here is a note hinting that he worked on the original letters. The maze of borrowings, revisions, and little ruses is quite bewildering. We can only marvel that he resorted to so many misdirections and mystifications in dealing with a simple matter. From the very first, he seems to have thought of writing as a masquerade![3]

The book, however, is very pleasant and one of Beyle's

[3] I am indebted to M. Anders, scholarly and obliging librarian at the Bibliothèque Impériale, for the following note which leaves nothing to be desired in clarifying the bibliographic riddle posed by M. Beyle's first book:

"Beyle's book on Haydn, published first under the pseudonym of Bombet (1814) and then under that of Stendhal (1817) is not merely a translation of Carpani's *Haydine.* Beyle rearranged the latter book to suit himself, disguising the plagiarism by means of alterations, additions, and transpositions which make it difficult to find the corresponding passages in the original.

"In Carpani there are sixteen letters; in Bombet we have twenty-two, because several letters were divided into two and entirely rewritten.

"It is to be noted that in some of the letters Beyle retained the original dates, while he changed them in others.

best in that it is one of the least disjointed. The art and
genius of Haydn, which gave us such splendid, rich, picturesque, and elevated music, are expounded in a simple
way, accessible to all. Beyle was the first to acquaint France
with the names of certain masterpieces which our nation
had been slow to appreciate. In his discussions of Cimarosa and Mozart, he admirably formulates the spiritual
qualities most favorable to the development of music.
When he speaks of Vienna and Venice, he shows that because the population was barred from political activity,
sensual enjoyment became the primary goal, and that music, the subtlest of sensual enjoyments, was pursued in a
carefree atmosphere animated solely by the passions. There
are very keen remarks on contrasting national tempera-
ments, as when he opposes Italian gaiety to French gaiety:
"Italian gaiety is a manifestation of happiness; in France,
such a manifestation would come close to bad manners: it
would be to flaunt one's own happiness, to demand that
others pay attention to one. French gaiety is supposed to

"Most curious of all is a note on p. 275 which says, 'The
author did his best to eliminate countless repetitions to be found
in the original letters.'

"It would seem that Beyle wanted to forestall the reproach
of plagiarism; but if so, why did he not give this indication at
the beginning of the book, in a short preface?

"The Life of Mozart is actually taken from a book by
Schlichtegroll, a well-known German author whose name has in
France been wrongly supposed to be a pseudonym. In addition
to works dealing with numismatics and archaeology, Schlichtegroll published for ten successive years a collection containing
biographies of prominent men who had died during the year.
The article on Mozart is to be found in Vol. II of this series
(Gotha, 1793), pp. 82–112. Beyle's translation is very free;
here too he left out many things and added others. Moreover,
he divided the biography into chapters,—a division that does
not exist in the original. Only the first four chapters contain details taken from Schlichtegroll. The last three are filled with
anecdotes extracted from another German book which Beyle
does not mention, but which had been translated into French as
*Anecdotes sur W.-G. Mozart, traduites de l'allemand par Ch.-Fr.
Cramer*, Paris, 1801; in 8°, 68 pages.

"Everything we find in Beyle from page 329 to page 354 is
taken from this pamphlet." (Note by M. Anders.)

show listeners that one is gay solely to please them. . . .
French gaiety requires a great deal of wit; it is the gaiety
of Le Sage and *Gil Blas;* Italian gaiety is based on sensibility, so that when there is no occasion to rejoice, an Italian
is not gay." Here Beyle launches his campaign against our
national character, insisting that vanity is its main incentive
and dominant trait. According to him, "Nature made the
Frenchman vain and keen rather than gay."

We may grant that every people has its own genius,
which is, of course, susceptible of growth and enrichment.
The Frenchman is sociable, and he is sociable primarily in
conversation; his favorite form is that which he gives his
thought when talking, reasoning, judging, and mocking;
music, painting, poetry come after conversation in the order of his preferences. More generally, any art, to please
him and to be fully successful in his eyes, must go halfway
to meet this primary disposition of his mind and identify
with it at least in passing. In Vienna, in Milan, in Naples,
sensibilities are different. However, when Beyle tries to explain this difference to us, to uncover the reasons for it,
and to explain its underlying principle in the manner of
Condillac and Helvétius, what is he doing himself if not
reasoning on the fine arts in the French manner while
scoffing at French taste?

When Beyle gives free rein to his taste and instinct in
matters of art he seems to me at bottom very much like
the Président de Brosses. He prefers gentle sentiments,
lightness of touch, gracefulness, facility in the divine:
Cimarosa, Rossini, the side of Mozart that makes him the
La Fontaine of music. He adores the charming Correggio
as much as Ariosto. His admiration for Petrarch is sincere,
though what he feels for Dante seems to me a trifle studied.
In these lofty, somewhat austere regions, his intellect
guides his feelings.

The essence of his taste and sensibility is what one might
expect of a refined Epicurean. "How foolish," he writes a
friend in Paris in 1814, at the end of his *Lettres sur Mozart,* "how foolish to be indignant and censorious, to begin

to hate people, to concern oneself with those great political interests which don't interest us a bit! Let the king of China order all philosophers to be hanged; let Norway adopt a wise or a ridiculous constitution—what is that to us? What an absurd self-deception it is, to assume the cares of greatness, and nothing but the cares! The time you lose in vain discussion is part of your life; old age is approaching, your good days are numbered: *Amiamo, or quando,* etc." And he repeats the voluptuous refrain of the gardens of Armida. One day, sitting on the steps of the church of San Pietro in Montorio in Rome watching a magnificent sunset, it occurred to him that he would be fifty years old in three months, and it was as though he were afflicted by some sudden misfortune. Like the Greek poet he believed that "the man who laments the end of his life and does not lament the end of his youth is very foolish."[4] He did not adhere to that severer, more difficult doctrine according to which the mind is elevated and perfected with age—the doctrine of Dante, Milton, Haydn, Beethoven, Poussin, and Michelangelo, which, even if it were an illusion, would still be a sublime illusion.

Beyle spent the greater part of the early Restoration in Milan and elsewhere in Italy; there he knew Byron, Pellico, and to a lesser extent Manzoni; he began to champion romanticism as he conceived of it. In 1817 he published his *Histoire de la peinture en Italie,* dedicated to Napoleon. There are two versions of the dedication, one which contains the name of the exile on St. Helena, and another, more enigmatic and more obscure, without the name. In both Napoleon is treated as an actual monarch, "the greatest of all existing sovereigns." Beyle argues that his aim in literature and the arts is to move forward, not to react against the Empire. This attractively written volume covers a variety of matters. Besides painting, Beyle touches on a great many other things—history, politics, mores. We recognize in him the opposite of the provincial whom he ridiculed, whose greatest fear in the drawing room is dis-

---

[4] He tended to think that death itself should be concealed, just as one conceals any unseemly function.

covering that no one shares his opinions. Beyle is fond of
contradicting this man at every turn, of expressing unexpected opinions on everything; he cannot endure conventional ideas on any subject whatever. He has no undue
faith in representative government, takes the part of the
Philosophes in their attacks on the Jesuits, but says that if
he were Pope he would not have suppressed them. He pro-
fesses a Machiavellianism which brings to mind the Abbé
Galiani, one of his spiritual ancestors (along with the Montesquieu of *Les Lettres persanes*). It would take us too far
afield, however, if we were to explain him in greater detail.
Bent upon breaking with tradition, he is often guilty of
confusions and contradictions. He does not go to the root
of certain prejudices, which are not necessarily errors for
being prejudices. There is a strong element of teasing in
him, he is witty, and his quips often disclose good sense,
but they are no more than quips and suggestions. Most of
all he regrets the golden age of Italy, the times of Lorenzo
the Magnificent and Leo X, of handsome seventeen-year-
old cardinals, and Catholicism before Luther: sumptuous,
indigenous, and favorable to the development of the arts.
He worships beauty and adores the land where people exclaim in a tone not to be heard anywhere else, *"O Dio!
com'è bello!"* when they are in the presence of something
beautiful. And at every turn he pauses to direct some more
or less aggressive remark at France.

. . . . .

We are beginning to understand how stimulating Beyle's
ideas were in the literary discussions of the time. Today
these ideas have lost much of their value. In literature as
in politics we have generally become cautious and con-
servative: the fact is, we see that we have made quite a
few miscalculations. Shakespeare was then continually being brought up in opposition to Racine, but the modern
Shakespeares failed to appear, while Racine and Corneille, incarnated by a great actress, have seemed once
again, to generations that had forgotten all about them, utterly if indefinably fresh and novel. This is not to deny all

merit or value to the modern theater: the new theories may
someday be justified by a dramatic genius, who, however,
will rely on his own powers, dispensing with all theories.
Such a genius, which it was never the task of criticism to
create, has not been forthcoming; there have been only a
number of second-rank talents, never too sure just where
they were going. At the present moment, out of weariness,
a kind of concordat has been signed between the opposing
systems, and the theoretical quarrels seem to have worn
themselves out. The future lies open, and it seems to have
fuller, vaster possibilities than in 1820, when critics like
Beyle waged a small war to clear the way for talent.

It is therefore only fair to credit Beyle with the services
he did render during the Restoration. His sharpest campaign was conducted in two pamphlets entitled *Racine et
Shakespeare* (1823–25). When I use the word "campaign"
and other military terms, I do no more than follow his own
lead. As early as 1818, during his stay in Milan, he had
drawn up a map of the theater of operations, showing the
positions of the two armies, "the classical" and "the romantic." The romantic army, led by the *Edinburgh Review,* constituted four full army corps: all the English authors, all the Spanish authors, all the German authors, and
the Italian romantics, not counting Mme. de Staël as an
auxiliary unit. It was camped on the left bank of a river yet
to be crossed (the river of "Public Admiration"). The right
bank was occupied by the classical army. I shall not, however, go into all the very ingenious details, which could be
explained only with a copy of the document in hand (re-
motely reminiscent of the *carte du Tendre*). When he returned to France, Beyle found himself on the right bank,
in more or less enemy country, and so he confined himself to daring skirmishes. In these pamphlets he attacks
two of the rules of classical drama—unity of place, unity
of time. Playwrights were then still urged to observe them
rigorously. He tries to show that spectators born after the
Revolution and after the wars of the Empire, who had not
read Quintilian, and who had taken part in the Moscow
campaign, require a larger scope of dramatic action than

that which was suitable for the noble society of 1670. According to his definition, a romantic author is merely one who is essentially of his time, who really lives in it and complies with its social requirements; the same author becomes classical only after a generation or two, when some of the elements of his work are dead. In this view, Sophocles, Euripides, Corneille, and Racine, "all great writers in their epochs," are just as romantic as Shakespeare was in his epoch, and it was only later that new dramatic productions were expected to take them for models: only later did they become classical. More accurately, "It is those who copy them instead of opening their eyes and imitating nature, who are the real classics." All this is said spiritedly and gaily. The *tirade*, the alexandrine, the descriptive or epic passages, and the elegant periphrases such as were to be found in contemporary tragedies were all targets of his mockery. He particularly resented the alexandrine, which, he said, often served as fig leaf to conceal stupidity. He demanded a "clear, sharp, simple, straightforward genre." He thought only prose could achieve such qualities, and for this reason he favored prose tragedies and dramas. It is to be noted that his insistence on a limpid, natural style seems to exclude poetry, color, the brilliant images and expressions that clothe passion and enhance the language of dramatic characters even in Shakespeare—I will go further and say especially in Shakespeare. In his demand for short words, he obstructed the dramatic development and dried up the flow of passion in moments when it finds an external outlet. Since then we have had dramas and tragedies in prose which realize M. Beyle's ideal, "which cover several months and the events of which occur in a number of places." And yet neither Corneille nor Racine has so far been surpassed. In these matters the critic's recipe is not enough; only genius can produce art. "May Heaven soon send us a talented man to create such a tragedy!" Beyle used to exclaim. We are still uttering the same wish, with this difference, that he seemed to blame governmental censorship and the taste of the French public for holding things up. "And these are the people one must please," he said in 1825. "Creatures so discriminating, so lightheaded, so impressionable, forever alert, forever at the mercy of a fleeting emotion, forever incapable of deep feeling. All they believe in is fashion. . . ." Alas! Chiding the public in this manner has gone out of style. The public, as we know it today, is not so difficult to please. Give it merely a bit of truth, something the least little bit moving, honest, natural, or profound, whether in verse or in prose, and you will see how it applauds you.

There are two very dissimilar aspects worth noting in the polemic that Beyle conducted with such spirit and such recklessness. When he comes to grips with adversaries of the moment, with those who speak about Shakespeare without knowing him, about Sophocles and Euripides without having studied them, about Homer having read him only in French—and whose classicism served primarily as a defense of their own works—Beyle is right, a hundred times right. He is very amusing at the expense of M. Auger, who, at a public meeting of the Academy, uttered the words "schism" and "sect." "Thus all Frenchmen who dare to think like the romantics are 'sectarians' (the term is *odious*, says the *Dictionnaire de l'Académie*). I am a 'sectarian!'" Beyle exclaims, and he develops this theme very gaily. To the list of the Academy he opposes a "counterlist" of persons who enjoyed public favor—most of these have since become members of the Institut. It was at such moments that Beyle was triumphant; everyone with a sense of humor was on his side. But when he expounds his plans for prose tragedy and comedy, he exposes weaknesses in his position and betrays embarrassment. He is at fault especially in the matter of comedy; he makes too little of Molière, still so very much alive, so close to us today. Classic that he was, Molière has aged very little and gives as much pleasure in 1850 as he did in 1670. Beyle cannot account for the fact that the author of *Les Femmes savantes* and *Le Misanthrope* contradicts his theory of "the partial death" of every classic work. Beyle himself sensed the difficulty, and in an as yet unpublished supplement to his pamphlet tried to deal with it. The objection is a valid one, even in a more general form. Beyle does not have sufficient faith in that which does not age in literature, in the eternal youth of genius, in the "immortality" of works—no empty word, and which resembles the immortality Athena suddenly spreads over Homer's hero upon his return to Ithaca.

However that may be, credit for having destroyed some of the prejudices and ingrained habits which in 1820 opposed all innovation, even the most moderate, goes to Beyle and to critics like him who contributed to our literary education. He contributed to it in his own way, not by flattering us with sweet nothings, like most of our teachers at that time, but by getting under our skin by his epigrammatic sallies. He did not try to resemble the La Harpes whom he combatted, but played the part of a casual amateur, keeping his tone light and bantering, that of a gentleman incognito writing for his own pleasure. As a critic, he did not compose books in the proper sense of the term; all his writings in this field are really one and the same work, and they can be read in almost any order. Wherever we pick him up, we find every sort of new idea and point of view. The taste for the true and the natural which he so often displays frequently looks like an act of defiance on his part; it is less a taste than a provocation, a gauntlet thrown down to those whose faults shock him. In a Russian bath, when you step out of the steam room, you throw yourself into the snow, and then you rush back into the steam room. Abrupt transitions from the academic to the natural genres, as Beyle practices them, seem to me to be of this kind. He subjects his disciples (for he had disciples) to this ordeal, and more than one temperament grew hardened in the exercise.

I have not mentioned his book *De l'amour,* first published in 1822, nor a number of other writings dating from those years. In a little pamphlet published in 1825 (*D'un nouveau complot contre les industriels*), he was one of the first to protest the exaggerated triumph of industrialism, the utilitarian school's habit of pinning medals on itself. I shall not go into the issues of the debate, nor shall I

ask whether he really understood the Saint-Simonian con-
cept of the *Producteur* which he had in mind. I shall only
observe that he insisted on the eternal value of devoted
feelings, of beautiful things that have come to be considered useless, of all that Italians sum up under the term of
la virtù.

Today I have confined myself to giving the reader some
idea of the literary services Beyle rendered us. To untrav-
eled people like myself (and there were many such at that
time) he disclosed many names, many foreign particularities; by his merest hints he stimulated the desire to see
and know more. He was lavish with familiar quotations
from the divine poets of Italy which we should be ashamed
not to know by heart. Thanks to him I (and I am sure I
was not alone in this) was able to enjoy the beauty of
Italian art and literature without leaving my room. He
stimulated the revival of old French literature as much as
he could; he teased and taunted the national laziness of the
pupils of Fontanes, in so far as Fontanes had pupils. Many
a man, if he were sincere, would admit that he was stimulated by Beyle—people profited from his epigrams more
than they acknowledged. In short, he urged us all to get
beyond our academic, narrowly French confines, and to
familiarize ourselves at least to some extent with what lies
outside. He was a critic not for the general public, but for
artists and for other critics. To repeat, he was a sort of Cossack, a Cossack who jabs with his lance as he gallops by,
but a friendly, helpful Cossack—that was Beyle as critic.

After Beyle the critic, we should discuss Beyle the novelist, but something must be said about a role that is perhaps uniquely his, the vocation at which he most excelled:
Beyle is a penetrating, pleasant, reliable guide in Italy. Of
the various works he published worth taking along when
you go abroad, we may especially recommend his *Promenades dans Rome*. It is very like the conversation of an intelligent cicerone with excellent taste, who points out beautiful things to you at every turn, but does not insist: he
gives you just enough to feel their beauty yourself if you

are capable of it. To what he sees he adds his own recollections and anecdotes in brief digressions that are instructive without ever being boring. In a land where "the climate is the greatest of all artists," the *Promenades* strike a lively, fresh, yet elevated tone. Read it in a carriage or on the deck of a steamship, or at night after you have been to see what the author points out to you, and you will find he has summed up the true ideal impression whether of Greek or Italian art. The author has flashes of natural sensibility and sincere emotion, which he shakes off quickly, but which he communicates to the reader. Beyle's failings are failings no longer when you take him in this way, in the role of traveling companion. By 1829 he had visited Rome six times. In July 1830 he was appointed consul at Trieste, but then, when Austria refused the exequatur, he became consul at Civitavecchia, and spent the last years of his life in Rome. When he returned to Italy after the July Revolution, he found it changed. In December 1834 he wrote from Civitavecchia: "Italy is no longer as she was when I adored her in 1815; she is in love with something she has not. The fine arts, for which alone she was made, are now no more than an expedient; she is wounded in the depths of her pride by the fact that she is not a sovereign nation like her older sisters, France, Spain, and Portugal. But even if she had a purple robe she could not wear it. She would first of all need twenty years under the iron rod of Frederic II to hang the murderers and put the thieves behind bars." He went on loving the Italy that was after his own heart, the Italy of the arts, without politics. He used to say that whenever politics turned up suddenly in a pleasant disinterested conversation, or in a literary work, it affected him "like a pistol going off during a concert." Anyone who visited Rome during the years he was consul at Civitavecchia could meet Beyle, and most visitors benefited from his knowledge and advice. Scoffer that he was, he was the most obliging of men. For all his unsparing criticism of the French, when a new arrival in Civitavecchia sought him out and proved to be intelligent, Beyle was happy to make up for a long dearth of French conversation. He would accompany the visitor to Rome and serve willingly as cicerone. When the learned M. Victor Le Clerc went to Italy —the witty Ampère was one of the party—Beyle kept the company continually amused with his sallies, while he escorted them around the Roman campagna. He was particularly helpful in bringing his erudite companions into closer touch with the local population. "Heaven gave me the talent for being persona grata to peasants," he would say. His friendly affability, his Silenus-like appearance (he had by then become plump) and a certain Satyr-like air which enlivened his remarks—all this endeared him to vintagers, harvesters, and the girls who drew water at the well of Tivoli just as in the days of Horace. This same man, who would have been quite at home acting in some ancient mime, found eloquent words to express the sublime grandeur of St. Peter's dome. I am speaking primarily of this distinguished man's high qualities: no one can deny that he had them.

. . . .

Beyle had a certain success as a novelist. I have recently reread most of his novels. The first in date was *Armance ou quelques scènes d'un salon de Paris,* published in 1827. It was not successful and was little understood. The Duchesse de Duras had shortly before composed pleasant novels or novelettes which were much appreciated in high society; in addition, she had given a reading of an unpublished short piece entitled *Olivier.* Inaccurate accounts of this reading fired people's imaginations, and there was a kind of malicious competition in treating what was wrongly supposed to have been the subject of *Olivier.* Beyle, following Latouche, made the mistake of attacking the same theme— a theme impossible to repeat and anything but pleasant to understand. His Octave, a rich, blasé, bored young man is, we are told, of superior intelligence, but capricious, impractical, and capable only of causing suffering to those who love him. He succeeds in being odious and arouses the reader's impatience. The salons the author had in mind are not portrayed truthfully in this work, for the simple reason that Beyle did not know them. Under the Restoration, there was still a demarcation line in high society. The Faubourg Saint-Germain was not open to all comers, and those who did not belong to it by birth were not admitted—as they have been since—on the sole strength of their intellectual accomplishments. A little later, M. de Balzac, among others, had only to express the desire to be admitted, but prior to 1830 there was no wangling an invitation unless one was of a particular political persuasion. Beyle frequented many a charming salon, literary and otherwise (those of Mme. Pasta, Mlle. Schiasetti of the *Italiens*, Mme. Ancelot, M. Cuvier, etc.), but he spoke of those of the Faubourg Saint-Germain as one speaks of some faraway land peopled with monsters. The specific portraits he attempted to draw (that of Mme. de Bonnivet, for instance) do not at all resemble their originals. His novel is enigmatic with respect to its subject and without truth with respect to detail, and as such exhibited neither genius nor powers of invention.

The Red and the Black, so titled no one knows why, referring to some emblem we can only guess at, was scheduled for 1830, but was not published until the following year. It is at least a novel with action. The first volume is interesting, despite the manner and the implausibilities. The author sets out to portray classes and parties as they existed before 1830. He begins by picturing a pretty little town in the Franche-Comté. There is M. de Rênal, the royalist mayor, a rich and influential man of less than average intelligence; his lovely wife is unsophisticated; they have two fine children. He wants a private tutor for the children, so as to outdo a local rival. The tutor chosen for this post is Julien, the nineteen-year-old son of a cabinet-maker, who knows Latin and is studying to be a priest. One morning Julien appears at the mayor's gate in a very white shirt, with a spotless lavender coat under his arm. He is received by Mme. de Rênal, who is slightly surprised at her husband's choice of a tutor for her children. Julien is a sensitive, passionate, excitable, ambitious young man, who has all the intellectual vices of a young Jean-Jacques

and nurses a poor man's envy of the rich and powerful. He
insinuates himself into the household, wins the mother's
heart without becoming attached to the children, and soon
is in full pursuit of a single aim, that of avenging himself,
out of vanity and pride, by tormenting the poor woman he
seduces but does not love, and dishonoring the husband
whom he hates as his superior. There is an idea behind all
this. Beyle was at bottom an aristocrat. One election day,
he began to wonder whether we should not eventually be
compelled to woo the lowest classes, as is the case in
America. He exclaimed: "If so, I shall quickly become an
aristocrat. I don't want to curry favor with anyone, but
rather less with the people than with a minister." Thus
Beyle was very much struck by the phenomenon of "making one's way in the world." He saw it as the barren passion of poor young men with education, a passion that
dominates and feeds on the normal interests of youth. He
personifies this passion truthfully enough in Julien at the
beginning of the novel. I am told that he had a model,
someone he knew personally, for the beginning of the
novel, and so long as he could follow the model closely
enough, the character was plausible. The introduction of
this timid young man into a society to which he was not
brought up, but had coveted from a distance; the streak of
vanity which distorts all his feelings so that even in the
touching tenderness of a weak woman he sees merely an
opportunity for coming into possession of the pleasures and
luxuries of a superior caste; the contemptuous, tyrannical
attitude he quickly adopts toward the woman whom he
should serve and honor; the protracted illusions about him
on the part of his fragile, interesting victim, Mme. de Rênal—all this is or at least would have been well rendered,
if the author had been less restless and less epigrammatic
in his manner of telling it. Beyle's deficiency as a novelist
was due to his taking up this type of composition only
after he had been a critic, so that he follows certain preconceived ideas; nature did not endow him with the talent
for composing narratives in which the characters are at
home and behave spontaneously, acting according to the

course of things. He forms characters by combining two or three ideas which he believes to be correct and above all *piquant,* as he reminds us at every step. They are not living beings, but cleverly constructed automatons; almost at every move they make, we hear the machinery grinding and realize the author is outside them, turning the crank. With the two or three ideas the author has given Julien, he very soon appears no more than an odious little monster, a criminal of the Robespierre type, who operates in ordinary life in terms of domestic intrigue. And in fact he ends on the scaffold. The author's portrayal of the parties and cabals of the period also lack the coherence and moderation in development which alone can make for a real novel of manners. I venture to suggest that Beyle had seen too much of Italy, that he had gained too deep an insight into the Rome and Florence of the fifteenth century, that he had read too much Machiavelli, not only *The Prince* but also his life of the clever tyrant Castruccio, and that all this had a harmful influence on him and made him misunderstand France, so that he was unable to offer her pictures of herself such as she likes and applauds. Although perfectly honest and honorable in his private manners and behavior, as a writer he applied moral standards different from ours. He saw hypocrisy where there was no more than a legitimate sense of propriety, nature reasonably and honestly observed—as we like to find it even in the portrayal of passions.

He did better in his novels and stories with Italian subjects. During his stay in the Roman state he made excavations, digging up black vases "which are 2700 years old, they say (but on this score as on others I have my doubts)." At the same time he used his savings to buy the right to copy manuscripts in family archives, which the owners protected jealously, the more so because they were illiterate and could not read their treasure. "As a result I have eight volumes in folio (but only one side of each page is filled), entirely true, written by contemporaries in a half-jargon. When I am poor again and living in a garret, I shall translate this *faithfully;* faithfulness to fact is the merit of the stories." He wondered whether he could entitle the collection, *Historiettes romaines, fidèlement traduites des récits écrits par les contemporains, de 1400 à 1650.* He hesitated (being a purist, he had scruples) over whether it would be proper to call a tragic story a *historiette.* His story *L'Abbesse de Castro,* published first in the *Revue des Deux Mondes* (February and March 1839), probably came from one of those somber, bloody family records. The author or translator takes pleasure in seeing in Helen's love for Jules Branciforte one of those *amours passionnés* which, according to him, no longer exist (in 1838), and which would be regarded as very ridiculous if one encountered them. Such love "feeds on great sacrifices, can subsist only when surrounded with mystery, and is always to be found in close proximity with the most horrible misfortunes." Thus Beyle seeks in the novel supporting evidence for his long-standing theory maintained to the last, which had inspired this saying: "Love is a delightful flower, but one must have the courage to go pick it at the brink of some dreadful precipice." *L'Abbesse de Castro* is a good example of the narrative of banditry, a genre popular in Rome, but we feel, literarily, that it becomes a genre like any other, and that it should not be done to death. In another story, *San Francesco a Ripa,* printed after his death (*Revue des Deux Mondes,* July 4, 1847), I find another anecdote about Roman passions. This time the scene is laid early in the eighteenth century: a jealous young princess takes revenge on an unfaithful French lover. The narrative is lively, raw, and abrupt. At the end there is a profusion of bullets. The faithless man and his valet were "each pierced with more than twenty bullets," such was the fear lest the master escape. In the more classical genre of Dido and Ariadne, in novels of the tone of *La Princesse de Clèves,* bullets and deathly blows are used less lavishly. Instead we have elegiac monologues, delicate thoughts, and fine shades of feeling. When we have exhausted one of the genres, we pass gladly to another to renew our appetite; but if we must choose between two abuses, a certain poetic excess of tender effusiveness is less tiresome to read.

The Charterhouse of Parma (1839) is of all Beyle's novels the one that gave a few persons the greatest idea of his
talent in this genre. The opening is graceful and genuinely
charming. It gives a picture of Milan between 1796, the
year of the first Italian campaign, and 1813, when the brilliant court of Prince Eugène came to an end. It was a
happy inspiration to show us the young Fabrice, all fire
and enthusiasm, running away from home on hearing that
Napoleon had landed at Juan-les-Pins in 1815, to fight in
France under the imperial eagles. But his bizarre Odyssey
has nothing artificial about it—Beyle took his idea from a
book of recollections by an English "soldier of the 74th
regiment," a man who witnessed the Battle of Vittoria without understanding any of it, more or less as Fabrice witnessed the Battle of Waterloo wondering afterward whether
he had really been in a battle and whether he could say
that he had actually fought in it. Along with his recollections of that book Beyle combined personal recollections of his youth, such as when he had left Geneva on
horseback to witness the Battle of Marengo. I like this beginning a great deal, though I cannot say the same of
what follows. The novel is less a novel than memoirs of the
life of Fabrice and his aunt, Mme. de Pietranera, who becomes the duchess de Sanseverina. Italian morality, which
Beyle abuses a bit, is decidedly too different from ours.
Fabrice, after his brilliant beginnings and his flash of enthusiasm in 1815, might have become one of those distinguished Italian liberals who nobly and perhaps vainly
aspire to a regeneration of their country, but who, by their
scholarly labors and unselfishness, share in our ideals (Santarosa, Cesare Balbo, Capponi). But Beyle did not so conceive his hero—lest he relapse into what is commonplace
on this side of the Alps. He made Fabrice a pure-blooded
Italian, bishop-coadjutor at an early age and then an archbishop without vocation, mediocrely and indolently witty,
libertine, weak (even cowardly). A perpetual pleasure
seeker, he falls in love with one Marietta, a provincial actress, and goes about with her everywhere without shame,
without consideration for himself or his status, without re-

gard for his family or for the aunt who loves him too much.
I am well aware that Beyle posits as a principle that a pure
Italian is totally unlike a Frenchman and has no vanity,
that he does not feign love when he does not feel it, that
he endeavors neither to please nor to surprise, nor to make
a good impression, and that he is content to be himself
in perfect freedom. However, what Fabrice is and appears
to be for almost the entire novel, despite his good looks
and figure, is very ugly, very insipid, very vulgar. Nowhere does he conduct himself like a man, but like an
animal at the mercy of his appetites or a libertine child
who indulges his every whim. There is no morality, no
principle of honor: he is only determined not to simulate
love when he is not in love. Similarly, at the end, when he
falls in love with Clélia, the daughter of a dreary general,
Fabio Conti, he sacrifices everything to her, even good
manners and gratitude to his aunt. In earlier writings Beyle
had defined *amour passionné* as almost the specific characteristic of the Italian and southern temperament generally; Fabrice is a character who supports that theory.
He goes out every morning in search of love and only at
the end is he allowed to experience it. Fabrice sacrifices
everything to it, just as earlier he had sacrificed everything
to pleasure. The pretty descriptions of landscapes, especially of Lake Como and its vicinity, cannot, in view of the
rest, ennoble a character so little worthy of interest, so incapable of honor, so ready to do anything—even to commit murder—for his momentary gain and for passion. In
fact, the one time Fabrice does kill, he does it in self-defense. He fights in a rather ignoble manner on the highway
with a certain Giletti, the actor protector of Marietta, who
regards Fabrice as her favorite. If we were to go into the
plausibility of the events in the novel, we might ask why
this highway accident has such a great influence on Fabrice's future fate; we might ask why he, the friend of the
Prince of Parma and of his prime minister (or so he can
consider himself), a bishop-coadjutor and very influential
in the little state, runs away like a criminal because he
happens to kill in self-defense, before witnesses, a lowly

actor who threatened and attacked him. Fabrice's behavior, his extravagant flight, and the consequences the author draws from it are all inexplicable if we were to look for plausibility or logic in this novel, which, except for the beginning, is nothing but a witty Italian masquerade. The love scenes, some of them rather good—those with the duchess who is Fabrice's aunt, and with the young Clélia —only half-redeem the impossibilities which leap to the eye and shock common sense. Truth there may well be in matters of detail, but it does not suffice to make me look upon this world as anything but a fantasied world, fabricated to the same extent as it is observed by a very intelligent man who has composed an Italian *marivaudage* in his own manner. The affectation and grotesqueness of the genre grow more marked as the novel develops. When I have finished it, I feel the need to reread some very simple, even-keeled work of fiction, which gives a broad, kindly portrait of human nature, in which aunts are not infatuated with their nephews, bishops are not as libertine and hypocritical as the Cardinal de Retz may have been as a young man, and are much less brilliant; where poisoning, lies, anonymous letters, and base actions of every kind are not part of ordinary behavior and are not all but taken for granted; in which, under the pretext of simplicity and avoidance of effects, I am not thrown into incredibly tortuous complications and intrigues more alarming than the labyrinth of ancient Crete.

Ever since Beyle began to chide France for the feelings we display in our literature and our society, I have more than once felt the desire to defend them. One of his principal theories, in accordance with which he wrote his novels, is that love is all but unknown in France—that is to say, love worthy of the name, as he understands it: *amour passion*, a lovesickness, which by its nature is something as special as is crystallization in the mineral kingdom (the comparison is his). But when I see what this love-passion develops into under Beyle's pen, in beings he seems to propose to us as models, in Fabrice when he finally attains to it, in the Abbess of Castro, in the Princess of Campobasso,

in Mina de Wangel (another of his novellas), I am persuaded that I like and respect love in the French manner.
Though physical attraction certainly plays its part, still
there are also moral elements—taste and inclination, well-
mannered gallantry, mutual esteem, enthusiasm, even reason and intelligence. Such love retains a little common
sense; society is not entirely forgotten, or is duty sacrificed to blind instinct and ignorance. Corneille's Pauline,
in my opinion, embodies the ideal of this type of love fairly
well. Though many diverse feelings are included in it,
honor and idealism are not silenced. Looking for somewhat
less exalted examples, we should find at least kindness and
a certain decency, whether in true loves or liaisons, perhaps even respectful, affectionate attachments—what we
call it is not very important.[5] Love-passion, such as immortal poets depicted it in Medea, in Phaedra, and in Dido,
is moving to see, thanks to them. But I have no patience
with the love-passion which has become systematic in
Beyle. A kind of animal sickness such as Fabrice serves to
symbolize at the end of his career is very ugly, and there
is nothing attractive about its semidemented conclusion.
After you have read this, you turn back very naturally, it
seems to me, to the French genre of novelistic composition or at least to a genre fuller in scope, which provides
an element of reason and sound emotion, true simplicity
such as is found in Manzoni's *I Promessi Sposi*, in every
good novel by Walter Scott, in some quite uncomplicated
but adorable short story by Xavier de Maistre. The rest is
merely the work of an intelligent man who went out of his
way to devise unexpected, piquant analytical paradoxes,
but the characters were not really products of his heart or
imagination. They do not live.

You can see how far I am from sharing M. de Balzac's
enthusiasm for *The Charterhouse of Parma.* Balzac, to put

[5] I like to visualize this French love or tender friendship, in
its various nuances, by evoking the names of Mme. de La Fayette, Mme. de Caylus, Mme. d'Houdetot, Mme. d'Epinay,
Mme. de Beaumont, Mme. de Custine. Gracefulness is never
absent from it.

it plainly, spoke of Beyle the novelist as he would have
liked to be spoken of himself. Yet even he had the faculty
of conceiving spontaneously and of bringing to life certain
beings which he then set in motion in his true or fantastic
world, and which are unforgettable. He praised highly the
character of Count Mosca, that intelligent minister of a
tiny despot state who, he supposed, was a true-to-life portrait of Prince Metternich. Beyle never had any such thing
in mind. Incidentally, no two novelists less resemble each
other than Balzac and Beyle. The former was as trusting
as the latter was mistrustful; Beyle was always diffident in
the presence of stupidity and feared above all that he might
appear vain. His constant concern was to avoid looking ridiculous, while Balzac scarcely supposed that he could.
When Balzac published his article on *The Charterhouse of
Parma* in *Lettres parisiennes*, Beyle wrote him a letter from
Civitavecchia (October 1840). After many thanks for
such an unexpected outburst of panegyric, he concluded:
"This amazing article, the like of which no writer has ever
received from another, I have read—I am bold to confess—
bursting with laughter. Whenever I came on a bit of excessive praise, and I did so at every step, I imagined the
faces my friends would make reading it."

Nor did the two writers differ less in their conceptions of
form, style, and good usage. In all such matters, M. de
Balzac was convinced that he had never done enough—
that there was always more and better to be done. In his
Mémoires d'un touriste, Beyle tells us—he was staying
somewhere in Burgundy: "In my room I found a book by
M. de Balzac, the *Abbé Birotteau* of Tours [*Le Curé de
Tours*]. How I admire this author! How well he enumerates the misfortunes and meannesses of provincial life! I
should prefer a simpler style, but then would the provin-
cials buy it? I suppose he composes his novels in two stages,
first reasonably, and then clothing them in a beautiful neo-
logic style, with such ornaments as *patiments de l'âme*
and *il neige dans mon coeur*." For his part, M. de Balzac
found something lacking in Beyle's style, and so do we.
Beyle either dictated or wrote hastily himself, just the way

he talked. Whenever he attempted to revise or correct his
first draft, he started all over again, rewriting entirely—
sometimes a third time—yet without necessarily improving
on the first draft. What he had not got down the first
time, he was never able to capture or develop later.
Though his style might gain in emphasis thereby, his
thought was not clarified in consequence. He had singular
ideas about how writers approach their task: "When I set
out to write," he says, "I am not at all concerned for the
ideal beauty of my words. I am assailed by ideas which
I feel the need of setting down. I suppose that M. Villemain is assailed by the forms of phrases, and that what is
called a poet, a M. Delille or a Racine, is assailed by verse
forms. Corneille was mainly interested in forms of dialogue." In short, he goes to a great deal of trouble to understand a very simple thing; he was not one of those to whom
the image is suggested by the thought, or in whom lyrical,
eloquent feelings burst forth and flow in natural, harmonious development. His early studies did nothing to correct this inadequacy; he had no teacher, no professor of
rhetoric—something it is always a good thing to have had,
even if one has to rebel against him later. In spite of his
elaborate theories on this score, he was well aware that
something was lacking. While he seemed to scorn style, he
was really very much preoccupied with it.

Though I have been criticizing Beyle's novels with some
outspokenness, I am far from wishing he had never written
them. If masterpieces are ever to be created again, writers
have to be willing to take risks—even to produce essentially unfinished works. Beyle has this kind of courage.
Around 1825 there existed an ultracritical, superrationalis-
tic school of thought which formulated the following as
guiding principle: "Our century will *understand* masterpieces, but it will not *produce* them. There are artistic ages,
and then there are others which merely produce intelligent people—if you like, supremely intelligent people."
Beyle replied to this despairing theory in a letter published
in the *Globe* (March 31, 1825):

"To try to be an artist in the wake of critics like La

Harpe takes iron courage. You have to disregard possible criticism even to a greater degree than a young cavalry officer charging into battle at the head of his company must disregard all thoughts of danger to life and limb. It is their total lack of just such *courage* that condemns all our poor poets to mediocrity. You have to write to give pleasure to yourself, as I am writing this letter to you: an idea occurred to me, so I took a sheet of paper. It is for lack of *courage* that we no longer have artists. Would anyone deny that Canova and Rossini were great artists? Few men have had greater contempt for critics. Around 1785, there was not a single art lover in Rome who did not make fun of the works of Canova, etc."

So, whenever Beyle had an idea, he took a piece of paper and wrote—not worrying about what others would say and never soliciting praise. In this he was a true gentleman. His novels are what they are, but they are not vulgar; like his criticism, they are destined primarily for other novelists. They have fresh ideas and blaze new trails. In studying the possibilities they open up, a novelist of talent may be helped to find himself.

In recent years, since M. de Balzac led the way, a number of writers have dealt with Beyle—his life, his character, his writings. M. Arnould Frémy, M. Paulin de Limayrac, and M. Charles Monselet have discussed him in turn. Their far-reaching analyses are instructive but, if they will allow me to say so, to gain clearer understanding of this rather complex man, and to avoid extremes of praise or blame, I still prefer to go back to the opinions of those who knew him in his best years and when he was just starting out: M. Mérimée, M. Ampère, and Jacquemont (or what the latter would have told me if he had been alive)—in short, those who knew and liked the man himself. As for his physique, though he was not a short man, at an early date his figure took on a certain sturdy compactness. His full face, above a short thick neck, was framed in sideburns and curly brown hair, no longer his own toward the last. His brow was a noble one, his nose turned-up, somewhat like a Kalmuk's. His lower lip protruded somewhat and conveyed something of his inner skepticism. His deep-set eyes were rather small, but very lively, and attractive when he smiled. As a young man he had a certain reputation at court balls for a well-turned leg—such things were noticed at the time. His hands were small and delicate and he was proud of them. In his last years he became heavy and apoplectic, but he took great care to conceal the signs of decline even from his friends. He died suddenly on March 23, 1842, at the age of fifty-nine, in Paris where he was then on leave. Continuing with originality and inventiveness the French literary tradition of Chamfort, Rulhière, and other wits whom he brings to mind by several of his characteristic traits, Beyle had an essential rectitude and sureness in personal relationships, which should not be forgotten when all the home truths have been stated.

II

. . . .

An opinion regarding Beyle is circulating today, which I see has been adopted and professed by a critic whose talent, vigor, and intellectual range I prize most highly—M. Taine. He declares that Beyle was a man of genius. However much I did and still do like Beyle, I cannot in all conscience agree with any such judgment, and I do not think anyone who knew him while he lived subscribes to it. I can understand how a man who has left behind completed works which went unappreciated or were little understood by his contemporaries should be proclaimed a genius when their truth and beauty finally become apparent after his death. What matter if, in his lifetime, he was looked upon as merely a distinguished eccentric? But Beyle is not a case in point. He left behind loosely constructed books, very remarkable in parts, but all in all a far cry from the monumental. In short his books are not such as to give us a higher idea of him than the one imposed by his living personality. Now, just what was that?

To revive and refresh my impressions on this score, I
have recently reread his *Correspondance*,[6] which is so
lively, so amusing, and to be wholly pleasing lacks only a
key, such as could easily enough be supplied (but haste is
in order!) to most of the proper names and a few nick-
names he used to designate his friends. Beyle had one
great, incontestable merit: under the Empire, when literature lagged behind the great actions and prodigious exploits of the regime, he felt the need for a different kind
of literature. This new literature, which would in turn be
great and original, would not compete with extraordinary
accomplishments in the historical sense; for, as he said, "a
nation is never great in more than one genre at a time."
Thus the victories of the spirit could only come after those
of the sword. Beyle provoked and prophesied the former.
He looked forward with impatience to the moment when
France would abandon its political, parliamentary preoc-
cupations, but although he waited a long time, the moment
never came. He believed that it is the way of life of a given
epoch which gives rise to truly living writing, and that all
else is merely hothouse production, suitable only for the
academies. According to his informal, privately expressed
definition, the principle and merit of romanticism was "that
it administers to a given public the exact drug calculated
to please it at a given time and place." He did not at all
imply that a drug proven effective in one case and one
country, would be equally effective elsewhere. The academies imagine that they possess universal recipes and formulas, but actually no formulas can be transposed from
one age, place, or nation to another. The merit of Manzoni (in 1819), he says, was to have sensed what the
Italian public was thirsting for. Let us use our own free
judgment with respect to France. (This is Beyle speaking.)
Let us be *ourselves*, let us not imitate. *Who will deliver us
from Louis XIV?* "Affectation did not make its appearance
until the seventeenth century; at the court of Henri IV

[6] *Correspondance inédite de Stendhal*, with an introduction
by M. Mérimée, a vol. in 8°, Michel Lévy, 2-bis Rue Vivienne.

there was still a great deal of candor; this fine quality of
the French was not completely annihilated until the reign
of Louis XIV. Since then France has had too many writers
emasculated by their desire to be admitted one day to the
French Academy." Beyle had no really exact knowledge of
literary history, and he failed to appreciate the essentially
solid, sober quality of the language under Louis XIV.
Where he was not mistaken, however, was in noting the
false imitations of that language, and particularly of Ra-
cinian poetry, which have proliferated since the seventeenth
century. Whereas Beyle was weak in his discussions of
the great classics, he was in his element when dealing
with the second- and third-rate. He called the alexandrine
a *"cache-sottise."* He asked why French poetry was so
proud that it employs only "a third" of the words in the
French language, while English poets can say whatever
they like. He maintained that Racine's verse had been
created deliberately for the use and in the likeness of the
haughty courtiers of Louis XIV. He did not shrink from declaring in 1818 that Racine was as superannuated as "the
royal coaches." He demanded the truth in all its simplicity,
not in its vulgarity; his pet aversions were vulgarity and
affectation—whereas the pet aversion of good society is
"energy" in any form. He pushed his taste for candor and
for "the unexpected" to the point where he took no further
notice of good society, which seemed to him too monotonous, too vapid. He even sought out bad society: it was at
this point that he came to grief. For what he meant—and
himself took with a grain of salt—others would take literally
and interpret as permission to indulge in crudeness. Refined Epicurean that he was, it is true that he spoke only
in the name of an elite. In a letter to Thomas Moore, he
says that he writes only for "the happy few," adding that
he was very much annoyed by the thought that the rest
of "the human rabble" might gain access to his private
musings. After Sieyès and the advent of democracy, he
took the attitude that only the literary aristocracy still
dared admire simplicity of expression and intellectual naturalness. He intended to stay a member of that aristocracy

and scoffed at all who were taken in by bombast, turgidity, pretentiousness in any form.

A man who thinks and feels this way is not a revolutionary, but at best a member of a secret conspiracy. He creates quite a stir, but behind closed doors and within a small circle. The fact of the matter is, Beyle celebrated his greatest triumphs when dining among friends, at Mme. Ancelot's Tuesday evenings, and M. Delécluze's Sunday mornings. What storms he could blow up! How much amusement he gave! How many moments of mingled rage and laughter he afforded with his probing frankness, observing his own principle "that nothing is as pleasant as an exchange of vigorous insults (between friends)." This man who passed as malicious among those who did not know him was dearly loved by his friends. I could cite countless instances of his generosity and delicacy. Because he lived in Italy, he grew somewhat estranged from the French atmosphere, out of touch with the ideas of the times, and because he feared pedantry, he contracted a particular species of it—that of trying to outdo nature, to carry naturalness to the point of affectation. It is not wise to be too willowy in your movements once you have acquired a paunch. But in his best years, what wit, what acumen! . . .

2 and 9 January 1854 (*Causeries du lundi*). 18 August 1862 (*Nouveaux lundis*).

The two-part essay was written on the occasion of the publication of the first collected edition of Stendhal's works. The later pages form part of Sainte-Beuve's review of *Souvenirs de soixante années,* by a French litterateur of the Restoration, Etienne-Jean Delécluze.

Sainte-Beuve's blindness to Stendhal's genius is a favorite theme of all his hostile critics. When we read his analyses of *The Red and the Black* and *The Charterhouse of Parma* we marvel that so much could escape him. But there they are, along with Flaubert's "I have read *The Red and*

the Black; I find it poorly written and neither its
characters nor its author's intentions are compre-
hensible to me." Apparently Stendhal was right
when he said that he would achieve fame only in
the twentieth century. Sainte-Beuve certainly did
not go beyond his own day in his opinions of his
contemporaries. Whether praising or blaming
Stendhal, he never comes to grips with the essential content and message. At best he deals
with secondary matters. On these latter, some
of his points are sufficiently well taken to make
his essay a useful corrective to present-day adulation of Stendhal.

BALZAC

To MAKE a real study of the famous novelist who has just died and whose sudden disappearance has aroused worldwide interest, would mean writing a book, and I do not think the time for that has come. Moral autopsies of this kind are not conducted while the grave is still new, especially not when its occupant was so full of strength and fertility and seemed to have many works and days yet in him. All we can do or should try to do for a great contemporary when he passes on, is to give a clear, brief account of his talents and of their value for us—of the variously subtle or powerful means by which he charmed and influenced his age. I shall try to do this for M. de Balzac, putting personal considerations out of my mind and speaking solely as a critic.[1]

M. de Balzac was indeed a painter of our times, perhaps the most original, the most capable, and most penetrating of all our painters. At an early date he chose the nineteenth century as his subject, as his field of observation: he plunged into it with ardor and he never again left it. Society is like a woman: it wants its features to be recorded for posterity by a painter, a painter all its own. Balzac was just that—he followed no tradition, but created new techniques and artifices of the brush to depict an ambitious,

[1] Cf. M. de Balzac's article about me in the *Revue Parisienne* for August 25, 1840. I have forgotten it, but I am not afraid to have it remembered by others. Such judgments judge only those who make them.

pleasure-loving society which took pride in having no ancestors and in being unlike any other. It cherished him all
the more for just these accomplishments.

Born in 1799, he was fifteen at the fall of the Empire;
thus he knew and felt the imperial epoch with the clear-
sightedness and special penetration of childhood which was
later complemented by reflection. Someone born at roughly
the same time has said: "As a child I felt things so keenly
that it was like a knife edge to my heart." He could have
said it himself. Childhood impressions, recaptured later in
reflections or descriptions, stand out by their special emotional coloring, and it is they that account for the subtlety
and liveliness in a work. A young man under the Restoration, he went through it, seeing it in its entirety from the
most favorable vantage point, i.e., from the bottom, as one
of the crowd, as a struggling artist, with all the vast yearn-
ings of talent and ambition. So placed, we are able to
divine, to imagine, and to penetrate things beyond our
immediate grasp over and over again—long before we have
ourselves experienced or possessed them. It was with such
feelings, the feelings of a lover, that M. de Balzac went
through the period of the Restoration. He was just beginning to achieve some reputation when the new regime
came to power in July 1830. He was able to view this
regime as an equal, even to look down upon it a trifle;
his judgments were delivered with utter frankness, and his
portraits of the age's various types were entrancing, especially his treatments of the middle class. Thus M. de
Balzac knew by his own *experiencing* of them the three
very dissimilar periods which together have made up the
first half of this century; to a certain extent, his work
mirrors them perfectly. Who, for instance, has depicted the
old men and the belles of the Empire better than he? Who
has given us more delightful limnings of the duchesses
and viscountesses of the last years of the Restoration, those
women of thirty who, having achieved high position, had
been awaiting their portraitist with a vague anxiety, now
found in M. de Balzac—as he found in them—an electric
thrill of recognition. Finally, who has better caught to the

life the genus *bourgeois* in all its rich detail, as it began
its victorious rise under the July dynasty? His portraits of
men like Birotteau and Crevel will live forever, though they
seem pale, alas, in comparison with their modern counter-
parts in real life.

The observation and depiction of an entire society is an
immense theme, and M. de Balzac from an early date never
shrank from the vastness of his task. Indeed, he covered
his chosen field very thoroughly, exploring every corner of
it, and even found it too confining for his gifts. Not content
to observe and to divine, he very often invented and
dreamed. Whatever we may think of his dreams, it was
primarily by his subtle and delicate observations that he
won the heart of the aristocratic society to which he always aspired. *La Femme de trente ans, La Femme
abandonnée, La Grenadière* were the elite guard with
which he first infiltrated the bastions of upper-class life,
and they made him master of the citadel at once. His
portrayal of the Woman of Thirty is not an entirely unexpected creation. In every civilized society, from time im-
memorial, women of that age have played an important,
even a leading role. However, the theory of the woman of
thirty, with her assets, her superiorities, her height of perfection, dates only from our day. M. de Balzac was the
man who conceived it, and this is one of his most real
discoveries in the domain of the novel of private life, *le
roman intime*. The key to his immense success lies entirely
in his first little masterpiece.[2] Women subsequently forgave him much, taking for granted that everything he said
was true, because he had divined them so well the first
time.

Rapid and great as was M. de Balzac's success in France,
it was perhaps even greater and more indisputable elsewhere in Europe. The details we could cite in this connection might seem fabulous, and yet they would only be
true. Yes, M. de Balzac portrayed his epoch, and his own

---

[2] I beg you to read it only in its first editions; the author
spoiled it for me by amplifying it later.

success may itself be regarded as one of its most interesting portrayals. More than two centuries earlier, in 1624, Honoré d'Urfé (author of the famous novel *L'Astrée*), who lived in Piedmont, had a letter very seriously addressed to him by twenty-nine princes and princesses and nineteen great noblemen and ladies of Germany. These personages informed him that they had assumed the names of the heroes and heroines in *L'Astrée* and had founded an Academy of True Lovers; they pressed him to write a sequel to that work. What happened to d'Urfé also happened to M. de Balzac. At one point, for instance, a number of people who happened to be together in Venice had the idea of assuming the names of his principal characters and of acting the parts. For a whole season one saw only Rastignacs and duchesses de Langeais or duchesses de Maufrigneuse, and we are told that more than one actor or actress in this little comedy played his part through to the end. Such is the law of reciprocal influences between a painter and his models. At first the novelist touches his readers to the quick, by exaggerating a bit, but then society feels honor-bound to imitate him, and so, what might at first seem exaggeration ends up literally true to life.

The same thing that took place in Venice occurred in varying degree at a number of other places. In Hungary, in Poland, in Russia, M. de Balzac's novels were law. At this distance, the slightly fantastic elements which mingle intimately with the realistic ones (and which keep more exacting minds from finding this author's success unalloyed) went unnoticed or served as an additional attraction. For instance, the rich, bizarre interiors he was so fond of, where at the urging of his imagination he would jumble together masterpieces from twenty countries and as many periods, actually became a reality after the fact. What seemed to us in France the daydreaming of a millionaire artist was elsewhere copied exactly: people furnished their houses "in the manner of Balzac." How could the artist remain deaf or insensitive to these multiple echoes of celebrity, and fail to hear them as evidences of his own fame?

He believed in his own fame, and it was his very ambition (which assumed a noble form in him) that drove him to exploit every aspect of his powerful inner resources and to produce many works of all kinds. M. de Balzac had the physique of an athlete and the fire of an artist infatuated with his own renown; he needed no less to be equal to the immense task he set himself. Only in our own day do we find such energetic, such Herculean figures making extraordinary demands of themselves in the way of production, and keeping up the pace for twenty years. When we read Racine, Voltaire, or Montesquieu, it does not occur to us to ask whether or not they were sturdy and possessed a powerful physical organization. Buffon was an athlete, but his style does not suggest it. In the more or less classical ages, authors wrote solely with their minds, with the higher, purely intellectual portion of their faculties, the essence of their being. Today, as a result of the immense labor that the writer imposes on himself and that society forces him to perform quickly if he is to make a strong, immediate impression, he lacks the time to be so Platonistic, so delicate. The writer's personality, his whole organism is involved in his works; he writes them not only with his mind, but with his muscles and bloodstream. The physiology, the way of life of the writer must today be taken into account in any analysis of his talent.

M. de Balzac took pride in being a physiologist, and he was one certainly, though with less rigor and exactness than he imagined; but physical nature—his own and that of others—plays a great part and makes itself felt continually in his moral descriptions. I am not blaming him for this; it is a feature that affects and characterizes all the picturesque literature of our age. One day M. Villemain was reading his charming eulogy of Montaigne to the Abbé Sieyès; it was the first eulogy he ever composed, and it is full of lightness and freshness. When he reached the passage, "But I should fear, when reading Rousseau, to linger too long over culpable weaknesses, which one ought always to shun . . ." Sieyès interrupted him with these words, "Not at all; it is preferable to let them come close, so as to be able to study them in greater detail." The physiologist, whose dominant trait is curiosity, was here at cross-purposes with the man of letters, to whom taste matters most. Shall I admit that I am like Sieyès in this respect?

This amounts to saying that I am also a little like M. de Balzac. But in two respects I do not follow him. In the more delicate parts of his style, I love the *efflorescence* (I am unable to find a better word) with which he infuses life into everything and makes the very page vibrate. But I cannot accept his continual abuse of this quality, under the guise of physiology. His style, often diffuse, tends to be flushed and enervated, veined with every shade of corruption. It becomes an Asiatic style (as our teachers used to say), more flawed in spots and more effete than the body of some ancient mime. Does not Petronius somewhere, in the midst of the scenes he describes, mourn the passing of what he calls the *oratio pudica*, or restrained style, which does not let itself become "fluid" with the flux of events it describes?

Another objection I have against M. de Balzac in his capacity as a physiologist or anatomist is that in this domain he imagined at least as much as he observed. A delicate anatomist of the soul, he certainly discovered new veins; he found and brought to life, so to speak, portions of lymphatic vessels which had previously gone unnoticed. But he also invented some. There is a moment in his analysis where the plexus of truth and reality ends and that of illusion begins; nor does he distinguish one from the other. Most of his readers, particularly his female readers, confuse the two just as he has confused them. This is not the place to insist on the distinction. But it is known that M. de Balzac admitted a weakness for the Swedenborgs, Van Helmonts, Mesmers, and Cagliostros of this world: in other words, he was subject to illusion. In short, to continue my physical, anatomic metaphor, I will say: When he grasps his subject by the jugular vein, his portrayal invests it with flesh-and-blood vitality, but when he mistakes a shadow for a substance, he proceeds no less vigorously.

M. de Balzac had scientific pretensions, but what he actually had was above all a kind of physiological *intuition*. M. Chasles has very justly stated, "It has been said over and over that M. de Balzac was an observer, an analyst, but he was something better or worse than that—he was a *seer*." What he did not take in at a first glance, he usually missed altogether; later reflection did not disclose it to him. Still, how much he did take in at first glance! In a gathering, he was sociable; although he was intoxicated with his work and seemingly so full of himself, he knew how to listen, and even when he had not been listening—when he had seemed to be caught up in his own thoughts—he would still have absorbed everything he wanted to know by the time he left, and later he would amaze you by describing it.

I have said that he seemed intoxicated by his work, and the fact is, from youth onward he never really got outside it; he lived in and for it. His world was one in every sense half-observed, half-created; the characters from every station of life which he endowed with vitality were every bit as real to him as the people he met in ordinary intercourse; the latter, in the last analysis, were to him but fainter copies of his own. He had dealings with his own characters, he lived and spoke with them, and on every occasion referred to them as to people of his and your own acquaintance. He had so powerfully and distinctly endowed them with flesh and blood that once "on their own" in his pages, they were inseparable from their author. He was surrounded by his own characters, and at moments of enthusiasm they formed a ring around him and drew him with them into the immense round of the Human Comedy —which makes us a little dizzy just to watch, but which dizzied its author first of all.

M. de Balzac's is essentially a rich, copious, opulent nature; he is full of ideas, types, and inventions, continually renewed and never exhausted. Such was the power he possessed; however, he lacked the supreme power of dominating his own creation. M. de Balzac may be said to have been devoured by his own work; his talent often carried

him away like a chariot drawn by four horses. I do not
expect writers to be the precise image of Goethe, always
serene above the battle. But M. de Balzac demanded
(and in writing) that the artist plunge headlong into his
work, "like Curtius from the edge of the precipice." This
type of talent implies a good deal of verve and passion,
but also the danger of mistaking smoke for fire.

To expound his actual literary theory, however, we need
only borrow his own words. For instance, in *Les Parents
pauvres*, his last novel and one of his most vigorous (published in this very newspaper[3]), the author's favorite ideas
and all his secrets, if he ever had secrets, are expressed by
one of his characters, Wenceslas Steinbock, a Polish artist.
According to him, "A great artist today is in the position
formerly enjoyed by a prince; fame and fortune are his."
But his fame is not acquired by playing or dreaming: it is
the reward of stubborn, laborious application: "You have
some ideas rattling around in your head? Is that all? Well,
I have some ideas, too. . . . What does it matter, what
you carry around with you, if you don't put it to some
use?" That is what M. de Balzac himself believed, and that
is why he never spared himself when it came to the hard
work of writing. To conceive a work, he said, "is to smoke
magic cigarettes," but until the work has been executed, it
remains an empty dream. He also said: "Constant work is
the law of art as it is of life, for art is idealized creation.
This is why great artists and poets never wait for commis-
sions or customers; they keep on producing, today, tomorrow, always. Thus they get into the habit of working hard,
of perpetually meeting and surmounting difficulties; this
keeps them in constant concubinage with the Muse, in
touch with her creative powers. Canova lived in his studio
just as Voltaire lived in his study. Homer and Phidias must
have lived the same way." I deliberately chose this passage
because, at the same time as it discloses M. de Balzac's
honorable virtues of courage and hard work, it also nakedly

[3] *Les Parents pauvres* was first published serially in the
Constitutionnel.

reveals what is so "modern" about him, the singular carelessness with which he derogated and did violence to the
very beauty he claimed to be pursuing. No, neither Homer
nor Phidias lived "the same way . . . in concubinage with
the Muse." *Their* Muse was always chaste and severe.

"Beauty is always severe," said M. de Bonald. Such authoritative statements are always necessary to me; they
stand like immutable sacred columns in the distance, and
I point to them merely to prevent our admiration and re-
gretful tribute to a wonderfully talented man from going
beyond all proper bounds.

M. de Balzac somewhere speaks of artists who know
"mad success, success of the kind that crushes people who
lack the physical and moral strength to bear it." And he
adds: "This is something, by the way, that often happens."
It is true that there is a test more redoubtable than the
great battle which decides the artist's success or failure: it
begins the day after he has triumphed. To sustain his
triumph, to preserve his vogue and not to be frightened or
discouraged by it, not to weaken and not to abdicate under its impact, as Leopold Robert did, one must possess
real strength. One must be able to recognize that one has
merely sought and found one's true level. M. de Balzac
possessed that kind of strength and proved it.

When people spoke to him of his fame, he accepted the
term, but taking it lightly; occasionally he himself joked
about it. "Fame," he said one day, "to whom are you
speaking about it? I experienced it, I saw it with my own
eyes. I was traveling in Russia with a few friends. When
night came, we asked for hospitality in a château. The
chatelaine and her lady companions received us courte-
ously; one of the latter left the drawing room at once to
get refreshments. Just then I was introduced to the lady of
the house, and we were starting to talk when the lady who
had gone out came back. She was holding a tray, about to
present it to us, when she heard the lady of the house say,
'And so, Monsieur de Balzac, you think that. . . .' She
was so startled and thrilled that she dropped the tray,

smashing the china and the glasses. Now, that is fame, don't you agree?"

Everybody smiled—he was smiling himself—and yet he enjoyed it. This feeling sustained him in his labors and spurred him on. The wittiest and most greatly missed of his disciples, M. Charles de Bernard, who died just a short time ago, lacked the same incentive. His irony and taste were such as to make him skeptical, and this affected his otherwise distinguished work. M. de Balzac's work gained in verve and warmth by virtue of the artist's own intoxication. An exquisite subtlety managed not to be wholly swept away by it.

All Europe was to him a sort of private park where he had only to go for a walk to run across legions of friends, admirers, and willing, lavish hosts. He would show you a little flower scarcely yet dry—he had picked it the other morning as he was leaving the Villa Diodati. The painting he was describing to you, he had seen it yesterday in the palace of a Roman prince. It seemed to him just a step from one capital to another, from a villa in Rome or Isola Bella to a castle in Poland or Bohemia. He had only to wave a wand to be transported there. In his case, such travel was not just in imagination: a devoted woman, one of those whom he had deified in passing, made possible for him in reality what has for so long been the dream of all poets.

All the artists of the age were his friends, and he portrayed almost all of them magnificently in his works. He had taste in art and a real passion for works of painting and sculpture, for period pieces of every sort. When he had the time (and he often found the time, spending his days as he pleased, and his nights in work) he liked to go hunting for what he called "fine pieces." He rummaged through all the curiosity shops of Europe and spoke of their contents as an expert. This is why, when he introduced masses of objects in a novel, they never seem mere inventory lists, as they would in so many writers, but have color and life. He described them with love. Even pieces of furniture are somehow alive, even the tapestries throb. He describes too much, but in most cases the spotlight falls where it should. Even if the final result falls short of accomplishing all he seems to have hoped, the reader is left with the impression of having been moved. Balzac has the gift for color and for crowded movement. This accounts for his appeal to painters, who recognize in him one of their own kind, transplanted by mistake to literature.

He had little respect for criticism; he imposed himself on the public almost despite it, and his passion, I believe, was not of the kind that can be moderated or guided. He says somewhere of a sculptor who became discouraged and lazy: "Having become an artist *in partibus*, he had a great success in the drawing rooms, and was consulted by many amateurs; he became a critic, like all impotent artists who are dishonest in the early stages of their careers." This last feature may be true with respect to a sculptor or painter who, instead of getting down to work, spends his time talking; but this observation of Balzac's which is often repeated by a whole school of young writers is (I beg their forgiveness for saying this) both an injustice and an error, intellectually speaking. However, since it is always a highly ticklish matter proving to people that one is or is not impotent, I shall not dwell on the point.

A really intelligent, sincere Aristarchus, could M. de Balzac have been able to put up with him, might have done a great deal for him, might have helped his rich, luxury-loving nature to contain and control itself. Three things must be considered in a novel: characters, plot, and style. M. de Balzac excels in setting up his characters; he makes them live and he analyzes them deeply and unforgettably. He exaggerates, he piles detail on detail, but no matter—they have plenty of substance on which to feed. He introduces us to keen, gracious, pleasure-loving, gay people; on other days to very mean persons. But once we have met them, whether they are of the former or the latter type, we are sure never to forget them. He does not content himself with portraying characters to perfection, he also invents singularly apt names for them, which engrave them forever in our memories. He attached the greatest importance

to finding the right names for his creations; following
Sterne, he ascribed to proper names a certain "occult
power" in harmony or in ironic contrast with the characters
designated. Marneffe, Bixiou, Birotteau, Crevel, and others are by their names invested with some sort of vague
onomatopoeic quality, thanks to which the person and the
name resemble each other. Next in importance after the
characters comes plot. In M. de Balzac it is often much
less strong, goes off the track, or is exaggerated. On this
score he is less successful than in his characterizations. As
for style, his is sharp, subtle, fluent, and picturesque,
without relation to tradition. I have sometimes wondered
what effect a book by M. de Balzac would have on a well-
educated man who had been nourished on ordinary good
French prose in all its frugality. Of course, no such man
any longer exists—one whose taste has been entirely formed
by writers like Nicole and Bourdaloue—on that simple,
serious, scrupulous style which "goes far," as La Bruyère
put it. Such a man would take a month to get back his
balance after reading a novel by Balzac. La Bruyère also
said that every thought has its own right way of being
expressed—and that one must find it. M. de Balzac seems
never to have heard of this remark by La Bruyère. He
employs numbers of lively, restless, capricious turns of
speech, but they never sum up a matter once and for all.
Rather they are experimental, groping expressions. His
printers were well aware of this—he was constantly revis-
ing, even in proof. Even the mold of his mind was in continual flux; it never took permanent shape. Even when he
had found the form he wanted, he kept on experimenting.

Could even the most benevolent criticism—that of a
friend and comrade like his Louis Lambert—have made
him accept a few relatively sober ideas, in the light of
which the rushing torrent of his talent might have been
controlled, contained, or regulated a trifle? Without at-
tempting utterly to deflect him from his self-imposed
paths, I should like him to have kept in mind a few axioms
I believe to be essential to every art, to every literature:

Precision is the classic writer's varnish (Vauvenargues).

The work of art must express only what elevates the soul, what gives it noble pleasure, and nothing more. The artist's feeling must concentrate on this alone—all the rest is false (Bettina to Goethe's mother).

Good sense and genius are of the same family; wit is merely a collateral (Bonald).

Finally I wish that he who had such admiration for Napoleon and was dazzled by his great example (as transposed and reflected in literature) just as were so many others, I wish that he might have put aside once and for all the thought of comparing himself to his hero or childishly emulating him.

However, we must make allowance for individual temperament, and since death has ended his career, let us be grateful for the opulent, complex heritage he has bequeathed to us. The author of *Eugénie Grandet* will live. The begetter (I was about to say the lover) of Mme. de Vieuménil and of Mme. de Beauséant will keep his place among every woman's favorite writers. Those who are looking for joyfulness, gaiety, and brightness—for the satirical, outspoken vein in this Rabelaisian native of Touraine—will not fail to appreciate the illustrious Gaudissart, the excellent Birotteau, and the rest of their tribe. As you can see, there is something for everyone. If I had more space, I should like to speak here about M. de Balzac's last novel, one of the most remarkable if not, as I see it, one of the most flattering depictions we have had of present-day society. *Les Parents pauvres* shows us this vigorous talent at its full maturity, holding nothing back. With his customary overabundance, he has flung himself into this work body and soul. Never before have we been brought closer to human wretchedness. The first part of this novel (*La Cousine Bette*) presents characters of great truth, but also exaggerations of the kind all but inevitable in this author. Bette, who gives her name to the novel, is the foremost among these exaggerations: it does not seem possible that this poor creature whom we first see as a simple peasant woman in the Vosges, shabbily dressed, rough of manner, and a little envious but not malicious or criminal—it does not seem possible that she should become a lady of society, almost a beauty, and moreover so devilishly perverse as to seem a female Iago or Richard III. This never happens in real life; this woman is of the race of Ferragus and of The Thirteen. Our spoiled and vicious society is not compatible with such atrocious hatred and thirst for revenge. To be sure, our sins are not minor or attractive, but our crimes are less gross. The other characters of the novel are profoundly true to life, however, above all Baron Hulot with his unbridled love of women, which step by step leads him first to dishonor and eventually to degradation. Crevel, too, is excellent in every respect. His tone, gestures, and jokes are well chosen to illustrate the bourgeois vice in full panoply and self-importance. Here, we must keep in mind, we are not dealing with failings, silliness, or even human folly; it is vice that supplies the motive, the substance of the novel is social depravity. The author plunges into it all with such verve that in spots, we suspect, he is enjoying it. Several scenes of elevated pathos wring tears, but the atrocious scenes predominate. Impurity here overflows its container—the infamous Marneffes infect everything they touch. If this remarkable novel were to be studied separately, it would suggest reflections that do not concern M. de Balzac alone, but all of us, offspring of a sensual literature that we are, whether we admit it or not. Some of us, true sons of [Chateaubriand's] René, have hidden our sensualism, burying it in a cloud of mysticism; others have torn off the mask.

M. de Balzac often thought of Walter Scott; the genius of the great Scottish novelist greatly stimulated him, he said. But was he aware of the universal charm of purity and wholesomeness, the breath of healthy fresh air that always blows through Scott's pages, even when human passions are in conflict? On finishing *Les Parents pauvres,* our first feeling is a need to go back to the older authors to acquire new strength, to plunge into the limpid pages of some more wholesome reading—to wash ourselves clean in some poem by Milton, in one of his "lucid streams."

In some less incomplete study, we would have to make careful comparison between M. de Balzac and his most famous contemporaries, Mme. Sand, Eugène Sue, and Alexandre Dumas. In an entirely different genre, but with a conception of human nature no prettier or more flattering, M. Mérimée might be regarded as his direct opposite with respect to tone and manner.

M. Mérimée has perhaps no higher opinion of human nature than M. de Balzac, and if anyone has ever seemed to slander it, he is not the one to rush to its defense. But he is a man of taste and tact, with a sense of accuracy and rigor, and even in the excess of the idea, preserves restraint and discretion. His personal sense of the ridiculous was as keen as M. de Balzac's was lacking, and in him, for all his admirable neatness, the vigor of his line, and the precision of his burin, we miss only a little of the verve which the other possessed to excess. We might say that in him, the accomplished man of the world, the *honnête homme*, as the old phrase had it, from an early date held the artist in check.

Mme. Sand—need we remind ourselves?—is a greater, surer, and a firmer writer than M. de Balzac; she never gropes in her expression. She is a great painter of nature and landscape. As for the novelist, her characters are often well captured and well drawn at the beginning; but they soon take on the features of a certain idealism which puts them in the Rousseau tradition, and which comes close to being systematic. Her people are not alive from beginning to end; there is a moment when they become types. She never slanders human nature, nor does she prettify it; she wants to enhance it, but she forces and inflates it though her aim is merely to magnify it. Her chief target of attack is society, and she disparages whole classes in order to show individuals to advantage; the latter remain, nonetheless, half abstract. In short, she does not possess the same masterful sureness in the realization of her characters as she does in expression and description. Let this be said with all appropriate reservations in view of so many charming and natural situations and scenes. As for style, it is in her case a gift of the highest quality, of the first water.

M. Eugène Sue (omitting the Socialist, speaking only of the novelist) is perhaps M. de Balzac's equal in invention, fertility, and composition. His grandiose frameworks are marvelously built; he has characters that are alive, too, and whether we like it or not, they stay in our memory; above all, he has plot and a dramatic skill, which he manages expertly. But the details are often weak; they are sufficiently numerous and varied, but less subtle, less profound, less original, and less new than those of M. de Balzac. He also has gaiety, and in this genre finds felicitous and natural types, but he likes eccentricities and is too fond of describing them. Both hold healthy natures to be of little account; they tend to focus on the spoiled and the factitious. Eugène Sue is not as much of a writer as Balzac, neither as good nor as bad—nor is his badness of so subtle a kind. And then, he has made the mistake of not following exclusively his own instincts; he sometimes draws upon systems of the day, and in his latest novels urges them upon us—something that M. de Balzac never did. At least Balzac remained faithful to his own instincts and pursued his own favorite inspirations, giving in to them ever more completely as an artist who does not compromise. In the matter of currents, M. de Balzac never followed any but his own.

As for M. Dumas, everyone knows his prodigious verve and facility, his felicitous way of setting the stage, and his witty, continuously animated dialogue. His light narration keeps flowing and succeeds in overcoming obstacles and space without ever weakening. He covers immense canvases without ever tiring his brush or his reader. He is amusing, he holds you, but he never grips you as Balzac does.

Of the last-mentioned writers, M. de Balzac is the one who gets the tightest grip on his subject and digs into it most deeply.

The February Revolution dealt a severe blow to M. de

Balzac. The whole edifice of refined civilization, such as he had always dreamed of, seemed to collapse. At one moment, Europe—his own Europe—was about to fail him as France had done. However, he was quick to recover and was planning to portray this new society—or rather the fourth form of it presented to him. I could outline here the novel he was planning—the last he projected, which he spoke of with great passion. But to what purpose? He died of a heart ailment, as today so many die who have lived too intensely.

The group of writers of whom Balzac was the most productive and certainly the most inventive created their own school and influenced their times. That school gave rise to some vigorous talents, almost gigantic in dimensions; today we may venture the opinion that its power, for better or worse, has passed its apogee. It is time now to call a truce, to pause and rest; society will be grateful for a respite after so many excesses, for an opportunity to restore some sort of order and to bring forth new painters of the contemporary scene. The spirit of frantic emulation and competition prevalent recently, and the vogue for serial publication, which has compelled the writer to overwhelm the reader in every fresh chapter, have driven the novel to an extreme, exasperating pitch of concentrated expression, which can scarcely be longer sustained. While admiring the use to which these men have put their gifts, we must keep in mind that circumstances prevented them from giving full scope to their best qualities. Let us hope that in the future our society will be given pictures that are no less vast, but calmer, more comforting. Let us hope that those who paint them will enjoy a more peaceful life, and that their inspiration will be not so much subtler as gentler, more wholesomely natural and serene.

2 September 1850 (*Causeries du lundi*).

Honoré de Balzac had died shortly before, on August 17, 1850, and Sainte-Beuve had consented to be one of the pallbearers at his funeral.

Hypocrisy or generosity? Perhaps both. There had been a long history of enmity between the two men, of which the causes have never been elucidated. Sainte-Beuve put the onus on Balzac, claiming that the novelist, who was never willing to admit the slightest stricture on his work, had been annoyed by a moderately written early article by the critic. Scholars, however, have suggested that the original cause of the difference was a woman. In any case, Balzac wrote and published in the *Revue parisienne* for August 25, 1840 a scathing and blatantly ignorant and biased review of Sainte-Beuve's *Port-Royal*. He is also supposed to have announced that in his novel *Le Lys dans la vallée* he was rewriting, as it should be rewritten, Sainte-Beuve's novel *Volupté*.

The torturous stodginess of this essay is thus certainly no accident. One may sympathize with many of Sainte-Beuve's objections to Balzac, but at the same time one senses that he was determined to leave no weakness unexposed. When he approves, he manages to introduce a hint that sours the approval. And how imperturbably, as though he knew no better, he proceeds to compare Balzac with Eugène Sue and the rest! For all that, the essay is remarkable for its restraint as measured against Sainte-Beuve's private feelings about Balzac, which he recorded in his notebooks, posthumously published: "Even in his best novels Balzac retains something ignoble, something of his sordid beginnings." And in these same notebooks Sainte-Beuve confesses: "Every critic has his favorite victim, whom he pounces upon and tears to pieces with particular relish. Mine is Balzac."

MADAME BOVARY
BY M. GUSTAVE FLAUBERT

I DO NOT forget that this work has been the subject of a discussion very different from a literary discussion, but what I remember best is the wisdom of the judges' conclusions. The work now belongs to the domain of art, and art alone; the only bar before which it need appear is that of criticism, and the critic can speak of it with complete independence.

This is what criticism not only can but must do. We often go to great pains to reawaken the past, to revive old authors whom scarcely anyone reads today, renewing interest in them and giving them a semblance of life. But when genuine and living works appear on the horizon and bear down upon us, sails spread, flags flying, fairly clamoring for our judgment, if we are real critics, if we have a drop of the blood that ran in the veins of a Pope, a Boileau, a Johnson, a Jeffrey, a Hazlitt, or even a M. de La Harpe, we find it hard to keep still, we itch to get our word in, to hail the new arrivals or to open fire on them with full batteries. Pindar said long since, in connection with verse: Long live old wine and young songs! Under the heading of the latter come also last night's new play and this morning's new novel, whatever catches the fancy of young people at the moment it appears.

I had not read *Madame Bovary* in its first form, in the magazine where it was published in installments. However striking the parts may have been, the work surely lost something, and particularly the general idea, the conception, must have suffered. The reader who had to stop abruptly after scenes bold in themselves must have wondered what more could possibly have been coming. The work might well have seemed more disorderly than it is, and the author might have been suspected of designs he did not have. Only when the work is read through, does each scene take on its real point. *Madame Bovary* is above all a book, a composed, thought-out whole, all of a piece, in which nothing has been set down casually, and in which the author—more accurately, the artist—has from first to last page had his way.

Clearly, the author has lived a great deal in the Norman countryside, which he describes with incomparable truthfulness. It is a strange thing, but writers who live a good deal in the country, long enough to acquire a feeling for nature and skill in portraying it, usually love it or at least present it in a beautiful light, especially after they have left it, and are inclined to make it a setting for an idyllic happiness or an ideal felicity that is no more. Bernardin de Saint-Pierre did not care much for Ile-de-France [today Mauritius] while he lived there, but having come back from those distant parts, all he could remember was the beauty of the place, the sweetness and peace of the dales, which served as setting for his most beloved characters in *Paul et Virginie*. Not so far away, in her native Berry, Mme. Sand probably found life dull. However, she never showed us anything but the more attractive sides of this place, she did not disillusion us about the banks of the Creuse, far from it. Situating characters of intellect and passion there, she infused the rural, pastoral landscape with a breath of ancient poetry. Here, with the author of *Madame Bovary*, we come upon something quite different— a different mode of inspiration, and, to speak bluntly, another generation. The ideal is gone, lyricism has run dry. We are soberer. A severe, pitiless concern for truth, the most modern form of empiricism, has penetrated even into art. The author of *Madame Bovary* has lived in the provinces, in the country, in villages and small towns; unlike La Bruyère's traveler, he did not go there for a day or two in early spring, just long enough to meditate on the top of a hill; he has really lived there. Now, what has he seen? Pettiness, squalor, pretentiousness, stupidity, routine, monotony, and boredom. The fields and villages, so natural and true, so full of the presence of the *genius loci,* will serve him only as a setting for portraying vulgar, banal, blindly ambitious creatures, totally ignorant or only semi-literate, whose love affairs are devoid of delicacy. The only person of refinement, the only one with an inner life whom fate has thrown there, and who aspires to something better, finds herself an alien, stifled. In the course of her sufferings, finding no one to understand her, she deteriorates, she becomes depraved, and in a vain pursuit of her dream amid ugly surroundings she comes step by step to her perdition and ruin. Is this moral? Is this comforting? The question does not seem to have occurred to the author. All he asked himself was one thing: Is it true? We must assume that he has observed something of the sort with his own eyes, or at least that in his tightly knit portrayal he has reported the condensed result of his various observations, against a general background of bitterness and irony.

Another equally remarkable particularity of this work is that among all these very real, very living characters, not one can be supposed to be representing the author. Not one has been studied by him save for the purpose of the most precise and crude description, not one has been spared as one spares a friend. The author has remained completely uninvolved; he is there only as spectator, repeating and describing everything; nowhere in the novel do we catch so much as a glimpse of him. The work is entirely impersonal. This is a sign of remarkable power.

Next to Mme. Bovary, the most important character is M. Bovary. Charles Bovary *fils* (for his father, too, is portrayed very much from life) first appears as a schoolboy; he is docile but clumsy, a cipher or incurably mediocre, a simpleton, without distinction, spirit, or incentive, born to obey, to be led step by step along some well-trodden path. Son of an ex-army barber-surgeon, who was a bad lot, he has neither his father's vices nor his enterprise.

His mother's savings enable him to obtain the diploma of *officier de santé* after laborious studies at Rouen. In possession of this title, all that remains for him to do is to decide where he wants to practice. He chooses Tostes, a small town near Dieppe. His family finds him a wife, a widow much older than himself, who is believed to have some independent means. He goes along with it all, not noticing even the fact that he is not happy.

One night he is suddenly called out to a farm some six leagues from Tostes to set Père Rouault's broken leg. The patient is a well-to-do farmer, a widower with an only daughter. The night trip on horseback, the surroundings of Les Bertaux (the name of the prosperous farm), Charles Bovary's arrival, his reception by the girl who is not at all a peasant, having received a polite education in a convent, the patient's behavior—all this is admirably described, rendered detail by detail as if we were on the spot: it could be Dutch, it could be Flemish, actually it is Norman. Bovary acquires the habit of visiting Les Bertaux, in fact he goes there more often than his patient requires, he keeps going back even after the latter has completely recovered. Without his realizing it, his visits to the farm have gradually become a need, a delightful interruption in his daily drudgery:

> On such days he would rise early, set off at a gallop, urge his horse; and when he was almost there he would dismount to dust his shoes on the grass, and put on his black gloves. He enjoyed the moment of arrival, the feel of the gate as it yielded against his shoulders; he enjoyed the rooster crowing on the wall, the farm boys coming to greet him. He enjoyed the barn and the stables; he enjoyed Monsieur Rouault, who would clap him in the palm of the hand and call him his "savior"; he enjoyed hearing Mademoiselle Emma's little sabots on the newly washed flagstones of the kitchen floor. With their high heels they made her a little taller; and when she walked in them ahead of him their wooden soles kept coming

up with a quick, sharp, tapping sound against the leather of her shoes.

She always accompanied him to the foot of the steps outside the door. If his horse hadn't been brought around she would wait there with him. At such moments they had already said good-bye, and stood there silent; the breeze eddied around her, swirling the stray wisps of hair at her neck or sending her apron strings flying like streamers around her waist. Once she was standing there on a day of thaw, when the bark of the trees in the farmyard was oozing sap and the snow was melting on the roofs. She went inside for her parasol and opened it. The parasol was of rosy iridescent silk, and the sun pouring through it painted the white skin of her face with flickering patches of light. Beneath it she smiled at the springlike warmth; and drops of water could be heard falling one by one on the taut moiré.

Can there be a fresher, sharper picture, more effectively arranged and better lit, where recollection of classical form is better disguised in the modern manner? The sound of the drops of melting snow falling on the parasol reminds us of the drops of ice tinkling as they fall from the twigs onto the withered leaves in William Cowper's "Winter Walk at Noon." One precious quality distinguishes M. Gustave Flaubert from the other more or less exact observers who in our time pride themselves on conscientiously reproducing reality, and nothing but reality, and who occasionally succeed: he has *style*. He even has a trifle too much, and his pen delights in certain curiosities and minutiae of continuous description which at times injure the total effect. The things or the persons who should be kept most prominently in view are a little dimmed or flattened by the excessive projection of surrounding persons and things. Mme. Bovary herself, so charming when she first appears as Mlle. Emma, is so often described to us in minute detail that I cannot visualize her physically as whole, at least not clearly and distinctly.

The first Mme. Bovary dies, and Mlle. Emma becomes the second and only Mme. Bovary. The chapter describing the wedding at Les Bertaux is a finished, full, almost too full picture, utterly true to life, a mixture of the everyday and the Sunday best, of ugliness and stiffness, coarse fun and gracefulness, of bombast and sensibility. The wedding, the visit to the Château La Vaubyessard and the ball which provides a sort of pendant to the wedding, and the whole scene of the agricultural show which comes later, are pictures which, if they were painted with the brush as they are written, would be worthy of hanging in a gallery beside the best genre paintings.

So Emma has become Mme. Bovary and has moved into the little house at Tostes. She occupies cramped quarters; there is a little garden, longer than it is wide, beyond which are open fields. She at once introduces order, cleanliness, and a certain elegance into the establishment. Her husband, who is bent on granting her every wish, buys a carriage, a secondhand buggy, so that she can take the air in it whenever she likes on the highway or in the surrounding countryside. For the first time in his life he is happy, and he feels it; busy all day with his patients, when he comes home at night he is ecstatic with joy: he is in love with his wife. He asks no more of life than that his peaceful domestic happiness should last. But she, who has dreamed of better things, and as a young girl in moments of boredom had more than once wondered how happiness could be achieved, realizes fairly promptly, during the honeymoon, that she is not happy.

Now begins a deep, thorough, subtle analysis, a cruel dissection that ends only with the book. We are led step by step into Mme. Bovary's heart. What is she really like? She is a woman; at first she is merely romantic, she has not been in the least corrupted. As he limns her for us, M. Gustave Flaubert does not spare her. Describing her dainty ways as a little girl and at school with the nuns, and showing her as given to extravagant daydreams, he exposes her pitilessly, and—shall I confess it?—we feel more indulgent toward her than he himself seems to be. Emma is unable to adjust herself to her new situation because she has one quality too many and one virtue too few: therein lies the root of all her transgressions, all her unhappiness. The quality is that she not only is a romantic nature but also has emotional and intellectual needs and ambitions, that she aspires to a higher, more refined, more elegant life than the one that has fallen to her lot. The virtue she lacks is that she never learned that the first condition of a good life is ability to endure boredom. She has a vague sense of something missing, the feeling that life ought to be more pleasant, more to her taste, and she is unable to resign herself in silence without showing anything, to create for herself an interest, a protective armor, a goal, a way of spending her time whether in her love for her child or in making herself useful to those around her. To be sure, she struggles, she does not turn away from the straight and narrow in a day: before plunging into evil, she will make many an attempt over many years to keep her head. However, every day she comes one step closer to her destiny, and in the end she has gone astray beyond recovery. But I am making a dry summary, whereas the author of *Madame Bovary* shows us his character's thoughts and actions day by day, minute by minute.

Emma's long solitary melancholy days, when she is left to herself during the first months following her marriage, her walks to the avenue of beeches at Banneville, accompanied by Djali, her faithful greyhound bitch, the days during which she questions herself endlessly concerning fate and imagines what *might have been*—all this has been seen clearly and set down with the same analytical keenness, the same subtlety as can be found in older novels portraying people's intimate lives, the novels that set us dreaming. Impressions of rural nature, just as in the days of *René* or *Obermann,* are mingled with sudden uprushes of capriciousness, spiritual boredom, and uncertain desires:

> Sometimes squalls blew up, winds that suddenly swept in from the sea over the plateau of the *pays de Caux* and filled the countryside with fresh, salt-smell-

ing air. The whistling wind would flatten the reeds
and rustle the trembling beech leaves, while the tops
of the trees swayed and murmured. Emma would
pull her shawl close about her shoulders and get up.

Under the double row of trees a green light filtered
down through the leaves onto the velvety moss that
crunched softly beneath her feet. The sun was setting;
the sky showed red between the branches; and the
identical trunks of the straight line of trees were like
a row of brown columns against a golden backdrop; a
terror would seize her, she would call Djali and walk
quickly back to Tostes along the highway. There she
would sink into an armchair and sit silent all evening.

It is about this time that a neighbor, the Marquis d'An-
dervilliers, who is campaigning for political office, gives a
grand bal at his château and invites all the important
and influential people of the region. He had by chance
made the acquaintance of Bovary when, no other doctor
being available, the latter had one day cured him of a
mouth abscess. During a trip to Tostes the marquis had
caught a glimpse of Mme. Bovary and had judged her
sufficiently presentable to be asked to the ball. Hence the
visit of the Bovarys to the Château La Vaubyessard. This
is one of the principal passages in the book, and one of the
most skillfully treated.

That evening Emma is received with the courtesy that a
pretty young woman can expect anywhere. The moment
she comes in she breathes the fragrant air of elegant
aristocratic life which she had been dreaming about, and
to which she believes herself to have been born. That evening she dances the waltz; though she had never done so
before, she senses the right steps and manages very well.
Her success goes to her head and will contribute to her
undoing. She is as though poisoned by the atmosphere;
the poison will act slowly, but now that it is in her blood
it will never leave her. All the circumstances, even the
most trivial ones, of this memorable, unique evening remain engraved in her heart and will secretly be eating

away at it: "Her visit to La Vaubyessard had opened a breach in her life, like one of those great crevasses that a storm can tear across the face of a mountain in the course of a single night." The morning after the ball, the Bovarys leave La Vaubyessard; back home at dinner time, they look around their little establishment, the modest table set with a steaming tureen of onion soup and a platter of veal with sorrel. Bovary is happy, he rubs his hands together and says, "How good to be home!" She gives him a look of ineffable contempt. Her mind had traveled a long way since the day before, and her thoughts had been moving the other way. Leaving for the party in their buggy, they were merely very different from each other; now that they have come back, there is a gulf between them.

I am abridging here a story that takes up many pages and covers many years. In all fairness to Emma, we must grant that she takes her time. In her effort to be virtuous she looks for help both inside herself and around her. But inside herself she has one serious defect: she lacks heart; at an early date her imagination had taken over and had absorbed it all. And she is unlucky in still another way. Poor Charles, who loves her, and whom at moments she would like to try to love, is not bright enough to understand her, to sense what is going on within her. If only he were ambitious, if he were bent upon distinguishing himself in his profession, upon elevating himself by study and work, upon achieving reputation, esteem! But he is not like that: he has neither ambition nor curiosity, he has none of the incentives that make a man step out of his narrow round, get ahead, and make his wife proud of the name she bears before the whole world. She finds it all aggravating. "It's pathetic!" she exclaims. "What a booby he is!" Once humiliated by him, she will never forgive him.

Finally she comes down with a kind of illness, one known as "nerves," a kind of nostalgia or homesickness for the unknown. Charles, blindly devoted, tries everything to cure her and can think of nothing better than a change of air. To this end he leaves Tostes and the practice he has begun to build up, and settles in another part of Normandy, in the *arrondissement* of Neufchâtel, in a good-sized market town named Yonville-l'Abbaye. What has gone before was only a prelude to the novel; the real story does not begin until after the scene has shifted to Yonville. Now the action moves faster, still, however, to the accompaniment of the closest and most detailed analysis.

At the time of this change of residence Mme. Bovary is pregnant with her first and only child, a girl. The child introduces an element of relative stability in Emma's life, at least for a time, postponing her downfall and inspiring momentary fits of tenderness. Emma is poorly prepared to be a mother, for her heart has been ravaged by unfulfilled desires and barren ambitions. She is incapable of natural, selfless feeling.

The part of Normandy where the Bovarys now settle adjoins Picardy, "a mongrel region where the speech of the natives is as colorless as the landscape is lacking in character." Flaubert describes it truthfully and unflatteringly. The town and its principal inhabitants—the priest, the tax collector, the innkeeper, the sacristan, the notary, etc.—are taken straight from life and remain fixed in our memory. Among the busybodies with whom we now become acquainted, the pharmacist M. Homais stands out. He is a creation of the novelist, and attains the quality of a universal type. We have all met a M. Homais and know all about him, but never before in so rich and ripe a presentation. He is the self-important, influential small-town figure, full of ready-made phrases for every situation, vain, and convinced that he is above vulgar prejudices. Aggressively commonplace, a shrewd intriguer, M. Homais raises stupidity to an art. He is the M. Prudhomme of half-knowledge.

On the day of their arrival in Yonville, M. and Mme. Bovary stop at the Lion d'Or and meet some of the principal inhabitants. Among the regular patrons of the establishment is a M. Léon Dupuis, who works in the office of the local notary. His conversation with Mme. Bovary in the dining room is very well rendered, at once natural and yet essentially ironic. We can see how the two are attracted to each other precisely by what is least genuine in them. They share a taste for vague poetry and romantic novels, but these are a cover for coarse sensuality. They are just beginning to be acquainted, but this first conversation ought to give pause to readers who believe in "the poetry of the heart." The secret of such sentimental effusions is here given away: never again will one be able to take this sort of love dialogue seriously.

The novel does not develop as predictably as the reader might expect. The notary's clerk does make headway in Mme. Bovary's affections, but not so soon, not yet. For quite a while Emma remains an honest woman, although in her innermost heart she is treacherous and unfaithful. M. Léon is not much of a conquest; however, he is young, pleasant looking, and he thinks he is in love. At moments, she too thinks she is in love. What sustains their feeling for each other is the fact that they cannot be seen together very often; it is difficult for them to arrange to meet, and they are both timid people. Though no one gives her credit for it, Emma really does struggle against temptation. "What exasperated her was Charles's total unawareness of her ordeal." One day she tries to open her heart to the good curé, M. Bournisien, a vulgar, insensitive man who does not begin to come close to grasping the nature of her moral conflict. Fortunately M. Léon must leave town: he is to continue his law studies in Paris. The constrained parting is admirably rendered and analyzed: the unspoken grief, the way each of them conveys what they feel to be despair. Emma's regret will increase after their separation, as her imagination busies itself. An undercurrent of irony is sustained throughout.

The day the regional agricultural show opens is a great day for Yonville-l'Abbaye. This is the third great set piece in the novel, and of its kind it is perfect. Mme. Bovary's fate is decided at the fair. A few days earlier, M. Rodolphe Boulanger de la Huchette, a gentleman who lives near Yonville, a kind of squire, had seen Mme. Bovary when he brought along one of his peasants to her husband for a bloodletting. Very much a ladies' man, whose mind is

never wholly off the chase, he told himself that Mme.
Bovary had beautiful eyes and would do very well. The
day of the agricultural show he never leaves her side.
Though a member of the jury, he gives up his place on
the platform in order to be with her. There is a very piquant, well-handled scene. While a high official who represents the authority of the *département* is delivering a
speech solemnly treating of weighty economic, industrial,
political, and moral matters, Rodolphe, sitting with Mme.
Bovary in a window recess at the *mairie,* whispers into her
ear the words that had so often helped him to seduce other
daughters of Eve. The pompous, turgid speech, which the
author has seasoned with pathos, is regularly interrupted
by sentimental cooings that are basically no less banal than
the official oratory. The scene is extremely effective, and
the irony beautifully sustained. What follows is the most
natural thing in the world! Mme. Bovary had been able to
resist Léon, but her heart had been torn, and she has re-
pented having resisted so much. She yields at once to the
newcomer, a man fatuous enough to imagine his success
wholly due to his own irresistible wooing. The illogicalities
and unexpected reversals of feminine behavior are excel-
lently observed.

Once she has taken the decisive step, Mme. Bovary
makes up for lost time. She falls madly in love with Rodolphe and is quite ready to expose herself to public censure in order to be with him. I shall not dwell on the
rest of the plot in such close detail. There is the episode of
the clubfoot. Her husband is persuaded to perform an unwise operation and bungles it. From this point on M.
Bovary ceases to exist in Emma's respect and affection. In
her frenzy she reaches the point where she cannot bear a
single day away from Rodolphe and asks him to run away
with her. She tells him how happy they would be in a tiny
cottage somewhere in the woods or in a cabin by the sea.
There is a deeply moving scene when Bovary comes back
one night from his customary rounds and stands by his
daughter's cradle, dreaming about the future happiness of
his little Berthe (the poor man suspects nothing!). His

wife lies in bed pretending to be asleep; actually she is imagining how she will be carried away the very next morning by a stagecoach drawn by four horses to a life of romantic happiness and world travel—the Orient, Granada (the Alhambra), etc. The portrayal of these parallel yet utterly different trains of thought—the abused father innocently summoning up a domestic happiness he does not possess, and the beautiful adulterous wife ready to destroy everything—bespeaks an artist who, once he gets hold of a theme, knows how to make the most of it.

The novel contains many expressions taken directly from life, which are memorable. One night Rodolphe comes to call on Mme. Bovary, and they meet in the consulting room, always empty at this hour. They hear a noise; Emma asks, "Do you have your pistols?" The question makes him laugh. The only person he would have to shoot is her husband, and he certainly has no desire to do that. No matter, the words have been said. Mme. Bovary spoke without thinking, but she is one of those women who will stop at nothing when carried away by passion. Later, after Rodolphe has deserted her—he enjoyed her as a pretty neighbor but had no intention of ever running away with her—she once again encounters Léon, while on a trip to Rouen. Léon has seen a bit more of life and is no longer timid. She, meanwhile, has given in to her baser instincts, has ruined her home, and contracted debts without her husband's knowledge. One day, threatened with foreclosure, she does not know where to turn and asks Léon to get 3000 francs for her at once. She says to him: "If I were in your place I'd know where to find the money!"—"You would? Where?"—"In your office!" Murder, and now theft—the ultimate degradation. Mme. Bovary does not shrink from suggesting crime to her lovers. They are not men to act on such impulses, but it is right that we should be reminded of such dreadful possibilities. These are only words, but they have real carrying power.

The second half of the book is no less well handled and carefully composed than the first. I should like to point out a drawback, however, to the author's approach, which becomes apparent in the second half. To describe everything in exhausting detail and with the same emphasis has led him—surely inadvertently—to include scabrous details sufficiently vivid to risk arousing sensual emotions. In our opinion he should have stopped short of this. After all, a book is not and can never be reality itself. There is a point beyond which description defeats its own purpose. Not only the moralist, but all serious artists should keep this in mind. I am aware that M. Flaubert has remained very sharp and ironic even in his most risqué and daring passages; his tone is never indulgent or suggestive—actually his treatment repels rather than attracts. But he has not taken French readers sufficiently into account: born with a streak of malice, they are quite capable of injecting it into everything within their reach.

Mme. Bovary's atrocious end—her punishment, if you will—is presented and expounded in inexorable detail. The author has not played down the wretchedness of it all—he rasps our nerves. Charles' death, which follows closely on that of Emma, is touching and arouses interest in this poor good man. Above I mentioned that the book contains spontaneous expressions which are terrible in their truth. Charles is grief-stricken at losing his wife, concerning whose misdeeds he has deceived himself as much as he could. He cannot forget her, she is ever-present to him. When he receives the announcement of Léon's forthcoming wedding, he exclaims, "How happy my poor wife would have been!" A little later he runs across a packet of love letters to his wife from Léon and from Rodolphe. But he forgives her: he still loves the ungrateful, unworthy woman who was his wife, and dies of sorrow.

At certain moments and situations in this book, the author could easily have superimposed a coating of idealism over his implacable realism. By so doing he could have "patched up" a character and rounded it off—that of Charles Bovary, for example. A few more pats, and the clay the novelist was molding could have turned out a noble and touching figure instead of a vulgar one. The reader would not have complained—indeed, he all but begs him to do so. But the author refuses: he will not do it.

When Père Rouault comes to bury his daughter, for all his grief and despair he utters a characteristically peasant-like remark, as sublimely natural as it is grotesque under the circumstances. Every year he had been accustomed to send a turkey to Charles Bovary in gratitude for the latter's resetting of his leg. Now as he leaves his son-in-law with tears in his eyes, his parting words are a gruff, "Don't worry—you'll always get your turkey!"

Although I appreciate the author's point of view—the keystone of his method, his poetics—I must reproach his book for the fact that there is no goodness in it. Not a single character represents goodness. The only person capable of disinterested, silent love—little Justin, M. Homais' apprentice—barely counts. Why has the author failed to include a single character capable of comforting and soothing the reader by a good action? Why is there no sympathetic character? Why lay oneself open to the reproach, "You know all there is to know about human nature, but you are cruel?" To be sure the book has a moral, one which the author has by no means dragged into it and which the reader must discover for himself. It is a rather terrible moral. But is it the duty of art to refuse all consolation to the reader, to reject every element of clemency and kindness under the pretext of being more truthful? Even granting that truth alone is a worthy goal, truth does not lie entirely with wickedness, with stupidity and perversity. These provincial lives may well abound in bickering, minor persecutions, mean ambitions, and pettiness of every variety. But there are also good people, people who have retained their innocence, perhaps more intact and more genuine than elsewhere. Modesty, resignation, devotion extending over long years—who among us has not seen examples of these virtues in the provinces? No matter how true to life your characters may be, they reflect the author's choice: it is he who has skillfully arranged the pattern of their shortcomings and absurdities. Why not arrange a pattern of good qualities—show us at least one character who captivates us or earns our respect? I once knew, in the depths of a province in central France, a woman still young, superior in intelligence, ardent of heart, and bored. Married but not a mother, having no child of her own to educate and love, what did she do to occupy the overflow of her mind and soul? She adopted the children about her. She became a benefactress, a civilizing influence in the somewhat wild country in which fate had placed her. She taught children to read, instructed them in moral culture. The villages were often far distant; at times she went a league and a half on foot; her pupil walked as far; and meeting, they had their lessons beside a path, beneath a tree, on a heath. There are such souls as that in the provinces, in the country: why not depict them, as well? This is uplifting, comforting, and makes for a more complete picture of mankind.

Such are my objections to a book whose merits, however, I value very highly—observation, style (save a few blemishes), design, and composition.

In all its elements the work certainly bears the mark of its times. Begun, we are told, several years ago, it has come at the right moment. It is certainly the book to be read when you come away from the theater with the clear, pointed dialogue of a comedy by Alexandre Dumas *fils* or *Les Faux Bonshommes* ringing in your ears. It is a book to pick up between two articles by Taine. For in many quarters and under various forms, I believe I discern signs of a new literature, exhibiting a scientific approach, a spirit of observation, maturity, power, and a certain tendency to callousness. These seem to me characteristics of the leaders among the younger writers. Son and brother of eminent doctors, M. Gustave Flaubert wields the pen as others wield the scalpel. Anatomists and physiologists, you seem to be everywhere!

4 May 1857 (*Causeries du lundi*).

This article appeared shortly after the famous trial of *Madame Bovary*. Flaubert had been acquitted of the charge of offending public morals (though he had been reprimanded by the judge). In a letter to a friend Flaubert ironically commented that Sainte-Beuve's article was "just right for the bourgeois"—meaning that it provided *Madame Bovary* with a certificate of respectability.

Indeed, the essay, while less uncomprehending than that on Stendhal, is particularly stuffy-sounding. Perhaps that was Sainte-Beuve's intention—to do Flaubert a good turn while appearing himself as a champion of chastity and morality, qualities not overpresent in his own private life.

BAUDELAIRE

I

THERE WAS, once upon a time (for I am speaking only of the dead), a very honest little literary magazine,[1] with very honorable editors, which helped young authors by printing their essays and diverted its readers with their poems. Eventually, however, it was afflicted with the most common, most regrettable of all literary vices: toward the last, envy raised its voice, and one day my very integrity, my conscience as a writer was doubted. . . . Why? Because I had spoken of *Fanny*. "Among the critics," said the article in question, "one of the best informed, not the most conscientious, but the slyest. . . ." This was myself, personally, and the flattering portrait concluded: "He can glorify *Fanny*, this honest man! and keep silent about *Les Fleurs du mal*." It is true that about the time *Fanny* appeared, the author of this slanderous article published an anodyne, fairly pleasant little book, *Les Païens innocents*. I had noticed that it had a certain amount of wit, though of the kind that attempts more than it achieves, and that it was full of involved phraseology. Now, I did not say a word about it to the public, and the latter, incidentally, paid little attention to it. Hence the anger of M. Babou, who apparently believes that his name rather than Feydeau's deserves to be on everyone's lips, echoing far and wide.

As for *Les Fleurs du mal*, which the austere critic reproaches me for having kept silent about, you know the

[1] *La Revue française.*

imperious reasons that forbade us to analyze it (not to
mention the fact that Edouard Thierry published an excellent review of it). Baudelaire is one of the oldest among
those whom I call my "young" friends: he knows how
highly I prize his subtle mind and his curious, clever talent.
If I had discussed his book, however, he would not have
been spared advice, remonstrances, and even chidings; he
would have been subjected to a sermon. Occasionally, he
forgives me such sermons. I would have said to him: "Let
me give you one piece of advice, which may surprise those
who don't know you: you are too distrustful of passion—of
natural passion; it is a theory with you. You rely too much
on the intelligence, on thinking things out. Let yourself go,
don't be so afraid of being like everyone else, of being too
common; your expression will always be refined enough
to set you apart."

Still, I should not have wanted to appear more prudish
than I am, or than is fitting in one who perpetrated his own
youthful poems and has read the poets of every age. I
should have added frankly: "I like more than one piece in
your volume. *Les Tristesses de la lune*, for example, is a
pretty sonnet that could almost be the work of some English poet, a contemporary of the young Shakespeare. Even
the stanzas of *A celle qui est trop gaie* seem to be exquisitely done. Why is this piece not in Latin—or rather, in
Greek—and included under the heading 'Erotica' in the An-
thology? The learned Brunck would have given it a place in
his *Analecta veterarum poetarum;* the Président Bouhier
and La Monnoye, that is to say, men of authority and
unimpeachable morality (*castissimae vitae, morumque in-
tegerrimorum*) would have commented it without embarrassment, and we should set our own seal to it, signaling
it to lovers of poetry, with Horace's line, *Tange Chloen
semel arrogantem.*" I would have told him all that and
many other things, making allowance for the fact that he
as well as some others (like Bouilhet and Joséphin Soulary,
recent author of some very distinguished sonnets,) come
late, when the school to which they belong has already
given and produced so much, when it is exhausted, so to

speak, when the old voices of the past are falling silent, save for one great voice.[2] These and a few others are honorably carrying on the tradition, adorning the decline and final sunset of the Pléiade. . . .

II

. . . . When M. Baudelaire presented himself as a candidate, some asked whether he was intending a practical joke on the Academy, making a kind of epigram. Some wondered whether his real purpose was not to remind the Academy that it was high time it considered admitting Théophile Gautier, his teacher, a distinguished writer, clever in all the genres of diction. M. Baudelaire's name had to be spelled for more than one member of the Academy, completely ignorant of his existence. It is not as easy as you might suppose to prove to Academicians who belong to political circles that *Les Fleurs du mal* contains some pieces truly remarkable for their talent and their art, nor to explain to them that among the author's little prose poems *Le Vieux Saltimbanque* and *Les Veuves* are gems, and that, all told, M. Baudelaire has managed to build for himself, out at the very farthest point of a neck of land reputed uninhabitable and beyond the frontiers of known romanticism, a bizarre kiosk of his own, ornate and contorted, but at the same time dainty and mysterious. Here Edgar Poe is read, exquisite sonnets are recited, hashish is taken for the purpose of analyzing the experience afterward, and opium and every other more dangerous drug is served in cups of the most exquisite porcelain. This kiosk, of a singular marquetry construction, expresses a deliberately composite originality and for some time now has been calling attention to the farthest outpost, to the Kamchatka of romanticism. I call it *"la folie Baudelaire."* The author is content to have done something impossible, to have reached

2 Victor Hugo, in *La Légende des siècles.*

a point no one supposed it possible to go. Is this to say, however, when it has all been explained to the best of one's ability to somewhat surprised, highly respectable colleagues, that such curiosities, novelties, and refinements are to be looked upon as conditions for admissions to the Academy? Does the author himself seriously believe so? What is certain, is that M. Baudelaire gains by being seen: where one may expect to meet a strange eccentric, one finds oneself in the presence of a courteous, well-spoken, exemplary candidate, a very nice young man, who has a fine feeling for language and is entirely classical in his forms.

Two extracts, the first from "La Morale et l'Art," 20 February 1860 (_Causeries du lundi_) and the second from "Elections de l'Académie," 20 January 1862 (_Nouveaux lundis_).

Would Sainte-Beuve ever have spoken of Baudelaire had he not been publicly chastised for his silence? He never devoted a full article to him; the two excerpts here translated are his only references. His language in his reply to the editor of _La Revue française_ suggests a certain embarrassment. When he says that there were "imperious reasons" for his silence, he obviously refers to the judicial condemnation of certain poems in _Les Fleurs du mal;_ but perhaps the silence was due also to a more personal reason, namely his consciousness of never having achieved greatness as a poet, for as the excerpt shows he was not insensitive to Baudelaire's power. He grudgingly admits his originality, but relegates him to Kamchatka—that is, the very limit of Siberia: there could be no clearer way of telling us that he does not want this new young poet close by. He also relegates him in time, speaking of him as though he were a survival, a last flicker from the dying embers of Romanticism.

As for the novel *Fanny*, the best work by Feydeau, even though no longer read, Sainte-Beuve spoke for his generation in devoting a *Lundi* to the moral problems of the "classical triangle"; but here too his personal interest, his experience with Adèle Hugo, may have influenced his judgment.

One is tempted to generalize: the striking contrast between Sainte-Beuve's judgments of older authors, which are so keen and illuminating, and his judgments of his contemporaries, which are almost always askew, reflects the presence of a disturbing subjective element in the latter case, and its absence in the former. Sainte-Beuve was aware of being influenced by personal motives; he also knew that this is one of the worst sins of a critic; but all too often his resentments carried the day in his reviews.

ON SAINTE-BEUVE'S METHOD

I HAVE often heard the reproach made to modern criticism, especially my own, that it has no theory to speak of, that it is entirely historical, entirely individual. Those who are most favorably disposed to me have been kind enough to say that I am a fairly good judge, but a judge without a code. However, I do have a method; and although I did not give it an a priori theoretical formulation, it took shape as I practiced my criticism, and I have found it confirmed by a long series of applications.

Beginning with my very first critical essays, I instinctively came upon this method. At a very early date it was already as though natural to me; and for years I have always followed it, varying it according to the subject treated. It never occurred to me to make a secret of it or to claim it as my discovery. No doubt it is related in some respects to M. Taine's method, but differs from it in others. It has been continually misunderstood by objectors who have regarded me as the most skeptical and wavering of critics, and as a mere entertainer. None of those has ever suspected the existence of the body of observations and positive principles that I shall now try to outline.

Literature, literary production, as I see it, is not distinct or separable from the rest of mankind's character and activity. I may enjoy a work, but it is hard for me to judge it independently of my knowledge of the man who produced it, and I am inclined to say, *tel arbre, tel fruit*—the fruit is like the tree. Thus the study of literature leads me naturally to the study of human nature.

In the case of the older writers, our information is inadequate. In most instances, we cannot reconstruct the man from his writings; especially is this the case with the truly ancient authors, those of whom we possess only mutilated statues. We are thus reduced to commenting on the work, to admiring it; we can only imagine the author, the poet, behind it. In this way we can reconstruct busts of poets or philosophers—torsos, even, in the case of a Plato, a Sophocles, or a Virgil—and endow them with lofty ideals. But this is as far as we can go in view of the incompleteness of our knowledge, the scantiness of the sources, the poverty of our information, and the difficulty of encompassing the historical background. A broad river, too deep to be crossed at most points, separates us from the great men of antiquity. We must be content to salute them from the hither shore.

The situation is entirely different in the case of the moderns, and the critic who adapts his method to his means has other duties here. To know another man, and to know him well, particularly if he is a prominent or famous man, is a great thing, not to be scorned.

Our study of human nature is still at the data-gathering stage; at best, we have descriptions of individuals and of a few types. Theophrastus and La Bruyère go no further. However, a day will come—I believe I have discerned its coming in the course of my observations—when a science of human nature will be constituted, and the great orders and species of minds will be sorted out. Then, on the basis of a mind's principal characteristics, it will be possible to deduce several others.[1] No doubt it will never be possible to achieve in the case of man what can be achieved in the case of animals and plants: human nature is more complex. It possesses what is called "freedom," and this always presupposes a great mobility of possible combinations.[2] How-

[1] "There is, in a character, a certain necessity, certain internal connections, such that a given principal trait implies given secondary traits." Goethe, *Conversations with Eckermann*.

[2] "Everything is to be found in this world, and the variety of combinations is inexhaustible." Grimm, *Correspondance littéraire*.

ever that may be, I imagine that eventually the science of the moralist will be constituted on a broader foundation; today it is at the stage where botany was before Jussieu and comparative anatomy before Cuvier—it is still anecdotal, as it were. What we achieve is mere monographs, detailed observations; yet I sense the presence of connections and relationships; and a more comprehensive, more luminous understanding, with a sharp eye for detail, will one day be able to discover the great natural divisions in which the various families of minds belong.

However, even once the science of minds has been organized along the lines here adumbrated, it will always be so delicate and so intricate a matter that only those with a natural vocation and talent for observation will be able to make much of it. It will remain an *art* requiring a skillful artist, just as medicine requires medical tact in the man who practices it, as philosophy should require philosophical tact in those who call themselves philosophers, as poetry is accessible only to poets.

Thus I conceive of someone possessing such talent, being able to make out groups or families of writers (for we are dealing with literature), being able, indeed, to make them out almost at first sight and capable of grasping their spirit and their life. To such a one this would be his true vocation; he would be a good naturalist in the vast domain of the human spirit.

Suppose we set out to study a superior man, or merely a man distinguished by his productions, a writer whose works we have read, and who is worth the trouble of being examined thoroughly. How should we go about it so as not to omit anything important or essential, and to progress farther than the old theoreticians, not being taken in by conventional phrases and fine sentiments? How can we arrive at the truth, as we do in the study of nature?

It is very useful to begin at the beginning and, whenever possible, to place the superior or distinguished writer in his own country, among his own people. If we knew his lineage thoroughly, physiologically speaking, including his remoter ancestors, we should gain much light on the essential hidden quality of his mind, but these deeper roots

most often remain obscure and elusive. Whenever they do
not escape us completely, we gain a great deal by observing them.

We surely recognize the superior man, at least in part,
in his parents, especially in his mother, the more immediate
and more certain parent; also in his sisters, in his brothers,
even in his children. In all these we encounter essential
traits which, in the great individual himself, are often
masked by being too condensed or too closely welded; his
own substance may appear more visibly, in a less complex
state, in others of his blood: nature herself has performed
the analysis. This is a very delicate matter, and needs to be
clarified by reference to actual persons and particular
facts. I shall mention a few.

Take sisters, for instance. Chateaubriand had two sisters.
According to him, one of them possessed imagination, but
it was superimposed upon an underlying stupidity, and
must have come close to pure extravagance. His other
sister, on the contrary, was divine (Lucile, the Amélie of
René). She possessed an exquisite sensibility and an affectionate, melancholy sort of imagination, without the sometimes compensating, and sometimes exaggerated features
that characterized Chateaubriand's own imagination. She
died insane, by her own hand. The elements which, at least
in his talent, were combined and linked and kept in a certain balance, were separated and disproportionately divided between his sisters.

I never met the sisters of M. de Lamartine, but I remember what M. Royer-Collard, who knew them, once said
about them—that in their early youth they were charming
and melodious, like a nest of nightingales. The striking
physical likeness between Balzac and his sister, Mme.
Surville, gives those who (like me) rightly or wrongly
withhold their full admiration from the famous novelist, a
somewhat more favorable idea of him: we are enlightened,
reassured, and reconciled. Julie, the sister of Beaumarchais,
whom M. Loménie revealed to us, certainly evokes her
brother by her propensity for gaiety and mockery, her
lively, pungent humor and irresistible flashes of wit, which

occasionally led her to the bounds of decency, if not beyond. This jolly, amiable woman died almost with a song on her lips: there can be no doubt that she was a sister of Figaro, his own flesh and blood.[3]

The same is true of brothers. Boileau-Despréaux, the satirist, had an older brother who was also a satirist, though somewhat platitudinous and vulgar; another brother, a canon, was very gay, clever in conversation, and highly spirited, but a bit grotesque, a little too elaborate in his humor. In Boileau, nature combined the features of his two brothers, but with refinement and distinction, and sprinkled the whole with a saltiness worthy of Horace. However, to those who are inclined to doubt Boileau's fertility and essential spontaneity, who deny him natural verve and see in him only cultivation, it may be not inappropriate to indicate those features of his background.

Mme. de Sévigné, as I have often pointed out, seems to have divided herself as between her two children: the lightheaded, scatterbrained chevalier, who possessed grace, and Mme. de Grignan, intelligent but somewhat cold, who inherited her mother's rationality. The mother had everything: no one contests her grace, but to those who would deny her seriousness and rationality it is good to show Mme. de Grignan, who was rationality personified, in all its solemnity and self-importance. In addition to what we find in Mme. de Sévigné's writings, this reminder is helpful and keeps us from being led astray.

Similarly, in our own day, the daughters of certain poets who died some years ago have helped me gain a better understanding and a more accurate picture of their fathers. At times I felt that I recognized in them their fathers' enthusiasm, warmth, and other qualities in a pure and integral state—preserved in virtue, as it were.[4]

That is sufficient to indicate my idea, and I shall not in-

---

[3] *Beaumarchais et son temps,* by M. de Loménie (V. I, pp. 36–52).

[4] For example, the countess of Fontanes, canoness, daughter of the poet.

sist on it. Once we have learned as much as possible about
the origins of an eminent writer, his parents and nearest
relatives, an essential point to be determined, after examin-
ing his education and studies, is his first *milieu,* the group
of friends and contemporaries among whom he was living
when his talent first manifested itself, took shape, and
matured. Whatever his subsequent achievements, he will
always show the influence of this early group.

Since I often use the term "group," it may be useful to
define the sense in which I do so. By "group" I do not
mean the fortuitous, artificial assemblage of men of parts,
but the natural and as it were spontaneous association of
young minds and young talents—not necessarily similar,
but of the same "flight" and the same spring, come to
flower under the same sun, who feel themselves to be born,
with variations of taste and vocation, for a common task.
Thus the little company of Boileau, Racine, La Fontaine,
and Molière about 1664, at the beginning of the *grand
siècle:* here you have the group par excellence—all geniuses! Thus, in 1802, at the beginning of the nineteenth
century, the set that included Chateaubriand, Fontanes,
Joubert. . . . Judging by the quality of their minds, this
latter group, too, was not weak, not to be scorned. To cite
not only French examples, there was the group of young
students and young poets at Göttingen in 1770, who published the *Almanac of the Muses*—Bürger, Voss, Hölty,
Stolberg, etc. Or in Edinburgh in 1800, the circle of critics
headed by Jeffrey, out of which came the famous *Review*
over which he presided. Speaking of an association to
which Thomas Moore had belonged as a young man at
the University of Dublin, a judicious critic wrote: "Every
time an association of young men is animated by a generous breath and feels called upon to accomplish great things,
its members stimulate and fertilize one another by private
associations. The professor at his desk communicates only
dead knowledge; the living spirit, the one that will constitute the intellectual life of a nation and an epoch, we
are more apt to find in young enthusiasts who gather to-

gether to discuss their discoveries, their hopes, and anticipations."[5]

I shall not elaborate on similar examples in our own day. The critical circle of the *Globe* around 1827, the poetic group of the *Muse française* in 1824, the *Cénacle* in 1828 are well known. None of the talents, then young, who belonged to one of these groups has passed through it without being affected by it. Therefore I say that in order to gain insight into a talent it is useful to determine the first poetic or critical center in which he was formed, the natural literary group to which he belongs, and to relate him to it exactly. That will supply the true date of his beginnings.

Very great individuals dispense with groups: they serve as centers themselves, people gather around them. But it is the group, the association or alliance, with its active exchange of ideas and spirit of perpetual emulation in the presence of one's equals, that provides a man of talent with his outward setting, all his development, and all his value. There are talents who belong to several groups, who never stop traveling through successive milieus, perfecting themselves, being transformed, or being deformed. In such cases of shifting affiliations, of slow or sudden conversions, it is important to note the hidden and constant spring, the persistent motive force.

Every work of an author seen in this way, after it has been situated in its framework and studied in the light of all the circumstances that attended its birth, takes on its full meaning—historical and literary—and discloses its true degree of originality, novelty, or imitation; and in judging it we do not run the risk of admiring it for qualities it does not possess, of missing the mark, as is inevitable when we are guided solely by rhetorical considerations.

This is not to imply that I reject rhetoric entirely, nor do I exclude judgments based on taste, on sharp, immediate impressions. I do not renounce Quintilian, I merely

[5] M. Fourcade, *Revue des Deux Mondes*, February 15, 1853.

assign him his proper place.[6] We should apply Bacon's method to the history of literature and to criticism; this seems to me a need of our epoch, and an excellent way of achieving greater sureness of judgment and greater enjoyment.

Criticism based on a first reading, on first impressions, will always be important, as well as the opinions of the fashionable and academic criticism. Such passion for thoroughness, as all this implies, is no cause for alarm: there are times and places for it, as well as times and places where it would be inappropriate. Laboratory methods are unsuitable for solemn celebrations and for certain publics. Academic or public speakers are obliged to show society and literature in a favorable light, stressing the sunny side. It is not indispensable nor perhaps very useful that the men whose function is to display and eloquently praise beautiful hangings and tapestries should look too closely at what lies underneath, or on the other side. This would be embarrassing.

However, analysis involves a kind of emotion, too; indeed, one might say that it has an eloquence of its own and even a poetic quality. Those who know a writer of talent and appreciate him only when he has been fully developed, or in his last works, who did not see him in his youth, at the moment when he first took wing, will never form a complete and natural idea of him, the only living kind. Vauvenargues gracefully expressed the pleasure an author takes in his first success, in a happy youthful debut: "The first light of dawn is not as sweet as the first smile of fame." Similarly, for the critic who studies a talent, there is no greater pleasure than to surprise it in its first fire, its first flights, to catch it in early morning, in all the freshness of youth. For the art lover and man of taste, the first state of a portrait is far more precious than anything that comes after. I know of no sweeter delight for the critic than to understand and describe a young talent, in

[6] "The knowledge of minds is criticism's charm; the defense of good rules is but its practical, utilitarian side." (Joubert.)

all its dewy freshness, all its directness and spontaneity, before acquired, perhaps artificial, elements have found their way into his works.

O first and fertile hour from which all else follows! O ineffable moment! It is among men of the same age and of the same period, or approximately, that the budding author most often chooses his companions, his witnesses, his emulators—also his rivals and adversaries for most of the rest of his career. Everyone creates his own "opposite number" and sets up his favorite target. There are rivalries, challenges, and fallings out between equals or near-equals, which can last a lifetime. But still, if we should find ourselves being outdone, to some extent, let us never desire a contemporary's failure and departure from the scene, even though he be a rival whom we look upon as an enemy. For if we possess true value, it may well be he who, if need be and as the occasion arises, will inform a new upstart generation of young insolents that we are an old fighter not to be scorned, not to be treated lightly. This is a matter of legitimate pride, for he who once pitted his strength against our own, knew us when we were at our best. Let me clothe my thought with illustrious names. Cicero, of all people, paid the noblest tribute to Hortensius. A saying by Aeschines has remained the finest eulogy of Demosthenes. And Diomedes, the Greek hero, speaking of Aeneas in Virgil, meaning to exalt him, said, "Take the word of a man who measured his strength against his!"

Nothing gives us as good an idea of a man's range and elevation as to see what antagonist, what rival, he chose at an early date. One serves as measure of the other. Calpe is as high as Abyla.

But if it is important to gain insight into an author at the moment of his first efforts, his first flowering, when he appears fully formed and more than adolescent, when he comes of age, there is also a second moment no less crucial, which must be noted if we are to grasp him as a whole—the moment when he weakens, disintegrates, declines, departs from his own norm. Choose the least shocking, the gentlest words when chronicling this moment, for it is one that comes to almost everyone. I shall refrain from giving examples, but in the majority of the literary careers we have studied, there is a moment when the maturity one hoped for fails to materialize, or, if it has been attained, it overshoots its mark, and the very excess of quality becomes a defect. Some writers stiffen and dry up, while others become careless. Some harden and grow heavy, while others sour; the smile freezes into a grimace. Next to the first moment when a writer's early promise flowers in his superb youth, we must pay most attention to this second, sad moment when it grows deformed and alters with age.

"Your talent has never been younger" is a compliment frequently paid in our day to those who are aging. Do not listen too much to such flatterers; a moment always comes when the age one has within is betrayed without. It must be granted, however, that in this respect there are great differences among talents and according to the genre practiced. Poetry and drama are like war: some men have only a single day, one shining hour, one victory, which remains associated with their names—and nothing else they do resembles it. They are like Augereau, who would have done better to die after Castiglione. Others have many successes of variable quality that are repeated season after season. As a rule, fifteen years fills out a career; to some it is granted to double this, to begin or even complete a second career. There are moderate genres for which old age is especially suitable—memoirs, recollections, criticism, a kind of poetry that comes close to prose; those who are wise will confine themselves to such works when they are old. Without taking the precept, *Solve senescentem . . .* too literally, without subsiding into inactivity—something an old man should do as late as possible—let him rather slow down gradually. It is the more becoming way. Certain exceptional minds, after long remaining incomplete or uneven, have seemed to improve with age and were never better than in their last years—such as Bonstetten, that amiable Swiss Voltaire, or Ducis, that quarter-genius. But these are exceptions to the rule.

There are never too many ways to go about learning to

know a man—man is a complex creature, by no means a pure spirit. What were his religious ideas? How was he affected by the spectacle of nature? How did he behave toward women? What was his attitude toward money? Was he rich, poor? What was his routine, his daily life? Finally, what was his vice or weakness? Every man has one. None of these questions is immaterial when it comes to judging the author of a book or the book itself (unless it is a treatise of pure geometry)—above all, if it is a literary work, for no aspect of human life is alien to literature.

Very often, an author, when writing, throws himself into the excess or affectation directly opposed to his vice or secret penchant, so as to disguise it, to conceal it. But this is still a perceivable, recognizable effect, however indirect and masked. It is too easy to take the opposite course to anything—we are only turning our defects upside down. Nothing is so like a hollow as a bulge.

Just as one may change one's opinions many times in one's life without changing one's character, so a writer may change his genre without necessarily altering his manner. Most talents have but a single technique, which they merely transpose when they change subjects, or even when they move to a different genre. Superior minds tend to put their seal on the corner of every page they write; others seem to be using a mold, into which everything they do falls indiscriminately, over and over again.

Up to a certain point it is possible also to study talents through their spiritual descendants, their disciples and natural admirers. Affinities may be acknowledged freely or betrayed inadvertently. The genius is a sovereign who creates his own people. Apply this to Lamartine, to Hugo, to Michelet, to Balzac, to Musset. Enthusiastic admirers are a little like accomplices: they worship themselves, with all their own qualities and defects, in their great representative. Tell me who admires and loves you, and I will tell you who you are. However, you must not confuse a writer's genuine public with the throng of vulgar admirers who merely repeat what their neighbors say.

The disciples who imitate the genre and the taste of

their model when they write are interesting to study, and they often illuminate him for us. As a rule the disciples caricature or parody the master without suspecting it; in the elegant schools they weaken him; in the picturesque or crude schools, they force him, push him to excess, and exaggerate him: they are magnifying mirrors. There are moments, however, when the disciple is warm and sincere, and we can actually mistake one for the other—as when we are tempted to exclaim, parodying the ancient epigram: "O Chateaubriand! O Salvandy! Which of the two has imitated the other?" Change the names, replace them with more modern ones, if you will: the epigram is eternal.

When the master is careless and the disciple spruce and wearing his Sunday best, the two can resemble each other; the days when Chateaubriand works shoddily and Marchangy does the best he can, there is a false similarity; from behind, at a distance, by moonlight, they cannot be told apart.

Not all disciples are necessarily copies and counterfeits; not all compromise the model. Some actually remove doubts we may have, unmistakably demonstrating their master's worth. This is what M. Littré did for Auguste Comte. Even in literature I could name admirers and disciples of such or such a daring talent who clarify him for me, and who teach me to respect the man whom I might have treated more lightly without them.

If it is right to judge a talent by his friends and natural followers, it is no less legitimate to verify one's judgment by the enemies he makes without intending to, those who are antipathetic to him or those who instinctively cannot suffer him. Nothing serves better to mark the limits of a talent, to circumscribe his sphere and domain, than to know exactly at what point revolt against him begins. In actual life this can be piquant to watch: in the domain of Letters there are people who detest one another all their lives, without ever having met. Such antagonisms merely reflect unbridgeable differences between intellectual types, differences of blood, of temperament, of early upbringing.

An excerpt from *Chateaubriand jugé par un ami intime en 1803*, 21 and 22 July 1862. (*Nouveaux lundis.*)

These are the pages Proust singles out for anathema in his *Contre Sainte-Beuve*, criticizing him for his emphasis on analysis at the expense of intuition.

The essay certainly invites attack if only for its pedestrian tone and looseness of organization (the latter is more apparent in the complete original text). Nevertheless, being Sainte-Beuve's only direct statement of his approach, it is often included in French anthologies and has considerable documentary interest. Whether Sainte-Beuve actually followed this method which he expounds is something else again. Statements by artists—and Sainte-Beuve is unquestionably a literary artist—about their ways of working can often be misleading. Perusal of this essay alone might leave one with the impression that as a critic Sainte-Beuve's main interest lay in studying a writer's inherited traits, upbringing, early influences, etc. Actually—as we trust the reader has seen for himself—these considerations play a subordinate role in his criticism, serving mainly to confirm or illustrate insights obtained from a close study of the works themselves.

BIOGRAPHICAL INDEX

Addison, Joseph (1672–1719). English essayist. 10

Aeschines (389–314 B.C.). Athenian orator, opposed Demosthenes; advocated appeasement policy with Philip of Macedon. 307

Aeschylus (525–456 B.C.). Greek tragic dramatist. 5, 67, 81

Alary, Pierre-Joseph, Abbé (1689–1770). Economist, founder in 1724 of a club for the discussion of economic reforms (*Le Club de l'Entresol*). The group was dissolved by order of Cardinal Fleury (q.v.). 158

Alembert, Jean le Rond d' (1717–1783). Natural son of Mme. de Tencin (q.v.), who abandoned him on the steps of the church St. Jean le Rond; author of scientific and philosophical essays; co-editor of the *Encyclopédie*. 146, 147, 149, 155, 158–60, 168, 169, 175, 177

Ampère, Jean-Jacques-Antoine (1800–1864). Son of the famous scientist; essayist and poet; author of *Histoire Romaine à Rome*. 240, 251

Ancelot, *née* Marguerite Charon (d. 1875). Playwright and novelist, wife of dramatist Jacques-Arsène Ancelot (1794–1854), who was a member of French Academy. 241, 255

Andrieux, François-Guillaume-Jean Stanislas (1759–1833). Poet and playwright, author of *Le Meunier Sans-Souci* (1797). 8

Anne (1665–1714). Queen of Great Britain and Ireland (1702–1714). 6

Anne of Austria (1601–1666). Daughter of Philip III of Spain, wife of Louis XIII, mother of Louis XIV; Queen Regent (1643–1661). 131

Argental, Charles-Augustin de Ferriol, Comte d' (1700–1788). Nephew of Mme. de Tencin, friend of Voltaire. 146

Ariosto, Lodovico (1474–1533). Italian poet; author of *Orlando Furioso* (1532). 10, 14, 28, 71, 231

Aristarchus (220?–150 B.C.). Alexandrian grammarian and critic, editor of *Iliad* and *Odyssey;* his name has become synonymous with critical severity. 267

Aristophanes (448?–380 B.C.). Athenian writer of comedies. 99

Aristotle (384–322 B.C.). Greek philosopher. 83, 112, 113

Arnaud, François, Abbé (1721–1784). Man of letters, contributor to literary journals; member of French Academy. 160

Arnauld, Antoine (1612–1694). "Le Grand Arnauld," theologian, vigorous polemical writer, adversary of Jesuits; one of the leaders of Port-Royal, author of several treatises, co-author with Nicole (q.v.) and Lancelot of *Logique de Port-Royal.* 16, 77

Arnauld d'Andilly, Robert (1589–1674). Lawyer, retired to Port-Royal in 1664; theological writer, translator of St. Augustine, Josephus, etc. 136

Arnim, Bettina von (1785–1850). Sister of German poet and dramatist Clemens Brentano, correspondent of Goethe. 269

Arnold, Matthew (1822–1888). English poet and critic. ix

Auger, Louis-Simon (1772–1829). Essayist, critic, editor of French classics; secretary of French Academy. 236

Augereau, Pierre-François-Charles, Duc de Castiglione (1757–1816). Marshal of France; distinguished himself by his courage at Lodi, Castiglione, and at the bridge of

Arcole; abandoned Napoleon in 1814, offered to rejoin him in 1815, but was rejected; subsequently rejected also by Louis XVIII. 308

Augustine, Saint (354–430). Church father and philosopher. 139

Aulus Gellius (123?–165?). Latin critic, author of *Noctes Atticae*, which contains fragments of Cato, Menander, and other authors whose works have not come down to us. 2

Babou, Hippolyte (1824–1878). Man of letters, author of *Les Prisonniers du Deux Décembre*, an interesting account of the coup d'état of 1851. 293

Bacon, Francis (1561 1626). English philosopher. 306

Balbo, Cesare (1789–1853). Italian historian and statesman, one of the founders of Risorgimento. 245

Balzac, Honoré de (1799–1850). Novelist. ix, 223, 241, 248, 249, 257–74, 302, 309

Balzac, Jean-Louis Guez, Seigneur de (c. 1597–1654). Writer of letters and essays; Malherbe's counterpart in the realm of prose. 29, 135, 143

Barbier-d'Aucourt, Jean (1635–1694). Lawyer; author of pamphlets against Jesuits; critic. 76

Baron, Michel (1653–1729). Actor; disciple and friend of Molière, author of seven comedies published in 1759. 122–24

Basil, St. (c. 329–379). Church father. 70

Baudelaire, Charles (1821–1867). Poet. x, 293–97

Bayle, Pierre (1647–1706). Philosopher, critic, historian; champion of religious tolerance; precursor of Age of Reason. 19, 22, 166

Beaumarchais, Pierre-Augustin Caron de (1732–1799). Playwright, author of *Le Mariage de Figaro*. 88, 89, 118, 302

Beaumont, Pauline-Marie, *née* de Montmorin, Comtesse de (1768–1803). Admirer of Chateaubriand. 248 n

Beauvau, Charles-Juste de (1720–1793). Distinguished soldier, governor of Languedoc (1763) and of Provence (1782). 160

Beethoven, Ludwig van (1770–1827). German composer. 232

Beffara, Louis-François (1751–1838). Author of studies on Molière and other dramatists. 103

Béjart, Armande (1642–1700). Actress, wife of Molière (from 1662). 116

Béjart, Madeleine (1618–1672). Sister of preceding, actress in Molière's company. 104, 106, 116, 117–18

Bellerose, Pierre le Messier (d. 1670). Actor in the theater of the Hôtel de Bourgogne; created the part of Cinna in Corneille's play. 104

Benserade, Isaac (1613–1691). Poet, author of the sonnet *Job*, which touched off a literary quarrel between his partisans and those of Voiture (q.v.); author of the sonnet *Uranie*. 132, 140

Béranger, Pierre-Jean de (1780–1857). Popular author of chansons. 64

Bernard, Charles de (1804–1850). Novelist, author of *La Femme de quarante ans*. 266

Bernardin de Saint-Pierre, Jacques-Henri (1737–1814). Essayist, novelist, author of *Paul et Virginie*. 213, 276

Bettina. *See* Arnim, Bettina von

Beyle, Henri. *See* Stendhal

Boccaccio Giovanni (1313–1375). Italian writer, author of the *Decameron*. 10

Boethius, Anicius Manlius Severinus (c. 480–524). Roman philosopher, translator of Aristotle; his best-known work is *The Consolation of Philosophy*, which he wrote in prison while awaiting execution. 2

Boileau-Despréaux, Nicolas (1636–1711). Poet and critic. 3, 8, 9, 67, 74, 75–78, 95, 101, 102, 107, 111, 115, 121, 122, 127, 130, 143, 193, 275, 303, 304

Bolingbroke, Henry St. John (1678–1751). English statesman and essayist. 6

Bonald, Louis-Gabriel-Ambroise, Vicomte de (1754–1840). Philosopher and political writer, champion of conservatism. 265, 269

Bonstetten, Charles-Victor de (1745–1832). Swiss essayist. 308

Bossuet, Jacques-Bénigne (1627–1704). Bishop of Meaux; preacher, author of theological, philosophical, and historical works. 84, 96, 102, 125, 139, 140, 143, 227

Boucher, François (1703–1770). Painter. 168

Bouhier, Jean (1673–1746). Magistrate, scholar, author of works on law and history; prolific but mediocre poet. 294

Bouilhet, Louis-Hyacinthe (1822–1869). Poet and dramatist; friend of Flaubert. 294

Bourdaloue, Louis (1632–1704). Jesuit preacher. 140, 268

Bouteville, François, Comte de Montmorency (1600–1627). Governor of Senlis; notorious duellist, fled to Brussels after killing the Marquis Desportes, the Count de Thorigny and La Frette; in defiance of Louis XIII's decree outlawing duels, returned to Paris to fight in broad daylight against the Marquis de Beuvron while his cousin Des Chapelles took on Bussy-d'Amboise. The two cousins were arrested by order of Richelieu and executed. 39, 132

Boyer, Claude, Abbé (1618–1698). Preacher, author of mediocre plays and pastorals; ridiculed by Boileau and Racine; admitted to the French Academy in 1666. 76, 90

Brancas, Charles de Villars, Comte de (1618–1681). Distinguished soldier, noted for absent-mindedness. 134

Brécourt, Guillaume Marcoureau, Sieur de (d. 1685). Actor in Molière's company, later at the theater of the Hôtel de Bourgogne; author of six comedies. 118

Brie, Catherine Leclerc, Mlle. de (d. 1706). Actress in Molière's company. 106, 117

Brosses, Charles de (1709–1777). Président (presiding

magistrate) at the Parlement of Bourgogne; scholar, author of witty *Lettres familières écrites d'Italie en 1739 et 1740*, and works on history, linguistics and ethnology. 145, 148–62, 231

Brunck, Richard-François-Philippe (1729–1803). Philologist, published critical editions of Greek and Latin classics. 294

Buchanan, George (1506–1582). Poet and historian; obliged to flee his native Scotland for having satirized Franciscans, spent some time in France; after return to England, tutor to James II; author of two Latin tragedies. 14

Buffon, George-Louis Leclerc de (1707–1788). Author of *Discours sur le Style, Epoques de la Nature,* and (with others) of the monumental *Histoire de la Nature.* 3, 194, 200, 207, 261

Bürger, Gottfried August (1747–1794). German romantic poet, author of famous ballads. 304

Burigny, Jean Lévesque de (1692–1785). Historian; author of a history of Russia and of biographies of Erasmus, Grotius, Bossuet, etc. 168, 171

Bussy-Rabutin, Comte Roger de (1618–1693). Cousin of Mme. de Sévigné; soldier, writer of letters, memoirs, and *Histoire amoureuse des Gaules,* for which he was sent to the Bastille and later exiled. 132, 133, 140

Byron, George Gordon, Lord (1788–1824). English poet. 7, 194, 232

Cabanis, Pierre-Jean-George (1757–1808). Physician, philosopher, disciple of Condillac. 225

Cagliostro, Count Alessandro di (1743–1795). Real name, Giuseppe Balsamo; notorious charlatan, involved in the affair of the diamond necklace. 262

Campistron, Jean Galbert de (1656–1723). Playwright, imitator of Racine. 87

Canova, Antonio (1757–1822). Italian sculptor; founder of neoclassical school. 251, 264

Capponi, Gino (1792–1876). Italian historian and statesman. 245

Caracciolo, Luigi Antonio (1721–1803). Author of biographies of Mme. de Maintenon, Joseph II, etc., and of *Lettres intéressantes du Pape Clément XIV*. 169

Carpani, Giuseppe (1752–1825). Italian librettist and dramatist; translated Haydn's oratorios into Italian. 229

Castro y Bellvis, Guillén de (1569–1631). Spanish dramatist, author of *Las Mocedades del Cid*. 34, 37, 48, 56, 61, 66

Catherine II (1729–1796). Empress of Russia (1762–1796). 164, 183, 193, 203, 204

Caylus, Marthe-Marguerite de Villette, Marquise de (1673–1729). Niece of Mme. de Maintenon, who took her away from her Protestant family to convert her to the Catholic faith; educated at Saint-Cyr; for her Racine composed his tragedy *Esther;* married the Comte de Caylus at the age of thirteen; Voltaire published her *Souvenirs* in 1769. 90, 211, 248 n

Cervantes Saavedra, Miguel de (1547–1616). Spanish novelist, author of *Don Quixote*. 10, 100, 103, 118

Chamfort, Sébastien-Roch-Nicolas (1741–1794). Moralist, dramatist, essayist; author of *Maximes*. 93, 252

Champmeslé, Marie Desmares (1644–1698). Tragic actress, brilliant interpreter of the roles of Bérénice, Iphigénie, Phèdre, etc.; mistress of Racine. 89, 90

Chantal, Baron de (d. 1627). Father of Mme. de Sévigné, died defending the Ile de Ré against the English. 131

Chapelain, Jean (1595–1674). Poet and influential critic; author of *La Pucelle*, epic ridiculed by Boileau; an original member of the French Academy; wrote, by order of Richelieu, the Academy's censure on Corneille's *Cid*. 65, 71, 132

Chapelle, Claude-Emmanuel (1626–1686). Author of light verse; disciple of Gassendi (q.v.); close friend of Boileau, Racine, Molière, and La Fontaine. 76, 117, 121

Charron, Pierre (1541–1603). Theologian, philosopher,

disciple of Montaigne; his best-known work is *Traité de la Sagesse* (1601). 197

Chasles, Philarète (1798–1873). Scholar and critic. 263

Chastellux, François-Jean, Marquis de (1734–1788). Fought in the Seven Years' War and in America under Rochambeau; close friend of Washington; follower of Voltaire, who got him elected to French Academy; author of critical essays, including an *Eloge d'Helvétius*, and a *Discours sur les avantages de la découverte de l'Amérique*. 168

Chateaubriand, François-René, Vicomte de (1768–1848). Author of *René* (1802), which initiated romantic movement in French literature, and other works; held posts of ambassador, and minister of foreign affairs. 168, 212, 215, 225, 270, 302, 304, 310

Châtelet, Gabrielle-Emilie, *née* Le Tonnelier de Breteuil, Marquise du (1706–1749). Author of scientific essays, an analysis of Leibniz's philosophy, a treatise on happiness; translated Newton's *Principia* into French; known for her liaison with Voltaire. 174

Chaulnes, Charles d'Albert d'Ailly, Duc de (1625–1698). Soldier, diplomat, ambassador to the Vatican. 141, 142

Chrysostom, Saint John (c. 345–407). Church father, author of important commentaries and letters. 70, 140

Cicero, Marcus Tullius (106–43 B.C.). Roman orator and philosopher. 2, 52, 100, 180, 204, 307

Cimarosa, Domenico (1749–1801). Italian composer. 224, 228, 230, 231

Cinq-Mars, Henri Coiffier de Ruzé, Marquis de (1620–1642). A favorite of Louis XIII; conspired against Richelieu; was betrayed by Gaston d'Orléans and beheaded with his friend De Thou. 104

Cizeron-Rival, François-Louis (1726–1795). Essayist and critic. 115

Clarke, Samuel (1675–1729). English philosopher; disciple of Newton; opposed pantheism, deism, materialism. 20

Colbert, Jean-Baptiste (1619–1683). Louis XIV's controller general of finance and minister of marine. 71

Comte, Auguste (1798–1857). Founder of positivism. 310

Condé, Louis II, Prince de (1621–1686). General, known as "the Great Condé"; he was twenty-two years old when he defeated the Spanish at Rocroi; friend of Molière, Racine, Boileau, Bossuet. 51, 121, 132

Condillac, Etienne Bonnot de (1715–1780). Philosopher, exponent of sensualism; close friend of Diderot and Helvétius; contributor to the *Encyclopédie*. 231

Condorcet, Antoine-Nicolas de (1743–1794). Philosopher, friend of Voltaire; president of Legislative Assembly (1792). Arrested as a Girondin, took poison and died in prison. His best-known work is *Tableau historique des progrès de l'esprit humain* (pub. 1795). 177

Confucius (c. 550–479 B.C.). Chinese philosopher. 9

Conti, Armand, Prince de (1629–1668). Brother of the Great Condé; soldier; married a niece of Mazarin; friend of Molière; author of a *Traité de la comédie et des spectacles* (1667). 105, 107, 132

Coras, Jacques (c. 1630–1677). Mediocre poet; author (with Leclerc) of a tragedy, *Iphigénie*, which was ridiculed in an epigram by Racine. 76

Corneille, Pierre (1606–1684). Father of French classical drama. 3, 4, 29, 31–66, 67, 74, 75, 83, 89, 93, 96, 126, 156, 233, 235, 248, 250

Correggio, Antonio Allegri da (1494–1534). Italian painter. 231

Coulanges, Christophe de, Abbé de Livry (c. 1607–1687). Uncle of Mme. de Sévigné. 132, 137

Coulanges, Marie-Angélique du Guy Bagnoles (1641–1723). Wife of Philippe-Emmanuel. 135

Coulanges, Philippe-Emmanuel, Marquis de (1633–1716). Cousin of Mme. de Sévigné. 135, 139

Courier, Paul-Louis (1772–1825). Hellenic scholar, edited and translated *Daphnis and Chloë* by Longus (1810);

political pamphleteer, champion of rights of peasants. 224

Cowper, William (1731–1800). English poet. 279

Creutz, Count Gustav Philip (1731–1785). Swedish diplomat and poet; served as ambassador in Paris (1766–1783). 169

Cromwell, Oliver (1599–1658). Lord Protector of England (1653–1658). 23

Custine, Delphine de Sabran, Comtesse de (1770–1826). Friend of Chateaubriand. 248 n

Cuvier, Georges (1769–1832). Naturalist, founder of comparative anatomy and paleontology. 241, 301

Damiens, Robert-François (1714–1757). Fanatic who made an attempt on the life of Louis XV; tortured, did not reveal names of accomplices; executed March 28, 1757. 202

Dante Alighieri (1265–1321). Italian poet. 2, 7, 10, 67, 88, 226, 231

Daru, Pierre-Antoine-Noël-Bruno, Comte (1767–1829). *Intendant général* of Napoleon's army; secretary of State (1811); author of a history of the Venetian Republic; cousin of Stendhal. 224, 226

D'Assouci or D'Assoucy, Charles Coypeau (c. 1604–1674). Author of burlesque poems (nicknamed *"Le Singe de Scarron"*) and memoirs. 105

Deffand, *née* Marie de Vichy-Chamrond, Marquise du (1697–1780). Her salon was frequented by the most brilliant contemporary writers; known for her wit, and her friendship and correspondence with Horace Walpole, Voltaire, Montesquieu, etc. 169, 170, 173

Delécluze, Etienne-Jean (1781–1863). Painter, novelist, critic. 255

Delille, Jacques, Abbé (1738–1813). Celebrated in his day for his didactic poem *Les Jardins*. 160, 250

Demosthenes (c. 385–322 B.C.). Athenian orator. 10, 307

Denis, Louise (c. 1710–1790). Niece of Voltaire. 153, 158

Descartes, René (1596–1650). Mathematician and philosopher. 23, 34, 53

Des Chapelles. *See* Bouteville. 39

Deshoulières, *née* Antoinette Ligier de la Garde (1638–1694). Poetess, author of idylls; her salon was frequented by Corneille, Ménage, Benserade, etc. 76–77

Destutt de Tracy, Antoine-Louis-Claude (1754–1836). Philosopher, disciple of Condillac; author of *Eléments d'Idéologie* (1801–1805). 225

Diamante, Juan Bautista (1626–1687). Spanish dramatist, author of a play based on Corneille's *Cid*. 64

Diderot, Denis (1713–1784). Philosopher, novelist, playwright, critic; editor of the *Encyclopédie*. 166, 183, 185, 187, 190, 201–2

Dryden, John (1631–1700). English poet. 101

Duché de Vancy, Joseph-François (1668–1704). Poet and playwright; Mme. de Maintenon admired his *Absalon* and other religious tragedies. 87

Ducis, Jean-François (1733–1816). Author of tragedies; first to introduce Shakespeare to the French stage; his garbled versions of *Hamlet* (1769), *Romeo and Juliet* (1772), etc., were extremely popular; successor to Voltaire at the French Academy. 308

Duclos, Charles Pineau (1704–1772). Moralist, novelist, historian, noted wit; friend of Encyclopedists. 194, 208

Dumas *fils*, Alexandre, (1824–1895). Best known for his play *La Dame aux camélias* (1852). 290

Dumas *père*, Alexandre, (1803–1870). Novelist and playwright. 271, 272

Duparc, Marguerite (d. 1668). Actress in Molière's company, later in the theater of the Hôtel de Bourgogne. 104, 106

Duras, Claire-Louise-Bonnie de Coëtnempren de Kersaint, Duchesse de (1778–1828). Author of two short novels;

presided over brilliant literary salon; close friend of Chateaubriand. 240

Enghien, Duc d'. Title of the Great Condé (q.v.) during his father's life. 62

Epinay, Louise-Florence, Mme. d' (1726–1783). Author of *Les Conversations d'Emilie* (1774) and interesting *Mémoires* (pub. 1818). 184–91, 203, 248 n

Ernesti, Johann August (1707–1781). German theologian and philologist. 180

Etienne, Charles-Guillaume (1777–1845). Journalist, dramatist, author of successful comedies. 65

Eugène, Prince (1781–1824). Son of Alexandre and Joséphine Beauharnais; Napoleon adopted him and made him viceroy of Italy in 1805. 245

Euripides (fl. 5th century B.C.). Greek playwright. 71, 81, 82, 235, 236

Fauriel, Claude (1772–1844). Historian, critic, translator. 62

Fel, Marie (1713–1794). Operatic singer. 182

Fénelon, François de Salignac de la Mothe (1651–1715). Archbishop of Cambrai; tutor to Louis XIV's grandson, for whom he wrote his celebrated *Télémaque*. 9, 20, 86, 95, 143, 207, 213

Feydeau, Ernest (1821–1873). Novelist; friend of Flaubert; his *Fanny* (1858) was his best and only successful work. 293, 297

Fielding, Henry (1707–1754). English novelist. 118

Firdusi (c. 940–1020). Persian poet; author of the *Book of Kings,* one of the great epics. 9

Flaubert, Gustave (1821–1880). Novelist. vii, 255, 275–91

Fléchier, Valentin-Esprit (1632–1710). Bishop of Lavaur and of Nîmes; member of the French Academy; noted for elegant funeral orations and interesting *Mémoires sur les Grands Jours d'Auvergne* (pub. 1844). 143

Fleury, André-Hercule, Cardinal de (1653–1743). Chief minister of Louis XV. 167

Foncemagne, Etienne Lauréault de (1694–1779). Historian; remembered for his polemics against Voltaire. 160

Fontanes, Louis de (1757–1821). Poet, held high post of *Grand-maître de l'Université* under Napoleon; translated Pope's *Essay on Man* into French. 238, 303 n, 304

Fontenelle, Bernard le Bovier, Sieur de (1657–1757). Nephew of Corneille; as a young man wrote undistinguished plays and pastoral verse; his *Entretiens sur la pluralité des mondes* (1686) and *Histoire des oracles* (1687) establish him as one of the precursors of the Enlightenment. 64, 76, 134, 161, 167, 172, 180, 194, 207

Fouquet, Nicolas (1615–1680). *Surintendant des finances* under Mazarin, patron of letters; tried for embezzlement in 1661, died in prison. 132, 133, 142

Franklin, Benjamin (1706–1790). American statesman, scientist, philosopher. 174, 182

Frederick II, "the Great" (1712–1786). King of Prussia (1740–1786). 145, 180, 181, 193, 199, 203, 239

Frémy, Arnould (1809–1882). Novelist and critic. 251

Gaillard, Gabriel-Henri (1726–1806). Historian. 160

Galiani, Fernando, Abbé (1728–1787). Italian economist and historian; noted wit; friend of Diderot, Grimm, Mme. d'Epinay, and Mme. de Geoffrin. 169, 182, 233

Gassendi, Pierre (1592–1655). Mathematician and philosopher, champion of empirical method and of doctrines of Epicurus, critic of Descartes; friend of Galileo and Kepler. 18

Gatti, Theobaldo de (d. 1727). Musician and composer. 169

Gautier, Théophile (1811–1872). Poet, critic, leader of the Parnassians. 295

Geoffrin, *née* Marie-Thérèse Rodet (1699–1777). 162, 163–77

Gibbon, Edward (1737–1794). English historian. 169

Gide, André (1869–1951). Essayist, novelist, dramatist. x

Girod, Jean-Louis, Baron (1753–1839). Magistrate and statesman. 152

Godeau, Antoine (1605–1672). Bishop of Grasse and Vence; author of sacred odes, moral epistles, a history of the Church, etc.; an original member of the French Academy. 140

Godefroy de Bouillon (1058–1100). Crusade leader, first King of Jerusalem. 177

Goethe, Johann Wolfgang von (1749–1832). German poet. 5–8, 181, 194, 264, 269, 300

Goldsmith, Oliver (1728–1774). English poet, dramatist, and novelist. 6

Gray, Thomas (1716–1771). English poet. 101

Grignan, François-Adhémar de Monteil, Comte de (1632–1715). Husband of the following. 132, 142

Grignan, *née* Françoise-Marguerite de Sévigné, Comtesse de (1648–1705), daughter of Mme. de Sévigné. 136, 139 n, 142, 303

Grimarest, Jean-Léonor Le Gallois, Sieur de (1659–1720). Earliest biographer of Molière. 121, 122

Grimm, Frédéric-Melchior, Baron de (1723–1807). Critic. 162, 168, *179–205*, 300

Gros-Guillaume (d. 1634). Real name Robert Guérin. Comedian, actor in farces at the theater of the Hôtel de Bourgogne. 104

Guasco, Octaviano de (1712–1781). Canon of Tournai; historian; friend of Montesquieu. 176

Guiche, Armand de Grassinet, Comte de (1638–1673). Soldier, fought under Condé. 117

Guimard, Marie-Madeleine (1743–1816). Dancer at the Opéra. 169

Hacqueville, Abbé d'. Close friend of the Cardinal de Retz and of Mme. de Sévigné. 134

Haller, Albrecht von (1708–1777). Swiss scientist, physician, and poet; wrote against Voltaire in defense of revealed religion. 156, 157

Harlay de Champvallon, François (1625–1695). Archbishop of Rouen and of Paris. 124

Haydn, Franz Joseph (1732–1809). Austrian composer. 226, 229–31

Hazlitt, William (1778–1830). English essayist. 275

Heliodorus (fl. 4th century A.D.). Greek writer. 70

Helvétius, Claude-Adrien (1715–1771). Philosopher, exponent of utilitarianism and sensualism; one of the Encyclopedists. 168, 201, 231

Hénault, Charles-Jean-François (1685–1770). Magistrate; author of tragedies, a history of France, and interesting memoirs; close friend of Mme. du Deffand. 158

Henri III (1551–1589). King of France (1574–1589). 131

Henri IV (1553–1610). King of Navarre (1572–1589); King of France (1589–1610). 20, 131, 253

Herder, Johann Gottfried von (1744–1803). German philosopher, historian, and essayist. 181

Hesiod (fl. 8th century B.C.). Greek poet. 9

Hobbes, Thomas (1588–1679). English philosopher. 198

Holback, Paul Thirty, Baron d' (1723–1789). Philosopher, champion of materialism and atheism; author of *Systèm de la Nature* (1770), and several other works; his houses were meeting places for the Encyclopedists. 166, 168, 169, 201, 221

Hölty, Ludwig Christoph Heinrich (1748–1776). German poet. 304

Homer. 2, 5, 8, 67, 99, 180, 194, 236, 237, 264

Horace, Quintus Horatius Flaccus (65–8 B.C.) Roman poet. 9, 12, 67, 100, 112, 113, 193, 198, 240, 303

Hortensius, Quintus (114–50 B.C.). Roman orator, leader of the aristocratic party. 307

Houdetot, Elisabeth-Sophie, Comtesse d' (1730–1813). Sister-in-law of Mme. d'Epinay (q.v.); remembered for her liaison with Saint-Lambert (q.v.), to whom she remained faithful until his death, and for J.-J. Rousseau's passion for her (described in his *Confessions*). 248 n

Huet, Pierre-Daniel (1630–1721). Bishop of Avranches. Mathematician and classical scholar; editor of Origen's *Commentaria;* author of philosophical and historical works. 3

Hugo, *née* Adèle Foucher (1800–1868). Wife of Victor Hugo. ix–xi, 278

Hugo, Victor-Marie (1802–1885). Poet, novelist, dramatist. vii, viii, x, 295, 309

Hume, David (1711–1776). Scottish philosopher and historian. 169

Ingres, Jean-Auguste-Dominique (1780–1867). Painter. 94

Jacquemont, Victor (1801–1832). Botanist; author of an Indian travelogue. 251

Jeffrey, Francis. Lord Jeffrey (1773–1850). Scottish critic, editor of *Edinburgh Review* (1803–1829). 195, 275, 304

Jelyotte, Pierre (1710–1788). Singer at the Paris Opéra. 182

Johnson, Samuel (1696–1772). English lexicographer and critic. 275

Joubert, Joseph (1754–1824). Critic and aphorist; friend of Fontanes and of Chateaubriand, who edited a selection of Joubert's *Pensées* in 1838. 304, 306

Jussieu, Bernard de (1699–1777). Botanist. 301

Juvenal. Decimus Julius Juvenalis (c. 60–140). Roman satirist. 157 n

Klopstock, Friedrich Gottlieb (1724–1803). German poet. 181

La Bruyère, Jean de (1645–1696). Moralist, author of *Les*

Caractères ou les Moeurs de ce siècle (1688). 9, 16 n, 111, 268, 276

La Calprenède, Gautier de Costes de (c. 1610–1663). Author of long historical romances (*Cassandre, Cléopâtre, Pharamond*) and sentimental tragedies and tragicomedies. 140

La Fayette, *née* Marie-Madeleine Pioche de la Vergne, Comtesse de (1634–1693). Author of *La Princesse de Clèves* (1678). 132, 134, 136, 248 n

La Fontaine, Jean de (1621–1695). Poet and fabulist. 3, 8, 9, 70, 72, 75, 96, 127, 130, 135, 137, 143, 217, 220, 231, 304

Laforest. Molière's faithful servant. 123

La Grange, Charles de (1639–1692). Actor in Molière's company; kept register of plays produced; helped prepare first edition of Molière's works. 113, 117

Lagrenée, Louis-Jean-François (1724–1805). Painter. 168

La Harpe, Jean François de (1739–1803). Dramatist, journalist, critic; friend of Voltaire. 176, 191, 250–51, 275

Lamartine, Alphonse-Marie-Louis de Prat de (1790–1869). Romantic poet and orator; minister of foreign affairs in provisional government of 1848. 302, 309

La Popelinière, Alexandre-Jean-Joseph Le Riche de (1692–1762). Financier noted for lavish living; patron of writers and artists; author of two licentious novels. 169

La Rochefoucauld, François, Duc de (1613–1680). Moralist; intrigued against Richelieu; took part in the Fronde; author of *Maximes* (1665); close friend of Mme. de La Fayette. 9, 16 n, 18, 105, 121, 125, 134, 136

La Tour, Maurice Quentin de (1704–1783). Painter; portratist of Mme. de Pompadour, Louis XV, Diderot, Voltaire, d'Alembert, Rousseau. 168

Lauzun, Antoine Nompar de Caumont, Duc de (1632–1723). Gascon gentleman; won favor of Louis XIV, who, after approving his planned marriage with the Grande Mademoiselle, changed his mind and sent Lauzun to prison where he remained ten years. On his return was restored to favor; commanded French troops at battle of Boyne. 117

La Vallière, Louis de la Baume le Blanc, Duchesse de (1644–1700). Mistress of Louis XIV from 1661 to 1674, when she was supplanted by Mme. de Maintenon and retired to a convent. 75

Lawrence, David Herbert (1885–1930). English novelist. ix

Leclerc, Michel (1622–1691). Dramatist; rival of Racine (*see* Coras). 76

Le Maître, Antoine (1608–1658). Nephew of Arnauld (q.v.); brilliant lawyer, retired to Port-Royal in 1638. 70

Le Maître de Saci, Louis-Isaac (1613–1684). Director of the Port-Royal community; spent three years in the Bastille; translator of the Bible and of Greek and Roman classics. 17, 29

Lemoine, François (1688–1737). Painter of historical pictures. 168

Leo X, Giovanni de' Medici (1475–1521). Second son of Lorenzo the Magnificent; Pope (1513–1521). 233

Le Sage, Alain René (1668–1747). Author of the novel *L'Histoire de Gil Blas de Santillane* (1715–1735) and the comedy *Turcaret* (1709). 118, 231

Lespinasse, Julie-Jeanne-Eléonore de (1732–1776). Natural daughter of the Comtesse d'Albon; companion of Mme. du Deffand for ten years, quarrelled with her in 1764 and founded her own salon; close friend of d'Alembert; best known for her love letters to the Comte de Guibert. 169

Lessing, Gotthold Ephraim (1729–1781). German dramatist and critic. 5, 64, 181

Littré, Emile (1801–1881). Lexicographer; disciple of Auguste Comte; author of monumental dictionary (1863–1872), *Auguste Comte et la philosophie positive* (1863) and other works; translator of Hippocrates. 310

Locke, John (1632–1704). English philosopher. 197

Longueville, Henri II, Duc de (1595–1663). Married the sister of the Great Condé in 1642; under her influence joined the Fronde. 144

Lorenzo the Magnificent (1449–1492). Son of Piero de' Medici; ruler of Florence, patron of arts and letters. 233

Louis XIII (1601–1643). King of France (1610–1643). 104

Louis XIV (1638–1715). King of France (1643–1715). 3, 6, 86, 102, 108, 114, 115, 121, 124, 130, 133, 143, 200, 253, 254

Louis XV (1710–1774). King of France (1715–1774). 131, 167, 202

Louvois, François-Michel le Tellier, Marquis de (1641–1691). Minister of war (1666), and after death of Colbert chief adviser of Louis XIV. 139

Lucian (fl. 2nd century A.D.). Greek satirist. 15, 78

Lucretius. Titus Lucretius Carus (c. 96–55 B.C.). Roman poet. 10, 198

Luther, Martin (1483–1546). German religious reformer. 233

Machiavelli, Niccolò (1469–1527). Italian historian and political philosopher. 107, 198, 243

Mademoiselle. *See* Montpensier

Maintenon, *née* Françoise d'Aubigné, Marquise de (1635–1719). Granddaughter of the poet Agrippa d'Aubigné; married poet Scarron in 1652; in 1669 entrusted with education of children of Mme. de Montespan and Louis XIV; secretly married to the King in 1684. 75, 83, 140, 166, 176

Mairan, Jean-Jacques Dortous de (1679–1771). Physicist, mathematician, man of letters; friend of Voltaire. 158, 167, 168

Mairet, Jean (1604–1686). Dramatist; protégé of Richelieu; violently attacked Corneille's *Le Cid.* 64

Maistre, Xavier de (1763–1852). Novelist; brother of the

moralist and Christian philosopher Joseph de Maistre; author of the *Voyage autour de ma chambre* (1794). 248

Malesherbes, Chrétien-Guillaume de Lamoignon de (1721–1794). Chief censor from 1750 to 1763; helped the *Philosophes,* with whom he sympathized; died on the guillotine. 221

Malherbe, François de (1555–1628). Official poet under Henri IV and Louis XIII; champion of purity, conciseness, and correctness of language; condemned the school of Ronsard. 2, 35, 143, 189

Malibran, *née* María Felicia García (1808–1836). Operatic contralto; her younger sister Pauline (1821–1910) was also a singer. 182

Manzoni, Alessandro (1785–1873). Italian poet; author of novel *I Promessi Sposi* (1825–1827). 232, 248, 253

Marchangy, Louis-Antoine-François (1782–1826). Magistrate, chief public prosecutor under the Restoration; man of letters; author of *La Gaule poétique* (1813) and the historical novel *Tristan le voyageur* (1824). 310

Marguerite de Valois (1533–1615). Wife of Henri IV; divorced by him in 1599; author of poems and memoirs. 20, 24, 143

Marin, François-Louis-Claude (1721–1809). Man of letters; served as chief censor; friend of Voltaire. 160

Marivaux, Pierre Carlet de Chamblan de (1688–1763). Author of plays, best known of which is *Le Jeu de l'amour et du hasard* (1730), and novels, both notable for keen psychology and realism. 168

Marlowe, Christopher (1564–1593). English dramatist. 119

Marmontel, Jean-François (1723–1799). Critic, author of plays and romances; protégé of Mme. de Pompadour; wrote literary articles for the *Encyclopédie;* successor of d'Alembert at the French Academy. 168, 175, 177, 191

Marot, Clément (1496–1544). Poet; protégé of Marguerite de Navarre; the suspicion of the clergy obliged him to leave France; died in Turin. Author of *ballades*, epistles, epigrams, translator of the Psalms. 76, 109

Mazarin, Jules. Giulio Mazarini (1602–1661). Cardinal, prime minister under Louis XIII and Queen Regent Anne of Austria (1642–1661). 129

Ménage, Gilles (1613–1692). Philologist, critic, author of etymologies of the French and the Italian language; frequented the Hôtel de Rambouillet. 132, 140

Menander (c. 340–291 B.C.). Athenian author of more than 100 comedies; only fragments of his works survive. 9, 99, 110

Mérimée, Prosper (1803–1870). Novelist, historian; author of *Carmen;* translator of Russian classics. 251, 253 n, 271

Mesmer, Franz (1734–1815). Austrian physician; originator of theory of animal magnetism ("mesmerism"); denounced as a charlatan. 262

Metternich, Prince Klemens Wenzel Nepomuk Lothar von (1773–1859). Austrian minister of foreign affairs (1809–1848). 249

Mézeray, François Eudes de (1610–1683). Author of a celebrated history of France (1643–1651). 78

Michelangelo Buonarroti (1475–1564). Italian sculptor and painter. 232

Michelet, Jules (1798–1874). Historian, ardent democrat; author of *L'Histoire de France* (1833–1843), *La Révolution Française* (1847–1853), and several other works. 309

Mignard, Pierre (1610). Painter whose works include portraits of Molière, Mme. de Sévigné, and Mme. de Grignan. 108, 118

Milton, John (1608–1674). English poet. 7, 10, 226, 232, 271

Molière. Real name Jean-Baptiste Poquelin (1622–1673). 3, 5, 8, 10, 28, 60, 63, 67, 74, 75, 76, 88, 89, 94, 95, 99–127, 130, 141, 143, 194, 236, 304

Moncrif, François-Auguste Paradis de (1687–1770). Author of comedies, tales, and *chansons;* friend of Voltaire. 158

Monselet, Charles (1825–1888). Literary historian and critic. 251

Montaigne, Michel Eyquem de (1533–1592). 7, 9, *13–29,* 140, 143, 164, 194–97, 209, 226, 261

Montesquieu, Charles de Secondat, Baron de (1689–1755). Political philosopher, author of *Lettres persanes* (1721), *L'Esprit des lois* (1748), etc. 3, 147, 164, 167, 172, 176, 194, 198, 200, 207, 220, 233, 261

Montpensier, Louise d'Orléans, Duchesse de (1627–1693). "La Grande Mademoiselle," niece of Louis XIII, first cousin of Louis XIV; author of interesting memoirs. *See also* Lauzun. 135, 144

Moore, Thomas (1779–1852). Irish poet. 254, 304

Morellet, André (1727–1819). Economist, man of letters, contributor to the *Encyclopédie.* 168, 177, 193

Mozart, Wolfgang Amadeus (1756–1791). Austrian composer. 63, 224, 229–31

Muret, Marc-Antoine de (1526–1585). Humanist scholar, teacher, author of a commentary on Ronsard and a play in Latin about Julius Caesar (1544). 14

Musset, Alfred de (1810–1857). Poet and playwright. 309

Napoleon Bonaparte (1769–1821). Emperor Napoleon I (1805–1815). 33, 232, 245

Nevers, Philippe-Julien Mancini-Mazarini, Duc de (1641–1707). Nephew of Cardinal Mazarin; author of satirical poems; supported Pradon against Racine. 76

Nicole, Pierre (1625–1695). Theologian, moralist, one of the recluses of Port-Royal; co-author with Arnauld of the *Logique de Port-Royal;* author of much-admired *Essais de morale et instructions théologiques* (1671). 76, 139, 268

Olivet, Pierre-Joseph-Thoulier d' (1682–1768). Critic,

translator, author of *Histoire de l'Académie Française* (1729). 87

Orléans, Charlotte-Elisabeth de Bavière, Princess Palatine, Duchesse d' (1652–1722). Second wife of the following. 75, 121

Orléans, Philippe, Duc d' (1640–1701). Only brother of Louis XIV. 108, 112

Ovid. Publius Ovidius Naso (43 B.C.–17 A.D.). Roman poet. 2, 14, 15, 28, 71, 100, 101

Paley, William (1743–1805). English theologian and utilitarian philosopher; adversary of the deists. 20

Palissot de Montenoy, Charles (1730–1814). Poet and dramatist; ridiculed the Encyclopedists in his comedies and in his poem *La Dunciade ou la Guerre des Sots* (1764). 150, 176

Pascal, Blaise (1623–1662). 3, 13, 16–19, 23–25, 28–29, 102–3, 140, 174, 207

Pasta, *née* Giuditta Negri (1798–1865). Operatic soprano. 241

Pellico, Silvio (1789–1854). Italian writer and patriot. 232

Pellisson, Paul (1624–1693). Secretary to Fouquet (q.v.); royal historiographer; author of a history of the French Academy down to 1652. 10

Pergolese, Giovanni Batista (1710–1736). Italian composer. 194

Perrault, Charles (1628–1703). Poet, critic; best known for his fairy tales; champion of the Moderns in the *querelle des anciens et des modernes*. 3

Persius. Aulus Persius Flaccus (34–62 A.D.). Roman satirist. 157

Petrarch. Francesco Petrarca (1304–1374). Italian poet. 226, 231

Petronius, Gaius (fl. 1st century A.D.). Author of *Satyricon*. 262

Phidias (fl. 5th century B.C.). Greek sculptor. 264

Philippe, Duc d'Orléans (1674–1723). Nephew of Louis XIV; regent during minority of Louis XV (1715–1723). 131

Pindar (c. 520–443 B.C.). Greek poet. 67, 70, 275

Plato (c. 427–347 B.C.). Greek philosopher. 2, 10, 70, 88, 300

Plautus, Titus Maccius (c. 254–184 B.C.). Roman playwright. 14, 100, 103, 110, 112, 116

Plutarch (c. 46–120 A.D.). Greek biographer. 26, 70, 82, 195, 196

Poe, Edgar Allan (1809–1849). American poet. 295

Pompignan, Jean-Jacques Lefranc, Marquis de (1709–1784). Poet and dramatist; opponent of the Encyclopedists; author of *Odes chrétiennes et philosophiques* (1771); ridiculed by Voltaire. 18, 158

Pomponne, Simon, Marquis de (1618–1699). Son of Arnauld d'Andilly (q.v.); minister of foreign affairs under Louis XIV (1617–1679). 132, 133, 136

Pope, Alexander (1688–1744). English poet. 7, 9, 101, 193, 204, 275

Poussin, Nicolas (1594–1665). Painter. 232

Pradon, Nicolas (1632–1698). Author of tragedies; his *Phèdre et Hippolyte* (1677) was praised by enemies of Racine as superior to the latter's *Phèdre*. 76

Prévost, Antoine-François, (1697–1763). Novelist; author of *Manon Lescaut* (1733). 101

Proust, Marcel (1871–1922). Novelist. ix, 177, 311

Quinault, Jeanne-Françoise (c. 1700–1783). Actress who maintained a kind of literary salon frequented by d'Alembert, Diderot, etc. 169

Quintilian. Marcus Fabius Quintillanus (fl. 1st century A.D.). Roman rhetorician. 140, 234, 305

Rabelais, François (1494–1553). 7, 76, 100, 116, 118, 140

Racine, Jean-Baptiste (1639–1699). ix, 8, 29, 46, 51, 59,

67–97, 102, 111, 116, 127, 130, 132, 143, 195, 227, 233, 235, 250, 254, 261, 304

Racine, Louis (1692–1763). Son of the preceding; author of didactic poems and memoirs of his father. 87

Rambouillet, Catherine de Vivonne, Marquise de (1588–1665). Her town house, on part of the site of the present Palais Royal, was the Hôtel de Rambouillet, one of the earliest literary salons. 53

Raphael. Raffaello Santi (1483–1520). Italian painter. 194

Raynal, Guillaume, Abbé (1713–1796). Historian, philosopher, leading freethinker; contributor to the *Encyclopédie;* his *Histoire philosophique et politique des établissements et du commerce des Européens dans les deux Indes* (1772), which attacks colonial policies, slavery, and religion, was publicly burned by order of the Parlement. 168, 183, 191

Régnier, Mathurin (1573–1613). Canon of Chartres; poet best known for his satires, which often anticipate Molière. 7, 143

Retz, Paul Gondi, Cardinal de (1614–1679). Archbishop of Paris, one of the leaders of the Fronde; imprisoned in 1652, made sensational escape; pardoned in 1662, retired to private life; author of *Mémoires*. 20, 121, 133, 247

Richardson, Samuel (1689–1761). English novelist. 194, 218

Richelieu, Armand-Jean du Plessis, Duc de (1585–1642). Cardinal, chief minister of Louis XIII. 39, 65, 129, 131

Richelieu, Louis-François-Armand de Vignerot du Plessis, Duc de (1696–1788). Grandnephew of the preceding; marshal of France. 145, 160, 167

Rollin, Charles (1661–1741). Historian and educator; author of a *Traité des Etudes* (1726–1728). 87

Ronsard, Pierre de (1524–1585). Poet, leader of the Pléiade, group of poets who undertook to reform French language and literature. viii, 138

Roquelaure, Jean-Armand, Comte de (1721–1818). Bishop of Senlis; author of funeral orations. 160

Rossini, Gioacchino Antonio (1792–1868). Italian opera composer. 231, 251

Rousseau, Jean-Baptiste (1671–1741). Author of odes much admired by his contemporaries; banished in 1707 because of some defamatory couplets ascribed to him; spent thirty years in exile. 87

Rousseau, Jean-Jacques (1712–1778). 3, 150, 159 n, 180, 184–90, 194, 197, 200, 201, 207–22, 261, 271

Royer-Collard, Pierre-Paul (1763–1845). Philosopher, statesman, noted parliamentary orator. 302

Rubens, Peter Paul (1577–1640). Flemish painter. 94

Rulhière, Claude de (1735–1791). Historian, author of light verse and epigrams; served as secretary to the French minister to Russia; author of an account of the Russian revolution of 1762 and a study on the causes of the revocation of the Edict of Nantes. 174, 252

Saci. *See* Le Maître de Saci

Saint-Evrémond, Charles de Saint-Denis, Sieur de (1613–1703). Soldier, essayist, moralist; fled to England in 1661, in consequence of a letter attacking Mazarin; friend of Buckingham, Hobbes, Cowley; buried in Westminster Abbey. 140

Saint-Lambert, Jean-François, Marquis de (1716–1803). Poet and philosopher; one of the Encyclopedists; friend of Voltaire, Mme. du Châtelet and Mme. d'Houdetot (q.v.). 168, 190

Saint-Pierre, Charles-Irénée, Abbé de (1658–1743). Economist, author of a *Projet de paix perpétuelle* (1713), and other essays on social, political, and economic subjects. 174

Saintsbury, George Edward Bateman (1845–1933). English critic. ix

Saint-Simon, Louis de Rouvroy, Duc de (1675–1755). Soldier, member of council of Regency under Louis XV, ambassador to Spain in 1721, after 1723 retired from court, devoting himself to his *Mémoires*. 124, 143

Sallust. Gaius Sallustius Crispus (86–34 B.C.). Roman historian. 161

Salvandy, Narcisse-Achille, Comte de (1795–1856). Soldier, statesman, author of historical and literary works. 310

Sand, George. Pseudonym of Amandine-Aurore-Lucie, *née* Dupin, Baronne Dudevant (1803–1876). Novelist; liaisons with Jules Sandeau, Musset, Chopin; in addition to numerous novels wrote critical essays, dramatic works, and an autobiography, *Histoire de ma vie* (4 vols., 1854–1855). 271, 276

Santarosa, Annibale de Rossi di Pomarolo (1783–1825). Italian patriot. 245

Sarrasin, Jean-François (1603–1654). Poet, wit, author of light verse and satires, and historical essay *La Conspiration de Wallenstein* (1643); banished by Mazarin in 1647. 108

Saxe, Maurice de (1696–1750). Natural son of Augustus II of Saxony; marshal of France; victor at Fontenoy (1745). 181

Scarron, Paul (1610–1660). Comic poet, novelist, dramatist; crippled from the age of thirty; in 1652 married Françoise d'Aubigné (*see* Maintenon, Marquise de); best known for his picaresque novel *Le Roman comique* (1651). 76

Scott, Sir Walter (1771–1832). Scottish poet, novelist, historian. 88, 89, 118, 248, 270

Scudéry, Georges de (1601–1667). Author of tragedies, poems, tragicomedies (best known of which is *L'Amour tyrannique*, which Richelieu considered superior to Corneille's *Le Cid*), and a critical essay against Corneille. 64

Scudéry, Madeleine de (1607–1701). Sister of preceding; author of romances *Le Grand Cyrus* (1649), *Clélie* (1654), etc. 64, 140

Sebond (Sebonde), Raymond de (b. 1431). Spanish theologian. 18–22, 25

Segrais, Jean-Regnault de (1624–1701). Poet and novelist; translator of Virgil; secretary to Duchesse de Montpensier; friend of Mme. de La Fayette. 110

Seneca, Lucius Annaeus (4 B.C.–65 A.D.). Roman philosopher. 79, 81, 196

Sévigné, *née* Marie de Rabutin-Chantal, Marquise de (1626–1696). 75, 121, *129–44*, 303

Shakespeare, William (1564–1616). 7–8, 28, 43, 47, 69, 88, 89, 92, 94, 100, 103, 118–19, 194, 195, 233–36, 294

Sieyès, Emmanuel-Joseph, Abbé (1748–1836). Political leader before and during French Revolution, best known for his pamphlet on the Third Estate (1789); helped Bonaparte in his coup d'état of 1799; exiled by Louis XVIII; returned to France in 1830. 254, 261

Siri, Vittorio (1608–1685). Italian-born historian, protégé of Richelieu and Mazarin; almoner and historiographer under Louis XIV; author of historical works and memoirs written in Italian. 78

Sirven, Pierre-Paul (b. 1709). A Protestant falsely accused of murdering his daughter; fled to Switzerland; sentenced to death in absentia in 1764; rehabilitated five years later thanks to Voltaire. 175

Solon (c. 640–559 B.C.). Athenian legislator. 9

Sontag, Henriette (1806–1854). German operatic soprano. 182

Sophocles (c. 500–406 B.C.). Greek dramatist. 6, 10, 81, 99, 194, 235, 236, 300

Soufflot, Jacques-Germain (1713–1780). Architect; designed Panthéon in Paris. 168

Soulary, Joseph-Marie, self-styled Joséphin (1815–1891). Poet, author of *Sonnets humoristiques* (1858). 294

Southhampton, Henry Wriothesley, Earl of (1537–1624). Shakespeare's patron. 119

Spinoza, Benedict (1632–1677). Dutch philosopher. 19, 26

Staël, Anna-Louis-Germaine, *née* Necker, Baronne de Staël-Holstein (1766–1817). Novelist, essayist, critic; precursor of romantic movement in France. 138, 139, 165, 225, 234

Stanislas Poniatowski (1732–1798). Last king of Poland (1764–1795). 175

Stendhal. Pseudonym of Henri Beyle (1783–1842). x, 223–56, 291

Sterne, Laurence (1713–1768). English novelist. 172, 268

Stolberg, Christian, Count (1748–1821) and his brother Friedrich Leopold (1750–1819). German poets whose works were published jointly. 304

Suard, Mme. Wife of Jean-Baptiste Suard (1733–1817), critic and dramatic censor. 166

Sue, Eugène (1804–1875). Prolific novelist, best known for *Les Mystères de Paris* (1842–1843) and *Le Juif errant* (1847–1849). 271–74

Sulla, Lucius Cornelius (138–78 B.C.). Roman general, dictator (82–79 B.C.). 23

Surville, *née* Laure Balzac (1800–1871). The novelist's sister; author of *Balzac, sa vie et ses oeuvres* (1858). 302

Swedenborg, Emmanuel (1688–1772). Swedish scientist, mystic, theosophist. 262

Swift, Jonathan (1667–1745). English poet and satirist. 6

Tacitus, Cornelius (c. 50–after 117 A.D.). Roman historian. 79–81, 85, 140, 195

Taine, Hippolyte-Adolphe (1828–1893). Philosopher, critic, historian. 252, 290, 299

Talma, François-Joseph (1763–1826). Tragic actor; author of memoirs (1826). 91, 93

Tasso, Torquato (1544–1595). Italian poet. 10, 67

Tencin, Claudine Alexandrine Guérin, Marquise de (1685–

1749). Author of three romances; maintained a salon frequented by Fontenelle, Marivaux, Montesquieu (*see* Alembert). 167, 168, 172, 174

Tencin, Pierre Guérin de (1680–1758). Brother of Mme. de Tencin, thanks to whose influence at court he was named cardinal in 1739, archbishop of Lyon in 1740, and minister of state in 1742. 146

Terence, Pubius Terentius Afer (c. 190–159 B.C.). Roman playwright. 9, 14, 95, 110, 116

Thales (c. 650–546 B.C.). Greek philosopher. 24

Theognis (fl. 6th century B.C.). Greek poet. 9

Theophrastus (d. c. 287 B.C.). Greek philosopher. 300

Thiériot (1696–1772). Friend of Voltaire, edited some of his works. 149, 161

Thierry, Edouard (1813–1894). Poet and critic. 294

Thomas, Antoine-Léonard (1732–1785). Author of mediocre poems and academic *éloges* of celebrities. 168

Thomas Aquinas, Saint (1227–1274). Medieval philosopher. 20, 71

Thou, François-Auguste de (1607–1642). Executed as an accomplice of Cinq-Mars (q.v.). 104

Thucydides (c. 470–400 B.C.). Greek historian. 52

Tibullus, Albius (54–c. 18 B.C.). Roman poet. 9

Tieck, Ludwig (1773–1853). German poet, novelist, critic. 119

Tournemine, René-Joseph (1661–1739). Jesuit scholar, historian, critic. 68

Tronchin, Théodore (1709–1781). Voltaire's physician; contributor to the *Encyclopédie.* 190

Trublet, Nicolas-Charles-Joseph (1697–1770). Canon of Saint-Malo; compiler, author of collection of critical essays; ridiculed by Voltaire. 174

Turenne, Henri de la Tour d'Auvergne, Vicomte de (1611–1675). Marshal of France. 144

Turgot, Anne-Robert-Jacques (1727–1781). Economist; finance minister 1774–1776; author of scientific and literary studies; contributor to the *Encyclopédie;* close friend of Condorcet. 177

Turlupin, real name Henri Legrand (d. 1637). Actor in farces at the theater of the Hôtel de Bourgogne. 104

Urfé, Honoré d' (1567–1625). Soldier, novelist, best known for his long romance *L'Astrée* (1607–1627). 260

Valmíki (fl. 3rd century B.C.). Author of the Sanscrit epic *Ramayana.* 9

Van Helmont, Jan Baptista (1577–1644). Flemish scientist and physician; author of *De Magnetica vulnerum curatione* (1621), in which he anticipates Mesmer (q.v.). 262

Vanloo, Carle (1705–1765). Painter. 168

Vatel. Steward employed by Fouquet and by Condé; committed suicide in 1671, believing himself dishonored because fish failed to arrive in time for a dinner given by Condé for Louis XIV. (Mme. de Sévigné, letters of April 24 and 26, 1671). 144

Vauvenargues, Luc de Clapier, Marquis de (1715–1747). Moralist and critic; author of *Introduction à la connaissance de l'esprit humain, Réflexions sur divers auteurs,* and *Maximes.* 10, 101, 122, 269, 306

Vendôme, Louis, Duc de (1612–1669). Grandson of Henri IV; governor of Provence. 133

Vernet, Claude-Joseph (1714–1789). Painter. 168

Vien, Joseph-Marie (1716–1809). Painter, teacher of David. 168

Villemain, Abel-François (1790–1870). Literary historian, critic, author of *Cours de littérature française* (1828); minister of public instruction (1839–1844). 250, 261

Villon, François (1431–after 1462). Poet. 109

Vincent de Paul, Saint (1576–1660). Founder of the Sisters of Charity (1634) and foundling hospitals. 20

Vinet, Alexandre (1797–1847). Swiss theologian and critic,

author of a *Etudes sur Pascal* (1848) and *Etudes sur la littérature française au XIXème siécle* (1849–1851). 38

Virgil. Publius Vergilius Maro (70–19 B.C.). Roman poet. 2, 9–10, 15, 67, 100, 140, 300, 307

Visé, Jean Donneau de (1640–1710). Critic hostile to Molière and favorable to Corneille; founder of periodical *Mercure galant* (1672) which later became the *Mercure de France*. 121

Vivonne, Louis-Victor de Rochechouart, Duc de Mortemart et de (1636–1688). Soldier, wit, patron of writers; friend of Molière and Boileau. 142

Voiture, Vincent (1598–1648). Court wit, author of occasional verse and a panegyric of Richelieu. 135

Volland, Louise-Henriette (d. 1784). Intimate friend and principal correspondent of Diderot, who called her "Sophie." 204

Voltaire. Pseudonym of François-Marie Arouet (1694–1778). 3, 10, 12, 18, 50, 64, 145–62, 175, 180, 190, 191, 194, 199, 200, 203, 204, 207, 261, 264, 308

Voss, Johann Heinrich (1751–1826). German poet and critic; translator of Homer. 304

Vyasa, the mythical "Arranger" of the Vedas and reputed author of *Mahabharata*, Hindu national epic. 9

Walckenaer, Charles-Athanase (1771–1852). Geographer, naturalist; biographer of Horace, La Fontaine, and Mme. de Sévigné. 136 n

Walpole, Horace (1717–1797). English man of letters. 170, 173, 182

Warens, Louise-Eléonore de Tour du Pil, Baronne de (1700–1762). Benefactress and mistress of J.-J. Rousseau. 217, 218

Xenophon (c. 430–355 B.C.). Greek historian and essayist. 10

ANCHOR BOOKS

BIOGRAPHY, AUTOBIOGRAPHY AND LETTERS

ANDRADE, E. N. da C. Sir Isaac Newton, A151

BEETHOVEN, LUDWIG VAN Beethoven: Letters, Journals and Conversations, trans. & ed. Hamburger, A206

BENDIX, REINHARD Max Weber: An Intellectual Portrait, A281

COLETTE My Mother's House *and* The Vagabond, A62

CONRAD, JOSEPH The Mirror of the Sea *and* A Personal Record, A207

DICKINSON, EMILY Selected Poems and Letters of Emily Dickinson, ed. Linscott, A192

ESSLIN, MARTIN Brecht: The Man and His Work, A245

FULLER, MARGARET Margaret Fuller: American Romantic—A Selection from Her Writings and Correspondence, ed. Miller, A356

GEIRINGER, KARL Brahms: His Life and Work, A245

—— Haydn, A361

GRAVES, ROBERT Good-Bye to All That, A123

HIMMELFARB, GERTRUDE Darwin and the Darwinian Revolution, A325

JONES, ERNEST The Life and Work of Sigmund Freud, ed. & abr. in 1 vol. Trilling & Marcus, A340

KEATS, JOHN The Selected Letters of John Keats, ed. Trilling, A70

KROPOTKIN, PETER Memoirs of a Revolutionist, ed. Rogers, A287

LEWIS, W. H. The Sunset of the Splendid Century: The Life and Times of Louis Auguste de Bourbon, Duc du Maine, 1670–1736, A355

LOWRIE, WALTER A Short Life of Kierkegaard, A273

NEALE, J. E. Queen Elizabeth I, A105

NEWMAN, JAMES R. Science and Sensibility, A357

NICOLSON, HAROLD Tennyson, A284

PHILLIPS, DR. HARLAN B., ed. Felix Frankfurter Reminisces, A310

RILKE, RAINER MARIA Selected Letters of Rainer Maria Rilke, ed. Moore, A223

SHATTUCK, ROGER The Banquet Years, A238

TAYLOR, A. E. Socrates, A9

TRELAWNY, E. J. The Last Days of Shelley and Byron, A225

WILSON, EDMUND A Piece of My Mind, A143

YEATS, WILLIAM BUTLER The Autobiography of William Butler Yeats, A142

LINGUISTICS AND LANGUAGE

HALL, ROBERT A., JR. Linguistics and Your Language, A201

JESPERSEN, OTTO Growth and Structure of the English Language, A46

ESSAYS, BELLES LETTRES & LITERARY CRITICISM

AUERBACH, ERICH Mimesis, A107

BARZUN, JACQUES Classic, Romantic and Modern, A255

BAUDELAIRE, CHARLES The Mirror of Art, A84

BERGSON, HENRI Laughter (with Meredith's *Essay on Comedy*) in Comedy, A87

BLACKMUR, R. P. Form and Value in Modern Poetry, A96

BLOOM, HAROLD The Visionary Company, A372

BRANDEIS, IRMA The Ladder of Vision, A320

BROOKS, VAN WYCK America's Coming-of-Age, A129

BURKHART, CHARLES, & TRASK, GEORGIANNE, eds. Storytellers and Their Art, A354

CARY, JOYCE Art and Reality, A260

CASTIGLIONE, BALDESAR The Book of the Courtier, A186

CHASE, RICHARD The American Novel and Its Tradition, A116

EDEL, LEON Literary Biography, A188

FERGUSSON, FRANCIS The Human Image in Dramatic Literature, A124

—— The Idea of a Theater, A4

FORSTER, E. M.   Alexandria: A History and a Guide, A231

FULLER, MARGARET   Margaret Fuller: American Romantic—A Selection from Her Writings and Correspondence, ed. Miller, A356

GRANVILLE-BARKER, H., & HARRISON, G. B., eds.   A Companion to Shakespeare Studies, A191

HOFFMAN, DANIEL, ed.   American Poetry and Poetics, A304

HOWARD, LEON   Literature and the American Tradition, A329

HYTIER, JEAN   Andre Gide, A307

JAMES, HENRY   The Art of Travel, ed. Zabel, A306

KAUFMANN, WALTER   From Shakespeare to Existentialism, A213

KAZIN, ALFRED   On Native Grounds, A69

KITTO, H. D. F.   Greek Tragedy, A38

KRONENBERGER, LOUIS, ed.   Novelists on Novelists, A293

LAWRENCE, D. H.   Studies in Classic American Literature, A5

MC CORMICK, JOHN, & MAC INNES, MAIRI, eds.   Versions of Censorship, A297

MEREDITH, GEORGE   Essay on Comedy (with Bergson's *Laughter*) in Comedy, A87

MONTAIGNE   Complete Essays of Montaigne, trans. Frame: 3 vols. A227a, A227b, A227c

MOORE, W. G.   Moliere: A New Criticism, A291

MORRIS, WRIGHT, ed.   A Mississippi River Reader, A299

NICOLSON, HAROLD   Tennyson, A284

NIETZSCHE, FRIEDRICH   The Birth of Tragedy *and* The Genealogy of Morals, A81

ORTEGA Y GASSET, JOSE   The Dehumanization of Art and Other Writings on Art and Culture, A72

ORWELL, GEORGE   A Collection of Essays, A29

ROURKE, CONSTANCE   American Humor, A12

SCOTT, A. C.   Literature and the Arts in Twentieth Century China, A343

SHATTUCK, ROGER   The Banquet Years, A238

SHAW, GEORGE BERNARD   Shaw on Music, ed. Bentley, A53

SYPHER, WYLIE   Four Stages of Renaissance Style, A45

TOKLAS, ALICE B.   The Alice B. Toklas Cook Book, A196

TRAVERSI, D. A.   An Approach to Shakespeare, A74

TRILLING, LIONEL   The Liberal Imagination, A13

VAN DOREN, MARK   Shakespeare, A11

WELSFORD, ENID   The Fool: His Social and Literary History, A262

WILLEY, BASIL   The Seventeeth Century Background, A19

WILSON, EDMUND   A Literary Chronicle: 1920–1950, A85

——— A Piece of My Mind, A143